Human
Resource
Essentials

Human
Resource
Essentials

Your Guide to Starting and Running the HR Function

2nd edition

Lin Grensing-Pophal, SPHR

Society for Human Resource Management
Alexandria, Virginia
www.shrm.org

Strategic Human Resource Management India
Mumbai, India
www.shrmindia.org

Society for Human Resource Management
Haidian District Beijing, China
www.shrm.org/cn

The Society for Human Resource Management (SHRM®) is the world's largest association devoted to human resource management. Representing more than 250,000 members in over 140 countries, the Society serves the needs of HR professionals and advances the interests of the HR profession. Founded in 1948, SHRM has more than 575 affiliated chapters within the United States and subsidiary offices in China and India. Visit SHRM Online at www.shrm.org.

Interior and Cover Design: Shirley E.M. Raybuck

Library of Congress Cataloging-in-Publication Data

Grensing-Pophal, Lin, 1959-
  Human resource essentials : your guide to starting and running the HR function / Lin Grensing-Pophal. -- 2nd ed.
    p. cm.
  Includes indexes.
  ISBN 978-1-58644-196-8
    1. Personnel management--United States. 2. Personnel directors--United States. I. Title.
    HF5549.2.U5G74 2010
    658.3--dc22
                        2010013648

                                                                10-0027

CONTENTS

PREFACE

The human resource (HR) profession has changed dramatically over the past several years from the days when HR departments were referred to as "personnel departments." In those days, personnel practitioners were relegated primarily to "pushing paper" and handling administrative burdens but were seldom involved in the truly strategic elements of what we call "human resource management" today.

Many organizations continue to consider human resources a function that covers compensation and salary administration, hiring and firing, training, safety and security, and employee facilities. Frequently, HR professionals are expected — perhaps even encouraged — to be reactive rather than proactive in their response to HR issues.

For example, employees involved in recruitment activities respond to job requests and are supposed to find applicants who meet the needs of managers. But HR staff may not be expected to determine whether the job specifications are valid. Likewise, a compensation analyst waits for a situation to surface and then applies a rule. In industrial relations, the emphasis is on waiting until someone has an issue to resolve. The thrust of contract negotiations is to avoid getting trapped into concessions. When the contract is drawn, the emphasis is again on applying rules. Situations are dealt with after they arise, in reaction to the demands and actions of others.

However, change is occurring. More than ever before, organizations are being forced to consider the very real value of their *human* resources. And more than ever before, organizations are turning to their HR staff members for strategic help. No longer charged with simply processing payroll, increasing numbers of HR professionals are being asked to be business partners along with other strategic planners in their organizations.

These changes, while good for the profession, also present challenges. In 2000, then-president and CEO of the Society for Human Resource Management (SHRM) Michael R. Losey, SPHR, said

> "The biggest problem that I see is the low barriers of entry into the HR profession. By 'low barriers,' I mean this: CEOs too often assign the im-

portant task of HR management to someone who has little or no background in the field, based on their assumption that 'anyone can do HR.' As we know, HR is a profession, with a body of knowledge. You can't 'do HR' with an empty head. We have too many people in the field who give us a bum rap. They are a great risk. The future — and even the present — demands higher degrees of competency."

Almost a decade later, corporate and HR thought leader Jack Welch had virtually the same advice during his keynote presentation at SHRM's 61st Annual Conference & Exposition: For HR professionals to be taken seriously by CEOs and other senior leaders, they have to deliver, he said. "Get out of the picnics/birthdays/insurance form business" and instead take action that makes a difference, he said to loud applause. "Nobody wants to see some crazy cheerleader in there while [the organization is] leaking." The recession, of course, was top of mind as 2009 drew to a close: "The one thing you have to do in a time like this [is] to communicate like hell ... so your people know every move that's going on," Welch added, and understand the actions the organization is taking, "because everyone is scared."

Many HR professionals have entered the profession from the ground up. The value of a broad understanding of an organization cannot be minimized. But HR professionals are challenged to ensure that the HR role is visible and credible — and that they enjoy a strategic relationship with the organization's leaders.

Successful implementation of an HR function requires following a defined course based on HR standards, overall management objectives, and company strategies. Despite the stated management objectives, the HR function must start with the basics, such as successful recruiting, performance appraisals, and corrective action. Strategic planning, projections, analysis, and organizational change come only after the basic areas are established and operational. Between these two extremes are the usual HR activities, which may include training and orientation, staffing and control of labor costs, automating processes, career development, and cross-functional processes such as quality teams and self-directed work teams. Where to start and how fast to act depend on the company's circumstances and the availability of resources.

The rapidly growing availability of technology and the Internet presents HR professionals with both opportunities and challenges. Technology can significantly improve productivity by automating what used to be labor-intensive processes. The Internet and the many emerging social media tools allow access to people from literally around the globe, but these tools take time to learn and manage and raise new questions about appropriate and inappropriate use, impacting HR professionals themselves as well as creating the need for new and revised policies for staff.

The HR profession is a broad one, encompassing many different activities and having an impact on every level and every function of organizations. The 21st century is an era in which decisions must be made quickly and implemented competently. The management of human resources is part of everyone's job. Decisions must be made when and where they occur at the line level; those closest to the action must know how to be firm and competent in carrying out their HR responsibilities. They need to have expertise and to understand their responsibilities. HR professionals not only must have the knowledge and information necessary to oversee the HR function, but also must be prepared to guide others within the organization who have line responsibility for the organization's *human* resources.

In October 2007, the World Federation of Personnel Management Associations (WFPMA), now the World Federation of People Management Associations, and Boston Consulting Group (BCG) conducted a worldwide study to identify and address key HR priorities. Eighty-three countries and markets were represented in the study. SHRM partnered with WFPMA and BCG in the collection of the U.S. data. To gain a better understanding of the human capital challenges that confront organizations, HR professionals were asked to identify priorities for their organizations now (2007) and in the future (2010-2015).

The most critical HR issues facing organizations were managing talent and improving leadership development, cited by approximately one-half of respondents each. Managing demographics, delivering on recruiting and staffing, and managing change and cultural transformation were the other leading HR challenges facing organizations. The least critical issues reported were providing shared services and outsourcing HR and managing corporate social responsibility.

HR management continues to be an evolving and multidimensional profession. Those in the profession must remain constantly ahead of the curve on laws, technology, and practice issues that impact their ability to manage critical organizational resources — human resources.

ACKNOWLEDGMENTS

Writing a book is always both an exciting and an intimidating prospect. This book was no exception. Certainly it's not an endeavor that can be taken on alone. Given the broad nature of the human resources field, the input of others was critical for this project, and I'm very grateful to the many human resource professionals who freely shared their time and expertise to provide valuable insights and examples.

Several individuals provided valuable insights and expertise, sharing their backgrounds and experience in response to frequently asked questions. They are noted throughout the book.

I am indebted to them and to the many supportive staff members at SHRM who shared information and resources, verified facts and references, and responded quickly and professionally to multiple queries throughout the project. I have found my relationship with SHRM to be a rewarding and enlightening one, and I continue to be amazed by the breadth of resources and information it has available, as well as by the professionalism and knowledge of the staff members with whom I have worked.

I would be remiss if I didn't mention the support of my family. My husband, Dave, tolerates the evenings and weekends I spend in front of the computer and makes occasional forays into my work domain to see how it's going, just to say hello, and often to bring me food! And my son, who wished to be acknowledged as "Justin 'Magnus Lionbane' Grensing — a beast of a man from the northwoods of Wisconsin who was invaluable to the completion of this book." Now almost 26, he's away at law school, but is a valued sounding board. He never ceases to amaze me by providing valuable and insightful opinions and feedback — and frequent comic relief. With this revision, I was able to call on him to help me out with checking and updating some of the content that required a bit of legal research.

I couldn't do what I do without either of them.

Lin Grensing-Pophal, SPHR

Introduction

Starting an HR function in a company of any size can be a daunting experience. You must be concerned about myriad issues, from the operational (establishing policies and procedures) to the strategic (designing a competitive compensation and benefits plan). And chances are that if you are faced with this challenge, you may very well be tackling it alone. For many small and emerging companies, the HR department is an HR professional — one individual charged with serving the company's HR needs. That is why, throughout this book, the terms "HR function" and "HR professional" are used instead of "HR department."

So, unlike your HR colleagues in larger organizations, you must be a generalist. You must understand every aspect of managing an HR function — recruitment and hiring, pay practices, benefits administration, termination, and a daunting number of legal issues that affect your day-to-day activities.

Adding to the challenges presented by the scope of issues you will need to address are the massive changes now taking place in the business world that will have impacts on HR management. SHRM's *Workplace Forecast* of 2008 identified the top 10 trends for 2008-2009. They are

- Continuing high cost of health care in the United States.
- Large numbers of baby boomers (born between 1945 and 1964) retiring at around the same time.
- Threat of increased health care/medical costs on the economic competitiveness of the United States.
- Aging population.
- Growing need to develop retention strategies for current and future workforce.
- Federal health care legislation.
- Preparing organizations for an older workforce and the next wave of retirement.
- Threat of recession in the United States or globally.
- Labor shortages at all skill levels.

- Demographic shifts leading to a shortage of high-skilled workers.

In response to these trends, the most common actions taken by organizations have been to

- Offer tuition reimbursement.
- Invest more in training and development to boost skill levels of employees.
- Implement an employee data privacy policy.
- Implement policies and procedures aimed at protecting employee and customer data from identity theft.
- Use nondisclosure/noncompete agreements for intellectual property.
- Invest in technology and services designed to protect company data in the event of disaster or cyber attack.
- Increase the use of technology to perform transactional HR functions.
- Increase technology training.
- Increase training in specialized skills.
- Implement preventive health programs.

The list is notably diverse, highlighting the vast array of issues the general HR practitioner must be aware of and must attempt to manage. Complicating these issues are the impacts of the severe economic downturn in 2008.

The population is aging. Some baby boomers will remain in or return to the workforce past normal retirement age, perhaps affecting health insurance and retirement plans, and presenting management challenges. However, despite the economy, many baby boomers will soon be leaving the workforce in droves. The good news is that the labor force is expected to increase, according to the Bureau of Labor Statistics (BLS).

In its *Occupational Outlook Handbook* for 2008-2009, the BLS (www.bls.gov) indicated that the civilian labor force is projected to increase by 12.8 million, or 8.5 percent, to 164.2 million between 2006 and 2016. This increase will be accompanied by an increasingly diverse population — with white, non-Hispanic people continuing to reflect a decreasing share of the labor force (from 69.1 percent in 2006 to 64.6 percent in 2016).

Hispanics are projected to be the fastest growing ethnic group — with growth of 29.9 percent expected during this time period. Asians also are expected to account for an increasing share of the labor force by 2016, growing from 4.4 percent to 5.3 percent. The number of black workers in the labor force is expected to grow from 11.4 percent to 12.3 percent.

While an increase in available talent initially sounds like good news, for HR professionals there are some factors that suggest otherwise. First, the aging of the baby boomer generation will cause not only an increase in the percentage of workers in the oldest age category but also a decrease in the percentage of younger workers. The increase in the number of workers 55 and older (from 16.8 percent to 22.7 percent of the labor force) and decline in the number of workers between 25 and 54 years old — the primary working age group — (from 68.4 percent to 64.6 percent) will have an impact on staffing.

In addition, 15.6 million jobs are expected to be added by 2016. And, of course, the types of jobs and skills these positions might reflect are unknown at this point. Technology, globalization, and increasing diversity among potential employees will all impact the roles of HR professionals over the next several years, creating both opportunities and challenges.

The changes are massive, their implications far-reaching. Despite the impacts of the recession, retention of qualified staff will continue to be a concern of companies and their HR professionals (see Figures I.1-I.3).

FIGURE I.1 The 10 Fastest-Growing Occupations, 1998–2008

[Numbers in thousands of jobs]

Occupation	Employment		Change	
	1998	2008	Number	Percentage
Computer engineers	299	622	323	108
Computer support specialists	429	869	439	102
Systems analysts	617	1,194	577	94
Database administrators	87	155	67	77
Desktop publishing specialists	26	44	19	73
Paralegals and legal assistants	136	220	84	62
Personal care and home health aides	746	1,179	433	58
Medical assistants	252	398	146	58
Social and human services assistants	268	410	141	53
Physician assistants	66	98	32	48

Source: Bureau of Labor Statistics.

FIGURE I.2 The 10 Occupations with the Largest Job Growth, 1998–2008

[Numbers in thousands of jobs]

Occupation	Employment		Change	
	1998	2008	Number	Percentage
Systems analysts	617	1,194	577	94
Retail salespeople	4,056	4,620	563	14
Cashiers	3,198	3,754	556	17
General managers and top executives	3,362	3,913	551	16
Truck drivers, light and heavy	2,970	3,463	493	17
Office clerks, general	3,021	3,484	463	17
Registered nurses	2,079	2,530	451	22
Computer support specialists	429	869	439	102
Personal care and home health aides	746	1,179	433	58
Teacher assistants	1,192	1,567	375	31

Source: Bureau of Labor Statistics.

FIGURE I.3 The 10 Industries with the Fastest Wage and Salary Employment Growth, 1998–2008

[Numbers in thousands of jobs]

Occupation	Employment		Change	
	1998	2008	Number	Percentage
Computer and data processing services	1,599	3,472	1,872	117
Health services, not elsewhere classified	1,209	2,018	809	67
Residential care	747	1,171	424	57
Management and public relations	1,034	1,500	466	45
Personnel supply services	3,230	4,623	1,393	43
Miscellaneous equipment rental & leasing	258	369	111	43
Museums, botanical and zoological gardens	93	131	39	42
Research and testing services	614	861	247	40
Miscellaneous transportation services	236	329	94	40
Security and commodity brokers	645	900	255	40

Source: Bureau of Labor Statistics.

Benefits will continue to be an important part of the total compensation package, and HR professionals will be challenged to meet employees' growing and diverse needs with ever-shrinking budgets (see Figure I.4).

FIGURE I.4. Factors Posing a Threat to Employee Retention

	Large Threat	Moderate Threat	Small Threat	No Threat
Career opportunities elsewhere	38%	48%	13%	1%
Better compensation elsewhere	31%	45%	23%	2%
Burnout	19%	48%	26%	7%
Dissatisfaction with potential career development at the organization	20%	36%	36%	8%
Not feeling appreciated	19%	31%	41%	9%
Better benefits package elsewhere	14%	36%	39%	11%
Difficulty balancing work-life issues	9%	32%	45%	13%
Poor management	15%	22%	47%	16%
Conflicts with supervisors	8%	30%	47%	16%
Boredom	7%	22%	46%	26%
Retirement	7%	19%	41%	32%
Child care issues	4%	13%	53%	30%
Conflicts with co-workers	3%	14%	54%	29%
Job security fears	8%	12%	39%	41%
Perceived unfair or discriminatory treatment	5%	12%	47%	36%
Return to school	2%	16%	46%	36%
Accompanying a relocating spouse/partner	3%	13%	50%	34%
Poor interpersonal relationships with co-workers	3%	10%	55%	32%
Health-related reasons	1%	9%	55%	34%
Conflict with organization's values or mission	4%	9%	40%	47%
Elder care issues	0%	5%	43%	52%

Source: SHRM/CareerJournal.com 2006 U.S. Job Retention Poll Findings. Available at www.shrm.org/Research/SurveyFindings.

Clearly, the role of the HR professional in any size organization will need to change and expand as companies are forced to deal with the changing nature of the environment in which they operate.

Whether your company is a "virtual" or a traditional firm, whether you recruit locally or internationally, many of your concerns are the same. How can you structure the HR function so that it is able to respond effectively to these changes while meeting the human resource needs of your company?

What policies/practices must you have in place to ensure that your company is getting maximum benefit from its human resources? How can you help your employer avoid legal liability? How can you aid in recruitment and retention?

This book will give you the information you need to design an HR function. It provides easy-to-follow instructions for designing a foundation for a reliable and productive employee relations strategy.

You will learn about ways that you might enhance the management practices of your company.

You will learn about how to comply with federal and state regulations that affect the management of human resources — and discover ways to make these regulations work for (not against) your company.

You will learn about reliable resources that you can use to find quick and up-to-date answers to your questions, because there is no doubt that the environment will continue to change rapidly around us.

To help you along, throughout the book are answers to "FAQs" (Frequently Asked Questions) and "Lessons from the Trenches."

In the FAQs, experienced HR consultants and practitioners give direct answers to some of the questions that they hear most frequently from HR professionals.

The paradox of working as an HR professional in a small business or start-up is that, while there are literally thousands of others out there just like you, it can be a very lonely and isolated experience. The good news is that you are not really alone. "Lessons from the Trenches" present the stories of just a few of the thousands of HR professionals who operate in solo or small-company environments. Their experiences are varied, but one thing is constant — their enthusiasm for and commitment to their jobs. Yes, there are countless issues to be aware of and seemingly endless tasks to juggle on any given day. But, as these professionals have discovered, managing an organization's human resources is both challenging and rewarding.

The management of human resources is as much an art as a science. You may question specific advice offered here based on your own experiences — your suggestions or recommendations for improvement are sincerely appreciated.

Essentials of Starting
A Human Resource Function

There are three important aspects to starting a successful HR function. As an HR professional, you must

1. Understand the impact that effective HR management has on the organization.
2. Assist the organization in following policies and practices that maximize the potential of its human resources.
3. Serve as a role model for the organization's leaders and managers, establishing and capitalizing on your own credibility and expertise.

As an HR professional, you can build a sense of confidence in your function by clearly linking HR strategies to the objectives of the company. For example, the development of a succession plan is directly tied to the company's need to develop a capable workforce. The establishment of a flexible benefits program may have an impact on the company's retention activities. All of these HR activities are interrelated, and each is affected by the company's strategic plan, goals, and objectives.

You also play a major role in helping your organization manage legal liability and risk. You need to be aware of these issues and develop methods of staying up-to-date on the changing legal environment in which you work, from national, state, and local perspectives. (A summary of the federal laws affecting human resources is provided in Appendix B.)

While you can and should look to HR colleagues in other organizations for assistance and advice, you should also keep in mind that programs and processes from one company may be difficult to apply, without modification, to another company. Company strategies and HR activities should be tailored to fit the unique needs of each organization.

Clearly, the HR professional of the 21st century must be a strategic partner in his or her organization. This means understanding the needs of the company and using those needs as the basis for all HR practices and procedures. Being a strategic partner also means working closely with line or operational managers to develop and implement HR processes. In many respects, as an HR professional you will serve in a consultative role to the managers and leaders of your organization. While you provide guidance and direction, the implementation of your HR policies and procedures will actually be driven by the line managers. It is crucial, then, that you develop strong relationships with these individuals, that they develop a sense of trust and confidence in your abilities and your counsel, and that you involve them as much as possible in establishing policies, procedures, and processes that will affect the operation of their departments and, ultimately, of the organization.

A number of HR activities affect the company's profitability and efficiency and, therefore, are as valuable to management as to the HR professional; among these valuable activities are staffing and succession planning, recruitment, selection, data analysis, reward and recognition, and advising on compliance with federal laws and judicial decisions. Your organization will develop a sense of the value of these and other HR activities if you, the HR professional, can clearly demonstrate and communicate the strategic importance of these activities.

Chapter 9, on Management Reports, offers ideas on how to communicate effectively with your organization's management and how to convey clearly the value of your activities.

If your company is concerned about reducing turnover, for instance, you may have a corresponding HR strategy of improving employee satisfaction through a variety of activities, including improved communication, increased career and job training, and management development. Not only do your actions aid in reducing turnover, but the resultant savings can be used to improve, strengthen, and accomplish other business objectives.

Informed employees are better able to provide effective customer service, which affects customer satisfaction and customer retention. Customer retention, in turn, saves money for the organization by reducing waste and the expense of prospecting for new customers — and provides the resources your organization needs for continuous improvement and internal quality activities. These activities create more money for education and employee relations strategies, which result in higher employee satisfaction. The customer service chain illustrates how a focus on human resources and employee relations can positively affect overall business profitability and create a good work environment.

Starting a Human Resource Function

HR professionals should be model leaders and managers. Understanding human resources is only one part of this role; being proficient in traditional management is another. You should not only be able to function as a key confidential adviser to the

CEO of your organization, but also be familiar with basic managerial responsibilities — sticking to budgets, showing that activities are profitable, and recognizing how long-range implications of management decisions can affect the organization's human resources.

As an advocate for the role of human resources (note: this does not necessarily mean that you are an advocate for employees), you must have the tenacity to advance employee relations strategies as you participate in the planning of all strategic activities that affect employees. This might include

- Advising management on the feasibility of acquisitions or downsizing.
- Identifying employee relations implications of plant relocations.
- Advocating appropriate selection requirements for top management.
- Championing workforce diversity as a competitive strategy.
- Discussing compensation and benefits limitations.
- Implementing safety and workers' compensation programs.
- Sponsoring productivity improvement or quality processes.
- Estimating the effect of remaining union-free.

Each of these activities has implications for employee relations. Historically, HR practitioners have not participated at the strategic management level in these activities. As we have already discussed, though, this is changing. Today, more and more companies are recognizing the impact the HR function has on the organization and are either calling for or responding positively to the involvement of HR staff in strategic planning issues. An experienced, knowledgeable HR professional, armed with the right information, credibility, and initiative, can lead the company in the right direction.

Human Resource Strategy and Its Relationship to Business Objectives

In recent years, enormous changes have taken place in the roles and responsibilities of what used to be called the personnel department. One significant change that has had an impact on the traditional HR function is the strategic planning process.

There are two aspects of strategic planning that HR professionals should be involved with: planning for their own function within the organization, and advising the CEO and upper management on the impact that other departments may be having on the success of the overall strategic goals. For example, you need to conduct planning that relates to the HR duties you and your department will perform to ensure that your activities are consistent with the goals of the organization. If, for instance, one major concern of the organization is retention of key staff members, you might have a goal to develop a comprehensive succession plan. You also need to plan for other impacts your department will have on the organization. For example, you may be aware that a production department is experiencing high turnover. Knowing that retention is a critical issue for the organization, and understanding the key role the production department plays in producing a sufficient supply to meet demand for the company's product, you might establish a goal to work with the leader of this department on tactics to reduce turnover.

Whether you are involved in strategic planning for the HR function itself or in concert with other parts of the organization, it is critical that you understand the goals and objectives of the company you work for. As the leader of the HR function, you need to determine how you can help to further those goals through your own department's activities. As an adviser to upper management, you need to understand how each of the functional areas in your organization affects the overall goals — and how HR can assist the departments performing those functions in being more effective. For example,

- Is the organization structured appropriately to meet its needs? Are the departments aligned properly to ensure smooth communication between workgroups that interact frequently?
- Are the right people in the right jobs? Are managers looking for the appropriate skills and experience when they fill positions?
- Do existing evaluation processes adequately measure staff members' ability to perform their assigned duties? Are there processes in place to improve or correct performance if needed?
- Are pay and benefits practices adequate to meet the organization's needs? Are they appropriately competitive with those of other businesses competing for the same qualified staff to ensure that your company retains a fully functioning workforce?
- Are there key functions that are not currently staffed? Are there non-key functions that are currently staffed that might be more appropriately handled through outsourcing?

The first step in any strategic planning process is determining what the overall goals and objectives are. The second step is conducting a SWOT analysis. SWOT stands for Strengths, Weaknesses, Opportunities, and Threats. It is a commonly used management tool that can be used at the beginning of a process to help identify the key issues affecting the process and future progress. A facilitator, who may be someone from the HR department, from another department, or from outside the organization, leads a group brainstorming process, working through each step by asking, "What are our strengths?" "What are our weaknesses?" "What opportunities lie before us?" "What threats must we be aware of?"

The SWOT analysis is most effectively conducted with a group of people, all bringing different perspectives to the discussion. In planning for the HR function, you would include any other employees involved in HR processes, as well as other key employees throughout the organization, key management staff, and so on. You would then engage in a discussion of your existing strengths (e.g., good recruitment program), weaknesses (e.g., high turnover rate), opportunities (e.g., forming a partnership with the local technical college to recruit for manufacturing students, utilizing social media for recruitment), and threats (e.g., a competitive business moving to town).

The next step is to determine how — given your existing resources — you can capitalize on your strengths, overcome your weaknesses, take advantage of your opportunities, and minimize or respond effectively to your threats. This may involve a discussion of priorities, again based on the overall goals and objectives of the organization.

The final step is to develop specific strategies and tactics designed to help you accomplish your goals. Specifically, *how* will you accomplish the tasks you have identified? At the end of the strategic planning process, you should have a plan that identifies both long- and short-term goals, based on your internal capabilities and resources.

We operate in an environment that is marked by continual change. Among the many forces that are currently affecting business and HR are these:

- Major demographic shifts that result in an aging, diverse, and shrinking workforce.
- Low basic skills of entry-level workers and a decreasing supply of qualified and competent employees.
- A need for higher levels of job skills and greater flexibility among employees.
- More laws and more regulation of a company's discretion to operate its business.
- An emphasis on value-added, bottom-line responsibility for HR functions.

Change is inevitable, and not as unpleasant as many of us tend to believe. In fact, those who have come to embrace change and take advantage of the opportunities that change often presents have discovered that it is not so much the change itself that we fear, but the thought that we will not be able to control the change — that it will *happen to us.* HR professionals who become strategic partners with the leadership in their organizations gain control over the change process.

Long-Range Planning

The specifics of the long-range planning process vary by company, industry, and competitive environment. But there are a number of ways HR can become involved in the company's strategic or long-range planning process. For example,

- Defining and developing qualified employees at all levels of the organization.
- Providing the necessary training and development programs for skills enhancement and for creating an atmosphere of trust and commitment.
- Retaining people through programs that build loyalty and a sense of community among employees.
- Developing fair, flexible, competitive compensation and benefits programs that meet legal requirements and encourage employee retention.
- Creating performance appraisal systems that are based on organizational objectives and that reward contributions to the organization.
- Evaluating managerial potential to identify — and develop — the leadership and professional qualities needed to meet the organization's strategic planning goals.
- Offering career management programs that merge the goals of the organization with those of the individual.
- Providing a management succession planning system that ensures management continuity.

The Human Resource Generalist

Several years ago, a common criticism of personnel professionals was that they focused too much on day-to-day operations and did not see the big picture. Today, HR is viewed as an important part of management and is increasingly counted among the more significant management functions. The transition from handling basic, administrative personnel activities to operating more proactively and more strategically has not come easily. Changes are made every day that require new practices in HR management. But the basic philosophy and organizational needs of companies have not really changed significantly.

The fundamental reasons companies start an HR function are to reduce costs, to comply with government regulations, and to compete effectively with other companies for scarce human resources.

In large companies, HR professionals have the luxury of specializing. In smaller organizations, though, and when charged with starting an HR function from the ground up, a generalist perspective is required. To be effective in the HR field, even in a large corporate environment, a generalist perspective can be extremely helpful. For example, developing a successful pay or benefits process requires an evaluation of the impact on other areas, which a compensation specialist may find difficult to do. Any changes in compensation programs must take into account the employee relations climate and strategies, the turnover rate, the complaint and grievance process, the promotion process, equal employment opportunity issues, diversity and affirmative action considerations, and legal and legislative issues.

Likewise, a new workers' compensation or safety and accident prevention program cannot be developed in a vacuum. It must factor in compensation issues, labor and employee relations links, legislative constraints, training and development problems, quality and productivity concerns, and even equal employment opportunity and diversity concerns. Starting a safety and accident prevention process without grasping how these other considerations affect business success can be disastrous.

But certainly, when initiating an HR function the professional *must* have a generalist perspective.

Becoming a Strategic Partner

To a greater degree than ever before, the HR function in any company must be linked closely to the overall performance of the company. Often, HR professionals feel hampered in their ability to facilitate change because they do not feel they have a strategic role.

The key is not waiting to be asked to be a strategic partner, but actively seeking opportunities to add value to the organization by partnering with the CEO and other top-level management staff to meet the company's strategic objectives.

Being a strategic partner does not involve waiting to be given the opportunity. It involves seeing the big picture, understanding the organization's goals, and determining the best method for HR to assist in moving the company to meet those goals. It requires confidence and commitment.

One of the key ways in which HR professionals can enhance their value to their organizations is by becoming knowledgeable about areas outside the scope of traditional HR functions. To be a member of the executive team, you need to contribute to decisions that affect every area of the organization. To do this effectively, you need to develop a working knowledge of operations, marketing, finance, and strategic planning — and understand how HR links into each of these areas.

Becoming a strategic partner is not an impossible goal, but it is not something that happens automatically or that HR professionals should view as their due. Involvement in the strategic issues of *any* organization occurs only as the result of demonstrating initiative, commitment, and an understanding of the needs and issues that affect the organization's success. Following are some practical tips and strategies for becoming a business partner:

Recognize that your purpose is to serve the needs of the organization — not the needs of your department or your position.

The people who have attained strategic roles put the needs of the organization first. Their decisions are based on what is best for the company, not on what is best for their department or for themselves individually. Taking that viewpoint is not always easy — and it is not always popular. But if you are not able to align yourself with the needs of the organization, you cannot expect to be taken seriously.

This does not mean that you must be a yes-person. It simply means that when you present a proposal or frame an argument, you need to do so in terms of how the organization will benefit from implementing your suggestion. To become a business partner, you need to have a broad business focus.

Learn about your organization and industry.

How do you develop a broad business focus? By learning about your organization and your industry. If your expertise is limited to HR, how can you expect that you will be treated seriously when it comes to making decisions that affect the entire organization? The most successful executives are those who have spent time in a variety of positions — finance, marketing, operations. What can you do to demonstrate your interest in the *entire* organization? Start by networking with co-workers in other departments and becoming involved in task forces or committees outside the scope of traditional HR duties. Read trade journals about your industry. Learn everything you can about the organization and the issues it faces.

Think of yourself as a consultant — not a decision-maker.

HR is a service department. It is a very important service department, but a service department nonetheless. What this means is that your role, as a member of the HR team, is to provide advice to management based on your expertise and experience. That is what you are paid for. Members of senior management are paid to make decisions based on the advice they receive from various internal and external advisers. Unless you are part of the executive leadership team, you are not a decision-maker and you should not be offended if your advice is not always taken.

Will this be frustrating from time to time? Certainly. But you will get much further in your career if you learn from the experience and consider how you could alter your approach or strengthen your position in the future — instead of feeling victimized or put upon because you feel "they never listen to me."

This is not to say that you should accept decisions that are against your values or that violate the law. Those are different issues. If you find yourself in an untenable situation at any organization because you are forced to support decisions that you feel are morally or ethically wrong, you may need to move to another organization.

Use data and objective information to back up your suggestions and decisions.

While it would be great if your opinion were so valued that no one ever questioned your judgment and always followed your recommendations, that is a highly unlikely situation to find yourself in. More likely, you will need to provide tangible evidence to back up your recommendations. You should not feel insulted by this; instead, you should recognize it as part of your job and learn to leverage your power and authority with the value of information and data you can provide from both internal and external sources.

There are very few HR professionals whose advice will have impact simply because of their stellar reputation. The longer you are with an organization, and the more you can establish a record as being someone whose advice is pertinent and valuable, the more you will find that you become someone who is listened to.

Disagree privately. Agree publicly.

You will not always agree with every decision that your management or your organization makes. It is your right — and often your responsibility — to share your concerns with the appropriate people. But there is a right way, and a right time, to do this. The right way is to present your opposing view respectfully and to back up your view with objective data and information. The *right* time is during the decision-making process. Once a decision has been made, and communicated throughout the organization, it may still be appropriate to present evidence to management that the decision may have been in error. But it is neither appropriate nor wise to express these views publicly. If you want to be considered part of the team, you need to support that team.

Build relationships.

Strive for diversity in the relationships you establish. Get to know people in all areas of your organization. Seek out people with different opinions. Purposefully pepper your committees with individuals who have dissenting viewpoints. Cultivate contacts at all levels of the organization — and outside the organization.

To lead effectively, you need to understand the views and needs of the people you deal with — not just people in the HR department, and not just people who are above you on the corporate ladder, but people throughout the organization. The broader your perspectives, the more accurately you will be able to "read" the organization and make proposals and recommendations that are strategic and appropriate.

And from a personal standpoint, you never know whose support may be important to you in the future — cultivating relationships can yield positive results at unexpected times.

Nobody is given a seat at the table — not even the top executives in an organization. Some are players; some are not. You have to *earn* your seat at the table, and you do this by demonstrating your understanding of the broad business issues of your organization and how your role supports those business issues. You do this by backing up your recommendations with sound data. You do this by being willing to take an unpopular stand and by publicly supporting the organization even when you yourself may not be 100 percent on board with a decision (as long as that decision is morally and legally appropriate). And you do this by establishing a wide range of personal and professional contacts both inside and outside your organization.

FAQs

See Appendix E for information about the experts who answered the FAQs throughout this book.

Why do companies need an HR function?

Patricia Fragen:

As soon as a company has non-owner employees, a formal HR system (not necessarily department) should exist to make sure that correct forms are provided and verified, and that there is a policy manual in place to ensure fair treatment for employees and to detail employees' obligations to the company. Benefits vary from company to company, but companies have a legal obligation to not discriminate against employees when providing benefits. Benefits plans require research and regular maintenance. If a company waits to create its HR function until things have gotten out of control, it has already exposed itself to great risk.

I have found through my consulting that most business owners are unaware of some of even the most basic HR record-keeping requirements (such as the I-9 form), much less the laws and regulations applicable in their own states. They have no idea that there are ways to go about firing an employee that results in no unemployment liability. They think they can offer certain incentives to one employee and not to others — which is occasionally the case, but rarely. Formalizing human resources forces the owners to either do the research themselves or hire an expert who can advise them so that they do not experience the many pratfalls of managing employees.

What are the critical first steps of starting an HR function?

Chris Laggini:

There are several critical steps to starting an HR function.

1. *Plan/Create.* Create the infrastructure with a vision of the company in both operational and cultural terms. Begin to prioritize functions, creating the building blocks of a plan in a structural order that is solid and that softens the

impact of so much change. Tasks must be done in an orderly fashion in order to create a solid foundation that can support future growth.

2. *Communicate.* Effective communication at each step of building the foundation is key. There is hard work involved in building these blocks, so employees or workers need to know the purpose and focus behind the tasks they are doing to build the structure.

3. *Evaluate.* Each block or piece of the structural puzzle must have future growth in mind. If pieces have a limited time frame attached to them, there will inevitably need to be changes in the future over and over as a reaction to growth. This constant change will have a negative effect on the productivity and growth of the company and the culture.

4. *Consider cultural impact.* Evaluate what the impact of each task will be on the employees directly. While the happiness of employees does not drive the business model, it is a strong factor in creating the stabilization of a company's foundation and culture. Create rules that are good for the company and that will, in turn, affect how people view management and the company.

William G. Bliss:

Steps crucial to a good beginning are these:

- Establish a mission and purpose for the HR function that directly supports the mission of the whole organization. The mission statement should include why the function exists, how its success or effectiveness will be measured, and to whom it will report within the company.

- Establish the focus of the function. Is it to be administrative, providing statistics, reports, and general compliance functions? Or will it be a strategic component of the business with a footing equal to finance, sales, manufacturing, and other key players?

- Establish key goals or objectives that must be accomplished within the first six to 12 months. Ensure that each member of the senior management team fully supports every goal or objective.

- Establish the qualifications needed for the person heading the HR function and ensure that the intended compensation is in line with the desired qualifications.

- Identify any potential conflicting expectations and resolve them as soon as possible. Once the head of HR is selected, he or she should meet with each member of the senior management team to fully discuss the goals, objectives, and expectations of the position and function.

- Allow a reasonable amount of time for the head of HR to learn the business, if he or she is hired from outside.

Why is it important for HR to demonstrate return on investment impact?

Paul Falcone:
Human capital, organizational talent, or "human resources," in the highest sense of those words, is the critical distinguishing factor between solid and stellar companies. When you think about what makes a McKinsey the leading consulting firm in the world or what makes a Google or Apple the leaders on the planet, by far it's the caliber of their people. Simply put, when you hire, develop, and retain the most talented individuals in your field, your company will thrive.

The key to managing this most critical resource, however, lies in measuring it successfully. And that, more than anything else, will help human resources attain the highest level of importance and impact that this functional discipline has experienced since its creation 100 years ago.

How can HR demonstrate return on investment impact?

Paul Falcone:
The first step lies in developing the questions that you want answered about your human capital asset. If we agree that the three action verbs associated with exceptional people management are to (1) grow, (2) develop, and (3) retain the strongest performers, then our questions will flow from there.

In short, if HR can create a scorecard or snapshot of the most promising talent, areas for development in terms of succession planning, and opportunities for strengthening leadership and communication within the enterprise, then HR will have achieved its highest goal: to maximize the productivity and performance of the organization's most strategic and critical asset.

What is HR's role during an economic downturn?

Patricia Peirce:
HR's role during an economic downturn can include
  • Suggesting a plan for reducing expenses related to the HR department.
  • Suggesting a plan for reducing expenses related to employee costs.
  • Managing any reduction-in-force programs, including planning a communication program for exiting and remaining employees, determining and recommending severance packages, providing support for managers, maintaining employee

relations, monitoring workflow change to make sure all important tasks are reassigned, revising job descriptions, and arranging training related to changes in responsibilities for remaining employees.

- Monitoring any changes in employee morale and company culture, and communicating them to senior management.
- Managing the performance review program to ensure that all employees are recognized for their contributions.

Janet Hirsch:

Layoffs and terminations are not the only responses to an economic downturn. HR can make the case for other solutions. One company in our area offered voluntary buyout packages for those close to retirement age. Aflac has made every effort to avoid layoffs by cutting costs, including salaries of top management.

Most companies cut out "perks" such as paid professional certifications and continuing education, company subsidies for vehicles and housing, birthday cakes, parties, and other social events. Many companies are placing emphasis instead on community service: food drives, Christmas cards for servicemen and women, charitable programs through local chapters of the Salvation Army and Goodwill. These activities give employees a positive feeling of helping others in less fortunate circumstances.

The key is to get buy-in from employees. If a company has an employee committee or general shift and team meetings, that is a good time to get employee input. It is also a good time to listen to employees and address their concerns with clear and open communication. If the company treats its employees fairly and openly, the employees feel more like partners and less like pawns in the economic viability game.

Lessons from the Trenches

Building From the Outside In

Michael Couch, president of Michael Couch & Associates, Inc., a Pittsburgh-based consulting firm, and the host of The Voice of Business Growth on the VoiceAmerica Business Network, says he has built several HR functions during his 30 years in the profession.

The starting point, he says, is understanding the business. "Build the function from the outside in and not from a typical internal, HR perspective. Get in front of customers and talk to executives. Build the function from the business's customers' and leaders' perspectives. Start with the results the business needs and build talent processes from there. Know the business measures you want to impact."

HR functions today must be much more clearly aligned with the business, notes Couch. The focus, he says, needs to be on building the capacity of the HR organization to match the business and *not* on completing day-to-day administrative transactions.

"The HR function of today must seriously consider outsourcing functions that don't directly contribute to building capability but that are needed to run a business — temp staffing, recruiting, benefits administration, pension administration, employee assistance program, etc.," he says.

Technology is a key consideration. Web-enabled, integrated and self-service are the buzzwords, says Couch. The tools available today are different from and more powerful than those of five or 10 years ago.

And the capabilities required of HR professionals are also much different. Today, says Couch, HR professionals must have the skills to be internal organizational effectiveness consultants and not just functional experts. They need to understand the new technology, be comfortable with analytic tools and measurement, and be expert facilitators.

The opportunity is great for HR professionals to build a function that is respected by the business and not "left in an administrative backwater," says Couch. "The pitfall is not developing the business case for the investment needed to build a modern HR function. That's why building from the outside in is important."

Staffing Plans and Legalities

aving the right people in the right jobs allows your organization to make maximum use of its HR investment. Any business — whether for profit or not for profit — exists to further its organizational mission and relies on employees to do that. The right employees, people who have the qualifications required to perform the critical functions of a job, can help further the mission efficiently and cost-effectively. This chapter discusses the characteristics of the hiring processes and its legal and practical implications.

Recruitment and selection are critical HR functions with great potential for risk if not handled effectively. A well-structured hiring process can help your company avoid exposure to employee relations liability. However, while ensuring that the hiring process is legally defensible is important, the need for an effective hiring process extends beyond concern for legal liability.

The Changing Nature of the Labor Market

The economic downturn that took much of the country by surprise in late 2008 has had a dramatic impact on the labor market. The sudden impact on the lives of employees — both those in the early and later stages of their careers — is significant and is causing workers at both ends of the spectrum to become introspective about their futures.

"I'm stuck where I'm at until someone dies or retires," laments a 34-year-old working as a graphic designer limited-term employee in a university setting. "My job is split between two offices, both of which consist of nearly all 50-somethings," she says. "The thought of people delaying retirement is really depressing."

She sees the economic downturn greatly affecting baby boomers' retirement plans. "I've heard older co-workers saying the downturn has changed their, or their spouses', retirement plans, which does not leave me feeling too hopeful about my job situation," she says. "If we have another child, how are we going to pay for the child care?

Would I have to give up my career? Will we ever be able to build our new house? Our plan had been three to five years. Now, looking at our investment portfolio, who knows? Am I ever going to get ahead?"

A 56-year-old IT specialist in a health care setting says she has watched her investments drop to less than half of what they were about a year ago. "I suppose I'm lucky to be employed where I am because it provides us a retirement plan that is self-funded by the organization," she says. "That plan alone, however, will not entirely fund our retirement."

"The fear of continued loss of personal investments, as well as the foreseeable loss in Social Security, makes the chance of early retirement, or even retirement at all, highly improbable. Unless we would severely alter our standard of living, we may be working as long as we are physically and mentally able. That's a big change from the dream of early retirement that we held in our early 40s," she says.

These perceptions are common and have the potential to significantly impact the work environment as employees who had been planning to retire, as well as those who had hoped to move into the resulting vacant roles, now find themselves in a holding pattern.

A SHRM poll conducted in July 2009 on the impact of the recession on employee retirement indicated a significant increase in the number of employees planning to delay their retirement (see Figure 2.1).

For HR professionals, these economic shifts present challenges as well as opportunities. Now more than ever there is a need to think strategically about employee engagement and workforce development options to create and maintain a healthy and productive work environment. Companies must grapple with how to keep their aging workforce engaged and committed in the face of a retirement that may now loom years in the future.

The needs of baby boomers and the needs of members of Generation Y and Generation X are often seen as divergent. Yet, in reality, their desires can be remarkably similar. Things like flexibility and work-life balance appeal to the older employee population as much as to their younger colleagues. And the desire to make a positive contribution to the workplace spans generations.

Despite the economic downturn, for the long term, employers must remain alert to the potential for a diminishing labor force, the impending retirement of baby boomers, and the increasing diversity of the labor population, discussed in the Introduction of this book.

These labor market changes represent challenges for HR professionals and the need for a continued emphasis not only on recruitment and retention but also on communication, team building, and the establishment of a culture that recognizes and values diversity. Companies of the 21st century must accommodate the needs of employees who represent a wide range of ages and demographic backgrounds. The competition for qualified and competent employees will continue.

FIGURE 2.1. The Impact of the Recession on Retirements
In the past 12 months, has there been an increase, a decrease, or no change in the number of employees ...

	Increase		Decrease		No change	
	2008	2009	2008	2009	2008	2009
Planning to extend their retirement date due to the recession?	–	68%	–	0%	–	32%
Reducing their 401(k) contribution?	–	67%	–	2%	–	31%
Suspending contribution to their 401(k)?	–	62%	–	2%	–	36%
Asking for advances on their 401(k) savings?	39%	49%	3%	1%	59%	50%
Requesting more guidance and information specific to investing/retirement planning?	–	47%	–	1%	–	52%
Reporting losing their homes (due to foreclosure/inability to pay rent, other reasons)?	14%	30%	0%	0%	86%	70%
Having their wages garnished by collection agencies?	26%	26%	6%	1%	68%	73%
Not rolling over their 401(k) savings after employment termination?	–	21%	——	3%	——	76%
Cashing out (i.e., prematurely before reaching retirement age) their 401(k) savings completely?	–	18%	–	0%	–	81%
Asking for advances on their wages?	20%	16%	2%	1%	77%	83%
Increasing their 401(k) contribution?	–	10%	–	35%	–	55%

Source: The U.S. Recession and Its Impact on Employee Retirement SHRM Poll Findings, Society for Human Resource Management, July 2009. Available at www.shrm.org/Research/SurveyFindings/Articles/Pages/RecessionImpactonRetirement.aspx.

Key Concepts: Work Requirements, Staffing, and Efficiency

HR professionals should consider work requirements, staffing, and efficiency as strategies that contribute to achieving the objectives of the company and to its profitability. Companies may be inefficient and unproductive if they do not focus on the activities that contribute the most value to their customers. The media are full of stories of companies, large and small, that are downsizing their workforces, cutting services, outsourcing operations, and closing facilities.

Neither HR professionals nor the leaders they work with enjoy implementing these strategies. Companies do not want to resort to activities that have negative impacts on their employees. Unfortunately, though, it is through their own actions that many organizations find themselves in a position of having to take these drastic actions. For instance, in the late 1990s, the bull market that buoyed hundreds of dot-com companies suddenly deteriorated into a bear market, and many organizations that had hired employees to meet growing demands for products and services found it necessary to downsize their workforces to cut costs. The ebb and flow of the economy struck again in the late 2000s, with layoffs and unemployment reaching levels not seen since the 1990s.

In times like these, only the operations that are absolutely essential to the functioning of a company can be justified. Human resources can play a significant role not only in helping the organization identify which positions can be eliminated during bad times, but also in staffing the organization based on a thorough analysis of the impact each position has on the essential functions of the organization. HR has a major impact here through maintaining efficient positions and hiring people who meet the essential qualifications for the job.

Maintain Only Full Positions

Organizations should hire only when there is a good business reason to do so. The addition of new staff members adds both burden and risk to the organization. The burden lies in increased costs for salary and benefits. The risk lies both in hiring the wrong person and in finding out down the road that the position is no longer necessary or can no longer be supported because of the company's financial standing.

Certainly, there is value in growing the business, and the addition of new staff members is often justified. But the decision to add staff should be made carefully. HR professionals can play a key role in working with the organization and the hiring manager to determine whether the addition is valid. Here are some questions that can help direct those discussions:

- Why is this job necessary? What are the critical tasks this employee will be performing?
- What value is added by this job? Is that value measurable in any way (e.g., "this new salesperson will be expected to generate $250,000 annually for the company")?
- What would happen if the employee never came to work for the company? What opportunities would be missed? What risks might exist?
- Is this a full-time job, or could the job objectives be accomplished in another way, such as through a part-time employee or a contractor?

Why is it important that employees have a full job? Companies want to spend their resources wisely — human resources can be costly. Your organization wants to make sure it is spending its HR dollars appropriately by hiring individuals who are necessary to the effective operation of the firm. Hiring additional staff — or replacing an employee who is leaving the company — is often a knee-jerk reaction. Taking the time to thoroughly evaluate the need for the position will benefit the company.

Here is an example.

The manager of an HR department requested two additional staff members. The department was doing so much that it could no longer provide effective HR services. The CEO refused the request, declaring that there would be no hiring. He told the HR manager to find ways to get things done with the current staff.

The HR staff were forced to reevaluate what they were doing. They identified two types of tasks: essential activities and requests received by others. These requests often were not essential and, members of the HR department felt, added no value for customers. Ultimately, they found that more than 50 percent of their activities were being conducted for other departments or did not have to be done at all. Based on this analysis, they decided not to add staff.

When considering whether to fill a position, ask the following questions:

- How does this position add measurable value to the product or service provided to the customer?
- If the position were not filled, how would the work be accomplished?
- Who could accomplish the required tasks, with or without some modification or accommodation?

Hire People Who Meet the Essential Qualifications of the Job

When staffing any position, your goal should be to find the best fit possible. That means finding someone who falls neither too far below nor too far above the requirements of the position.

Research and experience have shown that companies regularly inflate the credentials needed when advertising for positions. In preparing for litigation on an Equal Employment Opportunity Commission case, a legal consultant studied the job advertisements in a major Midwest newspaper. Although the consultant was searching for only a few specific job classifications, approximately 80 percent of the professional positions listed were filled by someone who did not have all the qualifications requested in the published advertisements. Even for hourly workers, where qualifications requested were basic, almost 20 percent of those hired did not have all the qualifications listed.

What does this mean? It means that the companies advertising for the positions asked for more than they really needed. The evidence is in the hire. When an employee whose qualifications are below the minimum required for the position is hired, it is a good indication that the qualifications were inflated. As an HR professional, your challenge is to work with your organization's hiring managers to ensure that the qualifications advertised accurately reflect the requirements of the position.

Strategic Staffing Plan

The development of a strategic HR staffing plan, tied to the organization's strategic plan, should outline your strategy for recruitment and retention, including such elements as compensation strategy, geographic market for recruitment, philosophy on recruitment from within versus recruiting from external sources, whether new hires will be sought from your own industry or whether you will encourage candidates from other industries, the role of the HR professional and the hiring manager in the recruitment process, and commitment to maintaining a diverse workforce.

Your strategic HR staffing plan should encompass these five key areas:

1. *Organization chart.* The organization chart should support your strategic plan, ensuring that departments and work teams are able to work together effectively and that staff are placed within appropriate workgroups. When organizations are poorly structured, resources may be wasted through ineffective reporting and communication channels, internal competition between workgroups, and so on.

2. *Job analysis and job descriptions.* Job analysis allows you to consider the need for a specific position, the critical functions of the position, and consequently the skills and knowledge required to support those functions. The job description outlines, specifically, the duties of the position.

3. *Workforce analysis and career paths.* Succession planning has been elevated to greater importance in organizations as baby boomers age and prepare to move out of the workforce. Examining your workforce needs — current and future — is an important part of the staffing process. What skills, knowledge, and abilities will your organization need as it changes and grows to meet the demands of a changing marketplace? What skills, knowledge, and abilities currently exist in the organization? Where are the gaps?

4. *Promotion from within.* Promoting from within can be a good way to reward employees and can be a boon for morale and commitment. It is not always possible, though, particularly in very small companies, to find the necessary talent within. At times, it may be necessary to go outside the organization for staff members. Clearly identifying your organization's strategy in this area and communicating that strategy internally can help avoid miscommunication and hard feelings when existing employees are overlooked for promotion.

5. *Strategic objectives, diversity, and turnover.* An examination of your workforce will help you identify areas where you are at risk to lose key employees (e.g., impending retirements) and can also point out issues related to diversity — or the lack thereof — among your workforce.

For the purposes of this discussion, this process is much simplified. The development of a strategic HR staffing plan is a lengthy and involved process requiring careful research and analysis, and requiring the involvement of a number of individuals throughout the organization. While it is appropriate for the HR professional to lead this process, it is not a process that should be undertaken without the involvement of other key professionals in the organization — or without the support and buy-in of the organization's CEO and top management.

Implementation of the plan also requires the partnership of many people throughout the organization — in particular, management staff. A close relationship between the HR department and the management function of the organization is critical to an effective recruiting, selection, and retention process.

The Legal Side of Hiring

In recruiting and selection, a company needs to be aware of the legal issues. Federal employment regulations affect most employment practices. In addition, HR professionals must be aware of the state and local laws that regulate recruitment, selection, hiring, and promotion. The primary focus of these laws is on preventing discrimination in employment and HR actions and on discouraging unfair work practices. As an HR professional, you should be very familiar with these laws — you have a critical role in helping your organization avoid legal liability. In addition, you need to take steps to ensure that hiring managers are aware of the laws that affect their role in the hiring process. This can be accomplished through training and education and also through the development of proscriptive hiring processes designed to guide managers through the recruitment and selection process and offering practical suggestions.

The following is an overview of the relevant federal legislation affecting the hiring process (additional details are provided in Appendix B):

- The **Fair Labor Standards Act (FLSA) of 1938** regulates the status of employees (versus independent contractors) and provides for a minimum wage and overtime unless the employee is exempt.
- The **Equal Pay Act of 1963**, an amendment to the FLSA, prohibits wage discrimination on the basis of sex.
- The **Age Discrimination in Employment Act of 1967** prohibits discrimination in employment for persons 40 and older.
- **Title VII of the Civil Rights Act of 1964** prohibits discrimination in all terms and conditions of employment (including pay and benefits) on the basis of race, color, religion, sex, or national origin. It requires that all persons of the same skills, seniority, and background be treated similarly.
- The **1978 Uniform Guidelines on Employee Selection Procedures** —

guidelines for carrying out Title VII of the Civil Rights Act — state that selection policies or practices that have an adverse impact on the employment opportunities for any race, sex, or ethnic group are considered discriminatory, and therefore illegal, unless business necessity can justify them. It defines "adverse impact."

- The **Fair Credit Reporting Act of 1970** governs the use of consumer reports and investigative consumer reports in all employment decisions.
- The **Vocational Rehabilitation Act of 1973** prevents employment discrimination against people who have physical or mental disabilities.
- The **Privacy Act of 1974** prohibits federal agencies from revealing certain information without permission from employees.
- The **Immigration and Naturalization Act of 1966** covers the hiring of resident aliens and new or prospective immigrants. Under a more recent law, the **Immigration Reform and Control Act of 1986**, every U.S. employer must require new hires to provide specific documents showing that they are who they claim to be and that they have the legal right to work in the United States. The burden of verifying that a new employee is eligible to work in the United States falls on the employer.
- The **Americans with Disabilities Act of 1990** and its subsequent amendments in 2008 protect qualified individuals with disabilities from unlawful discrimination in employment, public services and transportation, public accommodations, and telecommunication services. Discrimination is prohibited against a qualified individual with a disability if he or she can perform the essential job functions with or without a reasonable accommodation.
- The **Drug-Free Workplace Act of 1988**, amended by the Federal Acquisition Streamlining Act of 1994, mandates that firms that do business with the federal government must have written drug-use policies.
- **1965 Executive Order 11246** requires federal contractors and subcontractors and federally assisted construction contractors and subcontractors that generally have contracts exceeding $10,000 to comply with Title VII of the Civil Rights Act of 1964.

In addition to these federal laws, state and municipal regulations also limit employers' discretion in the hiring process.

FAQs

We are concerned about maintaining – and retaining – a productive, highly motivated staff. Where do we begin?

Beverly Kaye and Sharon Jordan-Evans:

Employers need to start treating people like the precious resources our rhetoric says they are. There are few HR or corporate mission statements that do not say something like "our people are precious." Yet people do not feel as though they are precious.

Even when the economy goes bad, a company will still have to keep its talent. And all of working life is about productivity, motivation, and retention. You do not achieve and keep that great workforce by tackling one part of the goal. You do it by working in many areas simultaneously: recognizing and rewarding individuals for good performance, training managers to be good managers, providing the tools that staff need to work effectively, giving employees constructive and timely feedback, living up to corporate commitments, communicating openly and freely, and so on.

How has the economic downturn impacted staffing plans?

Beverly Kaye:

Employees are staying longer, which presents companies with many opportunities. I think some organizations have undervalued their older workers and have some stereotypes or belief systems about them that are proving to be untrue. HR professionals have to invest time and effort in the care and nurturing of their baby boomer employees who are staying longer. These employees bring talent, brain power, skill, wisdom, and know-how, and they also have a very strong institutional memory. I think leaving a legacy is important to them. They can serve as coaches for the younger people in the organization — I think we need to be creative about the career paths inside organizations for the baby boomers and for members of Generation X and Generation Y.

What are the primary factors that retain employees?

Beverly Kaye and Sharon Jordan-Evans:

Most employees who leave did not start looking for other opportunities because of dissatisfaction with pay, perks, or benefits. They started looking elsewhere because of other reasons. The top four factors that influence an employee's decision to stay are these:

- Meaningful, challenging work.
- A chance to learn and grow.
- A good boss.
- The sense of being part of a team.

Recruitment, Selection, and Beginning Employment

A comprehensive recruiting policy can aid your company. Your recruiting policy should take into consideration the organization's unique goals, objectives, market, and culture and should identify your recruitment philosophy. The policy must be based on the qualities needed in every employee and must clearly identify the traits of those individuals who would be viable candidates. In addition, you should have clearly defined recruiting goals and should communicate these goals throughout the company. Obviously, your recruiting policy and goals should be based on your company's strategic plan.

The staffing plan processes described in Chapter 2 will, in turn, drive the specific activities involved in recruiting new staff members.

1. *Recruiting strategies and advertising.* Each company will develop its own unique methods of recruiting staff based on its staffing needs as well as the skills and knowledge available locally. In addition to selecting appropriate vehicles to use when advertising positions, you need to focus on the content of those advertisements, because potential applicants use that content to determine both their qualifications for, and their interest in, the available position. The rapid increase in the use of social media — e.g., Facebook, Twitter, etc. — by the general public has opened up an entirely new resource for HR professionals, representing both opportunities and risks.

2. *Prescreening activities.* These activities will include working with the hiring manager to prepare for the interview process — selecting a hiring team if this is the process used at your company, developing questions based on the requirements of the job, and so forth.

3. *Selection/testing.* Once applications/resumes have been received, they will be evaluated for appropriateness for the position. Candidates who meet the minimum requirements for the position will be contacted for interviews and testing as applicable.

4. *Employment decision.* Again, based on the requirements of the position, as well as the overall HR staffing plan, a selection decision is made.

5. *Offer/offer letter.* The selected candidate is offered the position.

The job of the HR professional is not over after a candidate has been offered a position. What happens *after* the offer has been accepted is as critical as the processes that preceded the offer.

1. *Postemployment testing.* Once the employee is on the job, testing may be required to gauge his or her level of knowledge and understanding of various work processes to determine where additional training and education may be needed.

2. *Orientation process.* The orientation process involves a range of activities, from basic introductions, to review of policies and procedures, to familiarizing the employee with the organization. While the formal orientation may take a few hours or a few days, an employee may require several months to be fully oriented to a new position — acclimated to the culture and understanding how his or her position contributes to the functioning of the company.

3. *Education, training, and development.* Various training and educational activities will occur throughout an employee's tenure with the organization. These activities may involve training specific to the organization (e.g., how to use the organization's data entry system), training specific to the employee's position (e.g., sales training), training on safety or service issues, or training on various soft skills (e.g., working effectively as part of a team, giving and receiving criticism).

4. *Initial employment evaluation.* After a specific period of time with the company, the new employee will be evaluated. This evaluation will be based on the requirements of the position and the employee's success in meeting those requirements and performing effectively in the job.

Feedback and recognition. In addition to the formal evaluation process, the employee should receive feedback and recognition throughout his or her tenure — both formal and informal.

Recruiting Candidates

How should the recruitment process work?

When a position becomes vacant, the HR professional and the hiring manager should review the job description to ensure that it is an accurate reflection of the position and its requirements. Based on this review, they should determine the best methods for recruiting qualified candidates. The hiring manager and human resources should agree on the recruiting strategy and the timetable for filling the position.

The discussion should include a comprehensive review of existing employees who may have the requisite skills or who could be trained to do the job. Content for any advertisements and announcements should be derived directly from the information contained in the job analysis and job description.

There are many sources from which to recruit applicants, depending on the company's recruiting and selection strategies and HR objectives, the level of the vacant position, the number of positions to be filled, the availability of qualified applicants within a reasonable recruiting area, the culture of the company, and the company's employee relations practices.

Advances in technology and the growing use of the Internet have had a marked impact on the traditional recruitment process. No longer are employers relegated to placing advertisements in the local newspaper's classified section — an expensive proposition, particularly if you are recruiting from a wide geographic area or in large metropolitan areas where the costs of advertising, even classified advertising, can be prohibitive. Today, HR professionals can choose from a broad range of recruitment options — still incorporating newspaper advertising if appropriate, but also using their own Internet home pages or online recruitment sites like Monster.com and a variety of other options, such as job fairs, campus recruiting, trade journal ads, and open houses.

In fact, as the use of social media has exploded, popular job sites such as Monster.com have lost some of their allure and traffic as recruiters find themselves able to advertise to and connect with potential job candidates directly.

Two polls conducted by SHRM in January 2001 generated information on how various search tactics are used by HR professionals and job seekers (pulled from the *CareerJournal.com* Job Alert list). The tactic most commonly used by job seekers was Internet job postings (96 percent), followed closely by personal contact/networking and newspaper ads (95 percent each).

HR professionals also relied on newspapers (96 percent), personal contact/networking (95 percent), employee referrals (91 percent), and Internet job postings (88 percent).

When asked to rate the effectiveness of each tactic, 61 percent of HR professionals rated personal contact/networking effective, followed by Internet job postings (58 percent), employee referrals/employee referral program (55 percent), headhunters (54 percent), and newspaper ads (47 percent). Job seekers rated personal contact/networking 78 percent, referrals from employees 65 percent, Internet job postings 48 percent, headhunters 45 percent, and temp-to-hire 43 percent.

A statistical analysis of the data and comparison between the two groups showed that HR professionals rated the following search tactics as significantly *more* effective than job seekers rated them: Internet job postings, headhunters, ads in newspapers, online or web site job applications, Internet advertisements, and employment agencies. Job seekers, on the other hand, rated personal contact/networking, employee referrals/employee referral programs, and places of worship as significantly more effective search tactics than did HR professionals.

Figure 3.1 shows the perceptions of both HR professionals and job seekers when using various job search and recruitment tools.

FIGURE 3.1. HR Professionals' vs. Job Seekers' Perceptions of Search Tool Effectiveness

Tool	HR Professionals		Job Seekers	
	N	Mean⁺	N	Mean⁺
Personal contact/networking	537	3.70*	414	4.07*
Internet job postings	493	3.62*	415	3.20*
Employee referrals/Employee referral program	515	3.51*	398	3.77*
Headhunters	413	3.47*	387	3.21*
Ads in newspapers	534	3.34*	416	2.83*
Online or web site job applications	273	3.21*	394	2.93*
Ads in professional and trade journals	373	3.17	337	3.05*
Internet advertisement (e.g., banners and links)	162	3.04*	295	2.15*
Temp-to-hire (consultant, independent contractor, temporary agency)	419	3.03	283	3.12
Employment agencies	424	3.03*	352	2.78*
Job fairs	391	2.76	331	2.70
Job hotlines	166	2.64	289	2.46
Radio/TV advertising	143	2.57	230	2.28
Minority job fairs	283	2.55	181	2.49
Community organizations	306	2.51	273	2.68
Open houses	203	2.33	300	2.19
Walk-ins	428	2.14	273	2.19
Ads in international newspapers	95	2.13	188	2.31
Places of worship	135	2.04*	206	2.50*
General public postings (supermarkets, movie theaters, etc.)	118	2.00	185	1.95

⁺ Mean ratings based on a scale where 1 is "not all effective" and 5 is "extremely effective."
* Statistically significant based on t-test results p≤0.01.

Source: SHRM/CareerJournal.com Search Tactics Poll.

The key when recruiting, obviously, is to get your message to your audience. If you are not already focusing on those tactics that job seekers view as effective, you may want to think about shifting your strategy slightly. While Internet recruiting can be effective, it may not be wise to focus on it at the exclusion of other, more traditional recruitment efforts.

With the exception of some information technology positions, if the position is hourly, nonexempt, or lower-level management, applicants probably can be found locally. In a small community, it may be appropriate to advertise locally for entry-level secretarial staff, but there may not be a large local supply of engineers, for example. Conversely, while the Internet can be a rich source of job candidates, using the Internet to recruit for secretarial staff when these candidates are readily available locally is not a good use of resources.

Communicating the opening to current employees and their friends and relatives often produces a sufficient number of qualified applicants. Newspaper advertisements may garner additional applicants.

You should exercise caution, however, when using these tactics so that your workforce does not become unbalanced by either gender or race. In discrimination investigations, the Equal Employment Opportunity Commission (EEOC) uses statistics to find probable cause of illegal hiring practices. When there are disparities between the company's workforce composition and available applicants within a reasonable recruiting area, probable cause may exist. Be aware that using referrals from current employees as the *sole* source of applicants can contribute to racial, ethnic, and gender imbalance.

Newspaper advertisements may not result in sufficient applications, especially from minority applicants. The readership of mainstream newspapers in minority neighborhoods is often 10 percent of that in nonminority communities. While some companies advertise in minority publications, often their publishing dates and lead times required are not consistent with a timely recruiting strategy. One way to increase employee diversity in terms of gender, race, national origin, or disability is to work with advocacy groups. Often, nontraditional recruiting sources such as neighborhood newspapers and grocery store bulletin boards are also successful vehicles for recruitment.

The company that is most successful in recruiting good employees locally has a recruiting policy integrated with its employee relations, marketing, and public relations strategies. The company is seen as a good place to work, with excellent people-oriented management, an acceptable pay and benefits package, and — especially in uncertain economic times — stability.

For certain positions, it may be appropriate to advertise outside the local market, perhaps even nationally. These decisions should be made carefully because the costs can be prohibitive, not only in terms of the advertising but also in terms of travel and relocation costs. For many small and emerging companies, the local market is a viable — and cost-effective — source of qualified candidates.

You may also want to consider recruitment or search firms for filling top-level or hard-to-fill positions. This approach can be cost-effective and efficient, especially for specialized professional or technical experts and top management with focused experience. Working with consultants is discussed in Chapter 10.

Online Recruiting

The Internet has changed the way we do business in many ways. We can have virtual storefronts, we can purchase goods and services online, we can interact with colleagues through forums and chat groups — and we can recruit employees.

The Internet offers a vast source of potential job candidates who are easy — and inexpensive — to reach. In addition to placing your job postings on your own Internet site, you will find numerous online recruitment sites you can use. Many sites allow users not only to post ads for open positions but also to search resumes posted online. Some sites also provide information on freelancers, contract workers, and short-term staffing arrangements, as well as helpful information on recruiting.

The best way to become familiar with the recruiting resources available on the Internet is to review the various services yourself, keeping in mind that you want to find one that is most advantageous for you. This may not necessarily be one of the major commercial sites like Monster.com. Smaller, more specialized services may be more appropriate for your needs, depending on the type of position you are attempting to fill. A quick and easy way to find information about the latest job sites online is to conduct a search using one of the many online search engines.

When recruiting online, you need to have the same familiarity with these services that you would have with any technical or professional journal you were advertising in. Who are the users of the site? What are their characteristics? How frequently is the site accessed? How widely does it advertise? Is the profession you are recruiting for well represented?

Determining keywords — the search words that online job seekers will enter to pull up your listing — is a critical and often overlooked skill. You need to tie the appropriate keywords to your ads. And you need to probe to make sure your ads are being coded properly. If you have posted ads and wonder why you are not receiving any inquiries, the coding process may be the culprit. Each search engine is different; you should take the time to learn how each site functions and what sort of patterns there are in putting the keywords together. Knowledge of how terminology is used in the field you are recruiting from is a must.

There are literally thousands of individuals searching online job sites for positions. Just as with any other form of recruitment advertising, while a very general posting may provide you with countless leads, the more specific you can be, the more clearly you can narrow the market to those candidates who are uniquely qualified to fill the positions you have available.

Social Media and Recruitment

As far back as November 2006, National Public Radio had a spot on its Morning Edition show about social networking — (see www.npr.org/templates/story/story. php?storyId=6522523) — and its benefits from a recruiting standpoint. Today, HR professionals are increasingly relying on social media sites for sourcing job candidates and checking credentials. In fact, three-quarters of hiring managers check LinkedIn to research the credentials of job candidates, according to a Jump Start Social Media poll on how social media is being used in the hiring process. Of the hiring managers surveyed, 75 percent use LinkedIn, 48 percent use Facebook, and 26 percent use Twitter to research candidates before making a job offer. Sixty-six percent of hiring managers visit LinkedIn, 23 percent visit Facebook, and 16 percent use Twitter to find job candidates to fill openings.

Raquel Garcia, an HR consultant and president of Silicon Valley Human Resources, says social media offers a number of benefits for recruitment. "You can learn a lot about your potential recruit from their social media pages, and you can find great passive talent online," she says. She has used social media both to source passive job seekers and to check candidates' profiles. She also posts positions she is recruiting for on Facebook and LinkedIn and says she gets "great responses and recommendations."

Jobvite, a San Francisco-based provider of next-generation recruitment solutions, published the results of its second annual Social Recruitment Survey in 2008, which found that employers were more satisfied with the quality of candidates from employee referrals and social networks than those from job boards. As a result, companies intended to invest more in these cost-effective candidate sources in 2009, rather than in job boards and other traditional sources, including search firms, according to the survey.

Because of the low cost of entry — there are no out-of-pocket costs associated with social media recruitment efforts — and constant media buzz about the popular sites, many companies are considering how they might turn to social media for everything from recruitment to marketing.

Time is money, of course. Some of the "fear" surrounding the use of social media is the time that may be required — or diverted — to learn about and "play with" these tools. Consequently, HR professionals considering this option should develop a strategy for their activities to avoid being overwhelmed by the amount of information and options available through these sites.

Lauryn Franzoni is executive director of ExecuNet, an executive business network, and frequently speaks to HR groups on the strengths and weaknesses of social media recruitment strategies.

The first step in using social networks to find staff, says Franzoni, is determining "what you really want to get out of it." She notes that there are "big, broad social networks out there — and there are also niche networks that support participating types of talent and various expertise." And, she notes, there are also company-specific networks.

"If I'm a hiring manager, I have to figure out the characteristics of the staffing we're going to need and how those characteristics match up with social networks." Franzoni says she has found that companies tend to be focused either on entry-level staffing, in which case the broad social networks can be useful, or on more skilled positions, where niche networks can be most helpful.

Much depends on the demographics of the company — and the type of candidates it wishes to recruit.

Social media can be used in three primary ways when recruiting.

- *Posting available jobs.* Franzoni cautions, though, that posting jobs too broadly can negate the social networking benefits of these sites. "If I go out and post a big message somewhere to thousands of people and send it out somewhat indiscriminately, I'm not networking," says Franzoni. "Networking is about really making a meaningful connection with someone. "It's not a numbers game."

- *"Trolling" for potential candidates.* Franzoni notes that the ability to search niche sites, particularly, can be helpful to HR departments and staffing managers who may be overwhelmed by the number of resumes they are receiving. "In today's economy, posting ads tends to get more responses than you can respond to," she says.

- *"Checking out" applicants/interviewees.* The Internet makes it easy to find information about applicants to augment the traditional reference-checking process. But, while the ability to learn about candidates by looking at online networking sites can be helpful, Franzoni recommends caution. "You may miss some very good candidates depending on whether you've been able to assess them on something relevant to the job, or you're rating them on personal characteristics," she says. "As much as we and many others counsel people to be careful about what they have on their profiles, it's proving to provide a lot more ammunition for hiring managers to rule people out — and they may actually be missing some very good candidates."

Patty DeDominic is a former professional recruiter who built, ran, and then sold a multimillion-dollar staffing firm. DeDominic says she recently posted a CEO position for an international organization on LinkedIn and received "quite a few qualified candidate referrals." She offers the following tips for recruiting:

- Communicate your need to a wide audience using every mean possible, including social media, online job boards, professional organizations, certification bodies, and educational/alumni associations.

- Tap into social networks and the people who love to connect and share resources. Referrals are like gold, and people love helping others become more successful.

- Find the connectors and the leaders of the networks. People involved in social networks know who the leaders are. With a few questions to a few active people, you can usually determine who are the connectors and leaders.

- Look for people who stand out. People who have spent years building their skills and professional reputations write and publish their findings and often their opinions. Their reputations and "networks" tell more about them than you can learn in five interviews.

15 Tips for Creative Recruitment

When it comes to recruiting high-caliber employees, small businesses are at a definite disadvantage. Often unable to offer the big benefits and top salaries of their larger competitors — and unwilling to spend substantial dollars on recruitment costs — they find their applicant pools shrinking, even when unemployment rates are rising. What to do? There are a number of creative recruitment techniques that small businesses have found successful — from job fairs, to employee referral bonuses, to creative public relations that are low-cost/no-cost and easy to implement.

1. *Existing applicants.* Many companies have a steady stream of off-the-street applicants who fill out applications expressing general interest in working for the company. Too often, though, these applications find their way into a filing cabinet, never to be retrieved again. Even if you do not have the resources to purchase a sophisticated applicant tracking system, you can set up a simple database on your computer to help keep track of applications received. Including fields for "date received," "job interest," "special skills," "education," and so forth will allow you to search and retrieve applicants easily when you are trying to fill a specific position. While you are building this database, also consider how you communicate with the applicants who contact you. These people are hot prospects. Do you follow up with them? Do you maintain contact? Do you inform them when positions open up that they are qualified for?

2. *Your employees.* Recruiting internal candidates for open positions offers a number of benefits, including the positive impact on staff morale. A well-organized succession planning process can help you identify talent within your organization and use that talent effectively.

3. *Friends of friends.* Do your existing employees know which positions you have

a difficult time filling? Do they have an understanding of how tight the labor market is? Do they recognize ways that they can help you identify potential applicants and fill those tough positions? Too often, HR departments fail to communicate with the staff at large about the challenges they face. Your employees can represent a ready source of recruiters — all you need to do is make sure they know what you are looking for and understand your recruitment and selection process — an easy task, but one that is far too often overlooked.

4. *General media.* You may have a steady relationship with the classified ad rep at your local newspaper. But how often do you communicate with the editorial staff? Articles about your company and its employment practices can provide you with good exposure and help build your image as a great place to work. Consider contacting the media about any special benefits your company may provide (e.g., on-site day care, concierge services), about your employees' involvement in community events, about any unique employee activities that you sponsor, or about tie-ins to national media issues related to HR. This exposure can help augment your other paid efforts to inform the public about your company.

5. *Job hotline.* A toll-free job hotline can be a good way to share information about job openings. The hotline number can be included in all of your recruitment materials, on your Internet site, and on business cards.

6. *Internet.* Even if you do not have a web site, you can take advantage of the many job sites on the World Wide Web. While you may not be looking for national applicants for every open position, certain positions (sales or information systems, for instance) may readily lend themselves to Internet recruitment. If you do have a web site, do some research to see whether your site could be linked to association sites that fit your recruitment efforts.

7. *Trade and lifestyle publications.* If you recruit through classified ads, look beyond your local newspaper. In addition to trade publications that appeal to various employment segments, there are a number of lifestyle or general publications that may target just the type of candidate you are looking for.

8. *Schools.* Area schools can be a great source of applicants — from high schools to technical colleges to universities. You may already have relationships with these institutions, but are you taking advantage of every opportunity to build strong relationships with students? Do representatives from your company regularly make career presentations? Are you involved in internship or school-to-work programs? Do you advertise job openings in school publications? Provide job postings for school bulletin boards? Attend job fairs at the schools? These efforts take time and resources, and results may be difficult to measure, but over time a strong relationship can help build your company's image — and your applicant pool.

9. *Job fairs.* Job fairs are becoming more popular as the labor market becomes more competitive. Be creative when you attend these fairs. Do not just show up. Consider ways you can engage attendees, capture their interest, and make a lasting impression. Arrange for mini-interviews on-site, or offer career counseling. Do not lose the information you gather here. Add it to your database of potential candidates for future follow-up.

10. *Open houses.* You do not have to wait for a job fair. Hold your own open house to attract candidates. An open house provides you with the opportunity to show off your organization and to gain the undivided attention of interested applicants. As with a job fair, be creative and make sure you are providing value to those who attend.

11. *Other employers.* Sometimes the problem is not getting applicants — it is getting the right applicants. An applicant who is not right for your firm, though, may be just the person a colleague down the street is looking for. Consider ways you can partner with other area businesses to share applicant information or make referrals.

12. *Word-of-mouth.* When you have an open position, or a particularly difficult area of recruitment, talk it up! Sometimes referrals can come from the most unexpected sources.

13. *Rejected applicants.* An applicant who was not right for one position may be perfect for another. But if you do not have a good mechanism for gathering and tracking data, these applicants can slip through the cracks. Make sure you have a reliable way of gathering and sharing information on all potential hires.

14. *Temporary services.* The temporary market is growing rapidly as more and more employees take advantage of the opportunity to try out various jobs. Employers can benefit, too, from trying out employees before they hire. While agencies have restrictions on exactly what you can and cannot do in terms of recruiting temporary staff, these individuals can be a rich recruitment source.

15. *Your customers.* Your frequent customers could be more than customers — they could be employees. Retail businesses often post "help wanted" signs, but other businesses can take advantage of this applicant pool as well.

Preparing the Advertisement

When recruiting to fill a position, you are, in essence, selling a product. That product is your company. Your goal with any recruitment ad, whether it appears in the classified section of your local paper, on your web site, or in a national trade journal, is to do the following:

- Accurately describe the position so that only qualified and appropriate applicants will respond.
- Present the benefits of both the position and the organization to attract as many of these qualified and appropriate applicants as possible.

Knowing what you want is critical. This involves a review of the job analysis, the job description, and the qualitative traits and characteristics of the type of individual who will fit your organization's culture. To determine these traits, consider your existing top employees. What are the traits that make them successful in your organization? Why does management consider them to be good employees? These qualitative traits are as important as the more quantitative job requirements outlined in the job description, and they should be included in the ad.

Your recruitment ad is selling the organization as well as the position. In a competitive labor market, you are competing against other organizations for scarce employee resources. Your ad should provide some indication of why applicants should want to work for you instead of for another company.

Consider also that your company is known by its products, services, and service — to customers and to the community. If your company is known within the field in which you are recruiting as a good place to work, your recruitment efforts will be boosted.

Above all, be honest in your recruitment ads. Do not oversell the position or the company. Recruitment is just the first phase of what you hope will become a long-term relationship. Turnover rates will rise if candidates are not fully aware of the true nature of the job, the organization, or its expectations.

Application Forms

Application forms are important documents. Every applicant for every position should be required to fill out and sign an application form. Because of the exposure to employee relations litigation and civil rights lawsuits, the application form should not be taken lightly. The primary value of the application form is that it requests and documents consistent information across all applicants. Unlike resumes, which vary widely in terms of the information included, application forms ensure consistency and provide a tool for gathering the information you need for both practical and legal reasons. For example, the application form may be your only source of information on the applicant's salary history.

In developing or selecting an application form, use caution in the type of information requested. For example, the form should not seek information about marital status, parental status, day care arrangements, or past workers' compensation claims.

All of this information could be used as evidence of discrimination. Information that is not specifically job related should not be requested on an application.

A model application form is included at the end of this chapter (Sample 1). SHRM also publishes a book of application forms that contains many examples for use by companies of all sizes. When choosing or developing an application form, select one that focuses entirely on job-related information that is required for the initial screening process. Once the number of applicants has been narrowed to those who meet the minimum qualifications, additional information can be requested.

The Hiring Process

Step 1: Developing Hiring Criteria

Before you can effectively and objectively review applications and resumes, you need to determine the criteria against which each applicant will be evaluated. This is a relatively simple process based on a review of the job analysis and job description, as well as the recruitment advertising that has been done. If you are recruiting a salesperson to sell computer components, for instance, the criteria might include these:

- Sales experience.
- Knowledge of computer components.
- Ability to work effectively with internal resources.
- Demonstrated ability to sell products in the computer industry.
- Demonstrated ability to process paperwork and handle administrative duties.

For each of the criteria developed, you might apply a ranking. For example, sales experience may be more important to the organization than the ability to handle administrative duties.

It is important, though, that you and the hiring manager take the time to complete this important step. It helps streamline the process and also ensures that your decisions are based on solid, job-related criteria.

Step 2: Reviewing the Application or Resume and Cover Letter

Developing Objective Criteria. Applications and resumes play different roles in the recruiting and selection process. Traditionally, companies want resumes, in addition to an application form, for professional positions, while they may use standard applications alone, in lieu of a resume, for hourly and nonexempt positions. The resume is a marketing tool for the applicant. If written well, it emphasizes the strengths of the applicant for the particular position while minimizing weaknesses and avoiding embarrassing topics or problem areas. Because applications provide the information in a more rigid form, they can be useful in identifying gaps in employment history, problem areas, and educational weaknesses. In addition to requesting a resume, it is a good HR practice to require applications even of applicants for professional positions.

Once specific minimum selection criteria have been determined, reviewing both resumes and applications is relatively easy. Remember, the essential job functions must be identified as well as the minimum criteria and the optional characteristics. This process will help focus attention on who should be hired. Keep in mind that the perfect candidate is seldom found.

A helpful first step, in consultation with the hiring manager, is to develop a simple grid or rating sheet that can be used to evaluate applications. Each applicant should be rated against the criteria you developed in Step 1. These criteria will include both the quantitative requirements of the position as outlined in the job description and any qualitative criteria you may have identified as critical for successful employees with your company. The rating sheet might look like the example provided in Sample 2 at the end of this chapter. Listed down the left-hand side of the form are the criteria you developed. Listed across the top of the form are individual candidates. Based on a simple scale of 1 to 5, you and the hiring manager could rate each candidate on these characteristics.

If desired, requirements could be weighted according to individual importance for the position. For instance, education might be valued twice as much as experience, or vice versa. The key is to develop a method of evaluation that helps to quantify the process and remove, as much as possible, the potential for subjective bias. The form is a good way to ensure that the focus for selection remains on the skills, knowledge, and abilities required for that specific job. A similar form would be used during the interview process. Results of the analysis help you narrow the number of candidates under consideration and also provide a basis of comparison across multiple raters.

Reviewing the Cover Letter. In addition to the objective criteria you will be considering when evaluating job candidates, there are some subjective considerations that can affect the decision whether to interview a specific candidate. Cover letters, for instance, can provide insight into an applicant's attitudes and abilities to do the job. The following questions can be helpful to ask yourself when reviewing cover letters:

- If the cover letter is the traditional kind (a paper copy sent by standard mail or hand-delivered), is it clean and typed or computer-prepared (not handwritten)? If sent electronically, is it well-designed and free of errors?
- Is it clean and specifically tailored to your organization?
- Is it addressed to a specific person in your organization, indicating that the applicant has taken the time to do some basic research on your company?
- Are the spelling and grammar correct?
- Does it clearly highlight the applicant's qualifications for the position?
- Is it persuasive, highlighting why the candidate would be a good fit with your organization and conveying the candidate's enthusiasm?

Reviewing the Resume. Like the cover letter, the resume can provide information that can be useful in narrowing the field of candidates. Along with the application form, you can use it to complete a form like the one in Sample 2. In general, a well-researched and well-written resume suggests a strong candidate. Conversely, a poorly written resume, despite experience and skills, suggests a poor candidate. In addition to a review based specifically on the position criteria, you might gain insight from the answers to the following questions:

- Are the spelling and grammar correct?
- Did the applicant anticipate a need for the pertinent data and provide them in the resume?
- Is the information presented easy to understand?
- Does the applicant meet the minimum educational requirements for the job? Consider only relevant, job-related educational qualifications. Check educational qualifications.
- Is there a list of significant accomplishments? Be cautious of lists of easily performed tasks or phrases, such as "involved in" or "part of."
- How long did the applicant hold each position? Are the titles valid?
- Does the applicant meet the minimum experience requirements for the job? Does the resume show how this experience fits your company's needs? Are the skills and accountabilities transferable?
- Is other information relevant to the job included, such as college activities, community involvement, awards, hobbies, and participation in sports? Consider only those items that have relevance to the position being applied for.

Reviewing the Application. When every candidate completes the same application form, comparisons are easier. Again, as with resumes, the reviewer should have a clear understanding of what the job entails. At this step, be sure to look for the minimum job qualifications, not necessarily the applicant with the most proficiency. Consider the following:

- *Clarity:* How clear are the answers to the questions? Did the applicant rush through the form or take time to do it right? Were the questions answered with relevant information?
- *Legibility:* Can the handwriting be read and does it fit within the lines? Are there a lot of erasures or mistakes? Was care taken to keep the application clean and neat?
- *Experience:* Does the experience listed match the experience required for the job? How is it explained? Can you get a good idea of the person's duties and responsibilities from the description? Does it sound reasonable?
- *Education:* As with experience, check for validity and credibility. Are the courses and degrees consistent with what you are looking for? Only education that is job related should be considered. Check/verify educational qualifications.

The Applicant Evaluation Form (Sample 2), included at the end of this chapter, is only an example and should be revised for use by your own company.

Step 3: Interviewing

The interview is a critical part of the hiring process. Your role as an HR professional is to provide hiring managers with the training, tools, and support they need to ensure that the interview is handled appropriately and professionally. This training may take place in group sessions or one-on-one, depending on the specific needs of your organization. For instance, a manager with little turnover would probably benefit most from training and coaching provided at the time a position needs to be filled. Managers who have more frequent hiring needs might benefit from a formal training session in addition to one-on-one coaching.

Procedures for employment interviewing vary according to the needs of the company and the level of hire. Some companies use a process in which an HR staff person conducts the prescreening and preliminary selection. The immediate supervisor then conducts interviews (sometimes with other managers or an HR professional) and makes the final decision. This approach can result in the hiring of an acceptable employee, but it offers limited opportunities for others within the organization to be involved in the process and consequently more committed to the hiring decision.

Many companies have been successful using a team approach to hiring, even with entry-level employees. For high-level and managerial positions, the team approach is especially useful. The ability to work well within the organization and to interact with a variety of people is important with these positions, and team interviews not only allow more people to be involved but also offer an opportunity to observe the candidate in an interactive setting. Each team member should rank each candidate based on the criteria developed in Step 1 and using a form adapted for your company from Sample 2. Candidates should be evaluated or compared with the criteria and not with each other. For this reason, it is a good idea to refrain from discussing any of the candidates until all interviews have been completed. Then rankings may be shared, individual opinions expressed, and a finalist selected.

The typical interview consists of questions about the applicant's work history, education, desires, and skills. Questions should be developed to obtain information that is directly related to the hiring criteria, and each candidate should be judged against the same criteria.

Managers and HR professionals are obviously concerned about hiring people who have the skills and experience to meet the needs of the job. In addition, hiring managers and HR staff are concerned about the fit of a candidate and look for specific behavioral traits such as the ability to interact effectively with others or the ability to handle stress and conflict. These traits can be identified and evaluated during the interview process through a behavioral interviewing model.

Behavioral interviewing is based on the assumption that past performance is a good indicator of future performance. In behavioral interviewing, instead of asking job candidates what they might do when faced with a particular situation, interviewers ask for examples of how they have handled certain situations. For example, if you have determined that the ability to work effectively as part of a team is a requirement of the position, you might use a behavior-based interview approach to develop questions such as these:

- Tell me about a time when you worked as part of a team.
- Thinking of a time that you were involved in a team effort, tell me about your role on the team and the part you played in the success of the project.
- What are some things you enjoy about being part of a team?
- What are some things that you find challenging about being part of a team?
- Give me an example of a time when you were not really sure about the goal of your task. What did you do about it?
- Give me an example of a time when you had to confront someone who was a peer.

These kinds of questions can be used to determine whether candidates have the right skills to fit the company's culture.

The purpose of the interview is twofold: to provide the company with an opportunity to evaluate the candidate and to provide the candidate with an opportunity to evaluate the company. Be prepared to share with the candidate information about the position and the company. Present the job accurately to convey a realistic picture of both the positive and the negative aspects of the job.

Prospective employees are also likely to have questions for you. For instance,

- What are my work hours?
- What time do I need to report to work?
- Will I be expected to work overtime? To work evenings? Weekends?
- Will I need to travel? How often? Will I be expected to make my own travel arrangements?
- What if a business trip interferes with my personal or family plans?
- How flexible are my work hours? If I need to take time off to attend a child's school event or take my dog to the vet, can I do that?

Additional Tips and Suggestions.
- Identify the questions that candidates will be asked and write them down. Ask the same questions of all applicants.
- Consider the setting; provide a quiet location free from interruptions that puts the applicant at ease.

- Tell the applicant that you will be taking notes. Do not be so focused on your note-taking, though, that you fail to make eye contact or fail to demonstrate interest in what the candidate has to say.
- Let the applicant do the talking. Do not dominate the discussion. The 80/20 rule applies — let the applicant do 80 percent of the talking.
- Maintain control of the interview and stay within the allocated time.
- Probe incomplete responses. If you do not feel that the candidate has adequately answered a question, ask for clarification.
- At the end of the interview, sell the company, but do not oversell the position. It is important to be honest with the candidate about the requirements of the job and the culture of the organization. Your goal is to make a hiring decision that will be beneficial for both the organization and the new employee.
- Write an interview summary or complete your evaluation form immediately after the interview.
- Maintain consistency when making hiring decisions. Review the recruitment and selection process to ensure that it meets affirmative action and equal employment opportunity requirements.
- Be able to document and explain the hiring decision. If you can clearly describe the reasons for the decision, it is likely that good selection practices were used.
- Use applicant evaluation forms to guide and document the decision-making process.
- Select one or two back-up candidates and do not send rejection letters to these candidates until an offer has been accepted. It is possible that your first choice, for whatever reasons, will decline the position and you will want to be able to make an offer to another qualified candidate.
- Move the process along as efficiently as possible. If a hiring decision is delayed, the first choice may take advantage of another opportunity and no longer be available.
- Respond to every applicant who has been interviewed, even if it was just a phone screening. If eliminated, the applicant should be notified as quickly as possible about his or her status in the interview process.

Questions to Avoid Asking. The information provided in Figure 3.2 is based on federal law and general practice; state and local laws may vary. In general, federal and state laws and regulations applying to equal employment opportunity prohibit inquiries that express, directly or indirectly, any preference, limitation, specification, or discrimination as to race, religion, color, national origin, sex, age, disability or handicap, marital status, sexual orientation, citizenship, or pregnancy. In most cases, you will be in compliance with these guidelines if you focus exclusively on questions that are specifically related to the requirements of the position. Check carefully in your state and local area for statutes that may give applicants other rights or that may limit your discretion in asking questions. The most basic advice: If it is not job related, do not ask!

The questions you ask should be directly tied to the specific requirements of the job. While it can be helpful to review sample questions as idea generators, make sure the questions you select are consistent for all candidates and are designed to elicit information from the candidate that will help you make the most informed decision possible.

FIGURE 3.2. Interview Questions

Subject	You may ask:	You should not ask:
Race or color		Anything, including about complexion or color of skin.
Religion or creed	Here are the time and work requirements of the position. Apart from religious observations, is there any reason that you cannot meet these requirements?	About religious denomination, religious affiliation, church, synagogue, parish, pastor, rabbi, or religious holidays observed.
National origin		About lineage, ancestry, national origin, descent, parentage, nationality, or nationality of parents or spouse.
Sex		No questions or inquiries are permitted.
Marital status		About marital status, living arrangements, spouse's occupation, children, child care arrangements.
Name		Have you changed your name? What is your maiden name? Have you worked under another name?
Age	If state child protective and safety laws apply, you may ask if the applicant is over that minimum age.	No other questions or inquiries are permitted. (*Certain public sector occupations may have bona fide age requirements.*)
Disability	Here are the job requirements of the position. Do you know of any reason why you cannot perform all the essential functions of the job with or without reasonable accommodation?	Do you have a disability? Have you ever been treated for the following diseases...? How many days were you out sick last year? What prescription drugs are you taking? Can you perform this job ___ with or ___ without reasonable accommodation (check one)?
Birthplace		About applicant's birthplace or the birthplace of spouse, parents, or other relatives.
Photograph		An applicant may not be asked to affix a photograph to an application or a resume at any time before actual employment.
Citizenship	Can you, after you are hired, verify your legal right to work in the United States?	Are you a U.S. citizen? In what country do you have citizenship? Are you a naturalized U.S. citizen? When did you become a citizen?
Criminal history	Were you ever convicted of a felony? (*This question can be asked only if the inquiry is job related and there is a significant business necessity.*)	Were you ever arrested? If so, when, where, and what was the disposition? How many traffic tickets have you received? Were you ever convicted of a non-felony? (*This question may be asked in some states; check your state law.*)

FIGURE 3.2. Interview Questions, continued

Subject	You may ask:	You should not ask:
Language	What foreign languages do you read fluently? Write fluently? Speak fluently? Do you speak and write English fluently? (Ask only if job related.)	How did you learn to speak (foreign language)? Do you speak (foreign language) at home? How did you acquire the ability to speak (foreign language)?
Education	About academic, vocational, or professional education or private schools attended.	Did your parents pay for your education? Did they help you pay for your education? Are your parents college graduates? When did you attend college? (Dates may provide information about applicant's age.)
Experience	About applicant's work history, experience, strengths,and weaknesses, and about any relevant unpaid/volunteer experience.	
Relatives	Do you have any relatives employed by this company	Names, addresses, ages, number, or other information on children or other relatives not employed by the company.
Military experience	(This area is not clear because some case law has found that using military service or type of discharge may have a disparate impact on minority service people. It is advisable to use military service as work experience.)	General questions about the applicant's military experience. id you receive anything other than an honorable discharge? Are you currently on reserve status?
Organizations	Are you a member of any professional organization that is relevant to the position for which you are applying?	About the clubs, societies, and organizations of which the applicant is a member.

+ Mean ratings based on a scale where 1 is "not all effective" and 5 is "extremely effective."
* Statistically significant based on t-test results p≤0.01.

Source: SHRM/CareerJournal.com Search Tactics Poll.

Step 4: Reference and Other Background Checks

Reference Checking. It has been estimated that as many as one-third of all job candidates alter their resumes or misrepresent their qualifications when applying for a job. Reference and background checks play a crucial role in the selection process, and you should always make the necessary checks for every employee hired.

Employers may be liable for negligent hiring if they fail to investigate an applicant's background adequately and, as a result, hire someone who commits crimes or other wrongful acts on the job. Employers need to make diligent efforts to obtain references on every employee hired in order to help prevent staffing disasters and negligent-hiring lawsuits.

Beyond the legal issues involved, reference checking is an important function of finding the best person for the position you are filling. The amount of screening necessary depends on the position and how critical it is to the smooth operation of your company.

Sample 3, at the end of this chapter, provides an example of a form that can be used in the reference-checking process.

Unfortunately, former employers face difficult issues in giving references and often are reluctant to provide information beyond employment dates, job titles, and ending salary. The following tips can help streamline the reference-checking process and increase the chances that the information you receive is valid and useful:

- Get from the applicant a signed permission to check references and a waiver of liability for the reference-giver. This can be done on the application form through a statement such as: "I authorize (company name) to make a thorough investigation of all statements contained in this application about my past employment, education, and other activities, and I release from liability all persons, companies, and corporations supplying such information."

- Have the applicant make the necessary arrangements for you to talk with the references that you chose. References may be more forthcoming when the applicant makes the initial request.

- Conduct a thorough reference check. Contact all references for a prospective employee. Never check just one reference. You want a total picture of the job applicant — one that will help spot both consistencies and inconsistencies. Ask each person you contact to provide you with additional names of people you should speak with.

- Always ask only for job-related information — even when talking with a personal reference. The collection of non-job-related information may provide the basis for a discrimination charge.

- Check references by telephone or even in person rather than using e-mail or form letters. A telephone call or in-person visit provides the advantage of listening to or observing the individual's response and can yield valuable information. In addition, direct contact is more efficient — few employers have the luxury of delaying the hiring process while mailing out and waiting for written responses, even if done via e-mail.

- Contact former supervisors rather than HR staff. Supervisors usually are more able and willing to discuss a former employee's performance. If you contact the line department and are referred to human resources, try the department again. (But be aware that many companies do not allow anyone — especially line supervisors — except trained staff to give company references.)

- Contact someone who has worked as a colleague with the applicant. Call the personal references listed on the application. People will often share valuable information after you have developed rapport with them. But remember to limit your questions to job-related information.

- Ask simple, nonthreatening questions before you inquire about job performance and potentially sensitive areas such as reasons for leaving and problem behaviors.

- Ask open-ended questions that encourage detailed responses, rather than those that elicit a brief answer such as yes or no.
- Offer to provide a hesitant reference-giver with a copy of the applicant's signed authorization and waiver of liability.
- Document the information you receive in writing. When and how did you obtain the information? Who gave you the information and what, specifically, did the individual say?

Educational Credentials. It is not uncommon for applicants to exaggerate their educational credentials. Although many companies check these credentials for professional and management positions, you need to make a value judgment about whether it is worth the time and effort involved. Some educational institutions will release graduation information only at the written request of the applicant. The longer an applicant has been in the workforce, the less relevant his or her education may be as a qualification for the position. However, knowing whether the applicant was truthful about his or her credentials could be worth the effort.

Fair Credit Reporting Act of 1970 and State Credit-Check Laws. If you feel it is necessary to use an outside agency or nonemployee to check an applicant's credit history and financial status or any other background information, the Fair Credit Reporting Act requires that you inform the applicant in writing that an inquiry will be conducted. You must also let applicants know if they are denied employment because of information obtained during the inquiry and you must provide the name and address of the third party who investigated them. Be cautious in the use of background checks. These checks must be in response to valid job-related requirements. Blanket credit checks of all employees might be found illegal if they are not job related, especially if the results show an adverse impact on protected classes.

State credit-check laws may impose additional obligations on companies using credit reports for employment purposes.

Background Checks. Many companies use agencies to conduct background checks of applicants. But with a few exceptions (e.g., high-level management positions, child care workers), the cost may not justify the results. In addition, the form used by these agencies often asks for information that could be considered evidence of discrimination or a violation of the Americans with Disabilities Act (ADA). Consider carefully any decision to use background checks as part of an employment screening process. Seek advice from knowledgeable HR practitioners, consultants, or an employee relations attorney.

Step 5: Physical Examination and Testing

This section provides some general information on testing and the types of tests that HR professionals commonly use. Only you and your company can decide whether testing is appropriate for you and whether to use tests as part of the selection process.

Testing as a selection method is popular with managers and HR professionals. The business community likes to include physical and psychological screening among its hiring tools. Whatever the reason a company decides to test, a clearly defined policy and a comprehensive plan need to be developed. Inconsistent application of the policy can alienate applicants and employees and put your company at risk for possible litigation and fines. Before you consider testing, you should get advice and direction from knowledgeable HR practitioners, consultants, or an employee relations attorney.

Preemployment Medical Examinations. Since the enactment of the ADA, it has been unlawful to require an applicant to submit to a medical examination until after a real offer of employment has been made. The offer can, however, be conditioned on the passing of a medical examination. A job offer is "real" if the employer has evaluated all relevant nonmedical information that it reasonably could have obtained and analyzed before it made the job offer to the applicant. In addition, companies are required to make "reasonable accommodation" for an applicant's disability unless that accommodation would cause an "undue business hardship." Post-offer medical examinations that are job related and that constitute a business necessity are lawful and can be very useful. An applicant with a disability that cannot be accommodated does not have to be hired.

A medical exam that is conducted after an offer but before the start of work can be used as evidence of preexisting health problems (e.g., hearing loss) for which the employer would not be liable under workers' compensation laws. Such physical examinations also can identify preexisting, work-related disabilities that in most states are covered by a "second injury fund." If a worker with such a disability is injured anew on the job, the employer must pay only for treatment for the new injury. The remainder of the benefits are paid from the second injury fund.

Drug and Alcohol Testing. For the most part, employers are not required to conduct drug screens, except for employees involved in commercial transportation and subject to Department of Transportation regulations and for government contractors who are subject to the Drug-Free Workplace Act. State laws may govern drug and alcohol testing, however, so be sure to check with the appropriate state office. Drug testing can be legally conducted before a conditional offer of employment, but alcohol testing is considered a medical exam and may not be conducted until after a conditional offer has been made. Most employers using both drug screening and medical examinations combine the two and conduct them after a conditional offer of employment.

If you decide to conduct drug screening, you must notify applicants and employees of your intention. If company management does not see the value of screening or is not committed to it, you should avoid conducting these tests. The courts have generally upheld the legality of drug and alcohol testing conducted after a conditional offer but before employment. Less clear but also generally upheld is mandatory testing for cause, especially as part of safety and accident prevention programs. The practice of random testing is the one most open to questions and objections from employees. Before you consider drug and alcohol screening, seek advice from knowledgeable HR practitioners, consultants, or an employee relations attorney; develop a comprehensive plan; and discuss the process with employees.

Honesty Screening. The Employee Polygraph Protection Act of 1988 was passed in response to abuses by employers using the polygraph both for employment screening and to determine the honesty of employees. The Act restricts most employers from using lie detector tests without reasonable suspicion of workplace theft or other misconduct. The Act recognizes that such tests are unreliable and often inaccurate.

In response, employers began using paper-and-pencil honesty tests in which applicants or employees write responses and make signed statements about their behaviors and values. Accuracy has been the main controversy with these tests — in fact, these examinations have been found unreliable and inaccurate. The test developers and publishers contend that there is a correlation between test findings and performance on the job and personal honesty, but the courts have routinely discounted the relationship and ruled against companies that use them.

The EEOC's Uniform Selection Guidelines ("the Guidelines") require that each instrument a company uses be validated for use in that particular company. An instrument used by one company with no adverse impact may have an adverse impact in another company, even if it is used on a similar workforce applicant base. If the use of a particular selection device results in adverse impact, the company may not use the instrument unless the selection device, the process, or its component procedures have been validated in accordance with the Guidelines, or the user otherwise justifies them in accordance with federal law.

A company should consider carefully before it uses these instruments and should seek professional human resource and legal advice.

Handwriting Analysis. Handwriting analysis has been popular in Europe and is slowly gaining acceptance in the United States. It involves a review of the physical characteristics of an applicant's handwriting compared with that of other individuals. As with other paper-and-pencil instruments, the courts have found little evidence of a correlation between results of the analysis and job performance or honesty.

Psychological Testing. Many companies are looking beyond traditional technical criteria when hiring employees to consider various soft skills. Popularized by Daniel Goleman as "emotional intelligence," the concept is hiring based on the ability of an applicant to fit a company's culture. Most agree that hiring based on cultural fit is a legitimate business goal as long as the company finds an acceptable balance — both legally and practically — in avoiding inadvertent underutilization of various types of employees and ensures that the profile is not so restrictive that it hinders the influx of new ideas and perspectives. The validation provisions of the EEOC's Uniform Selection Guidelines are designed to be consistent with the generally accepted standards of the psychological profession. A study by the American Management Association in 2000 showed that nearly half of 1,085 employers polled used at least one form of personality or psychological assessment in their interviewing process.

Skill and Aptitude Testing. These tests measure the applicant's ability to do a task or use a skill. They usually involve a combination of written tests and demonstrations of ability. Although these tests can predict job performance, some may have an adverse impact on certain protected groups, which may make them illegal under the provisions of the Uniform Selection Guidelines. For example, written tests may be difficult, if not impossible, for applicants who are illiterate. While the candidate could perform the task, he or she may not be able to complete a written test that poses questions about performing the task.

Step 6: Making the Hiring Decision

The hiring process can be long, complex, and challenging for both the HR professional and the hiring manager. If the process has been carefully outlined, and if the HR professional plays a role in helping to coach the hiring manager through the process, it can be much simplified, resulting in a timely and valid decision.

Efficiency is important, particularly in competitive labor markets. Taking too long to make a decision can result in the loss of the most highly qualified applicants, who may quickly find a job with another employer. In addition, an efficient process will ensure that the department with the job opening is able to quickly return to maximum production capacity.

There is certainly some stress involved in making any hiring decision — even when selecting an internal candidate who is well known to the organization. The question always lingers: "Have we made the right choice?" In reality, there is no one right choice — no perfect candidate. There are simply multiple options to consider. By considering these options in relation to established selection criteria, the HR professional and the hiring manager can feel more comfortable about the decision that is ultimately made. When working with the hiring manager, you can help facilitate this process if

- The position has been analyzed and the essential functions identified. Both required and desired characteristics have been listed.
- The prescreening process identified candidates who met the essential qualifications of the position.
- Interviews of applicants who passed the first cut distinguished among those who were not suitable, those who were acceptable, and those who were extremely qualified. A second round of interviews might then be scheduled for those who were extremely qualified.

- Of those who were extremely qualified, experience, education (if relevant), and job history were verified. Any other selection devices, such as written tests or psychological profiles, were conducted. (None of this group of candidates should be eliminated at this step.)
- The hiring manager enlisted the help of his or her peers to participate in the hiring process, using an evaluation tool to rank candidates according to the data gathered and each evaluator's perceptions.

Based on careful analysis, a top applicant will eventually emerge. This candidate should then receive a conditional offer of employment. Any salary negotiation should take place at this step. The applicant should be given no more than a few days to consider the offer. If the applicant accepts, a physical should be scheduled, if applicable. If the applicant declines, the next-ranked applicant should be offered the job. This process continues until an offer is accepted. (Note: Second-, third-, and fourth-choice applicants should not be notified of their rejection until an offer of employment has been accepted by the top applicant.) All applicants should be sent a letter notifying them that the position has been filled.

While few small-business owners, managers, or even HR professionals are trained in hiring techniques, you can learn to make sound, well-reasoned decisions. Following are some common selection mistakes you should take steps to avoid:

- *Inadequate screening.* Before you can decide who you *do not* want to hire, you have to know who you *do* want to hire. Develop specifications before you even look at the applications you receive so there is no chance that your decision will be swayed by candidates who are impressive but nevertheless unsuitable for the position.
- *Inadequate preparation.* Take the time to hire right. Invest as much time as necessary in performing the critical tasks of developing sound specifications, making well-reasoned decisions about where to advertise the position, carefully reviewing all applications, selecting only those candidates who meet your requirements, preparing interview questions based specifically on the requirements of the job, and making a selection decision based solely on the specifications and requirements of the job.
- *Lack of knowledge of the position to be filled.* Whenever possible, it is best to have the person who will be the immediate supervisor of the new employee involved in the interview. That is the person who should understand best what levels of experience, education, knowledge, and interpersonal skills are needed to succeed in the job.
- *Unintentional coaching.* Applicants may reasonably expect to receive general information about a job right away. However, be cautious about revealing too many details before an interview. For example, assume you are looking for a

supervisor to lead a group of independent, professional employees and prefer a flexible, "hands-off" management style. You should not share this information with candidates before asking the question "What approach do you use in managing professional employees?" In addition, avoid leading questions such as "You don't mind working overtime, do you?" This wording signals to the candidate the response you are hoping for, which is called "telegraphing responses."

- *Ineffective use of questions.* Use open-ended instead of closed-ended questions as much as possible. Instead of asking, "Have you had experience with budgeting?" say, "Tell me about your budgeting experience." Do not ask candidates to tell you what they *would* do; ask them to tell you what they *have done*. "Tell me how you would handle a conflict situation" only requires that the candidate devise a good response. A better way to word this question would be to say: "Tell me about a situation when you had to handle a conflict with a co-worker. What did you do? What was the outcome?"

- *Dominating the interview.* A good rule of thumb suggests that an applicant should be talking about 80 percent of the time. To encourage the candidate to share information, use questions that require in-depth responses, probe for clarification and expansion of answers, and be an active listener.

- *Stereotyping the candidate.* We all have biases that can affect our judgment when we make hiring decisions. Be aware of your own personal biases and work to overcome them during the interview process. The best defense against a bad hiring decision is a solid understanding of the requirements of the position.

- *Failure to probe for depth.* Many interviewers will accept superficial or ambiguous answers from job candidates. By failing to ask for clarification, you risk making incorrect assumptions. Do not back down. If you need to know, you need to ask.

- *Evaluating solely in relation to other candidates.* All hiring decisions should be based on a comparison of applicants to preestablished job standards. Refer to the standards you established, and compare each and every applicant in relation to these standards — not to each other.

- *Premature evaluation and selection.* Many interviewers automatically judge applicants immediately after the interview — sometimes sooner. Resist the temptation to do this. Keep an open mind. Do not make a decision until after you have interviewed all applicants.

Step 7: New Employee Orientation

When a selection has been made and the company's offer accepted, it can be tempting to feel that the hard work is over. In reality, it has just begun! The habits and patterns that an employee establishes during the first few weeks of employment will have a strong influence on that employee's attitude, productivity, and team spirit for months and years to come.

Once bad habits and unacceptable standards of performance are developed, they are hard to change. Employees tend to fall into good or bad patterns early in their employment. Steering new employees along desirable paths is a primary responsibility of management. The HR staff can play an important role in advising managers on how to orient the new hire effectively.

What new employees experience in their first days on the job can determine whether their tenure is long- or short-lived. What employees really need and want to know during those critical first days is often very different from what their organizations focus on. Employees first need to know about the issues that affect them individually and to feel secure on a personal level before they can look beyond their needs to the needs of the department or organization. That is why the first day on the job probably is not the best time to talk in any detail about the organization's strategic goals, budget, or competitive strategies. The new employee simply is not ready to hear it.

Orientation, therefore, can be viewed as a three-step process, from the specific (where should I park?) to the general (what are the organization's long-range goals?). Employees are first interested in the things that affect them personally. Next, they want to know about the things that affect them as members of their department. Finally, they are interested in the things that affect them as members of the organization. You can set the stage for an employee's initial experience with your organization even before he or she walks through the door on the first day at work. Consider some of these basic bits of information that can be important to your new employees:

- What time should I report for work?
- Where should I park?
- What should I wear?
- Where should I report?
- Whom should I ask for?

The more you can do to respond to some of these questions, the more relaxed and comfortable the employee will be.

Having a sense of belonging is important to the new employee. Be sure that the employee has a home — a place to sit and a place to put his or her things. Provide the initial tools and supplies that the employee will need to do his or her job. Something as simple as having a name tag or a nameplate in place can send a positive message to a new employee and make him or her feel welcome. It can also be helpful on the new employee's first day to have someone assigned (a buddy) to invite the new employee to go to breaks and lunch and to show the employee around.

The new employee will need to learn how things get done. For example, new employees will be concerned about administrative issues such as how to use the telephone and the computer. These may seem basic, but the employee may have been used to an entirely different system. Also, the new employee cannot know about your organization's idiosyncrasies, such as how you want the phone to be answered. It is frequently these little things that create stress and uncertainty for the new staff person — and it is also these things that often are overlooked by the organization during the orientation process. Other questions may pertain to the approval processes that the new employee should be aware of — whether he or she can sign off on invoices, and up to what dollar amount.

New employees want to begin working as soon as possible. They want to become involved quickly and feel some sense of contribution. The first big question new employees have is "What, exactly, will I be doing here?" That question encompasses a variety of issues, such as these:

- Who are the people I will be working with?
- Who are the people I need to get to know in the department and in other departments?
- What kind of work will I be doing?
- Where will my assignments be coming from?
- How will my work be judged?
- How does my work fit in with what the department does? How does it fit in with the organization's goals?
- Who are the movers and shakers in the organization?
- Are there opportunities to serve on special committees or task forces? How can I find out about them?
- If I have ideas, suggestions, or concerns, what are the channels I use to share those concerns?
- How do people prefer to communicate in this organization (face-to-face, e-mail, phone)?
- How does what I do in this department affect the organization?

Only after employees' individual needs for information are satisfied will they be able to look beyond their own interests to the interests of the organization, with some of the following questions:

- What are the organization's mission, vision, and values (and how does my department fit into this)?
- Do we have a strategic plan? What does it entail?
- Who are our competitors?
- How are we positioned in relation to our competitors?
- What are the major external issues that affect us?
- Do we have strategic partners? Who are they?

- Are we financially sound as an organization?
- What are our priorities?
- What are our long-range goals?
- What are employees rewarded and recognized for? What are they ostracized for?

Work with the new employee's manager to ensure that the manager is attuned to the new employee's need for information and individual capacity for learning. Some new employees may want to move quickly beyond the basics to learn about the broader issues affecting the organization, while others may have many more questions about the practical details of the daily routine that will affect their individual work lives.

In most organizations, the orientation process is short. It focuses primarily on filling out personnel forms, reading the job description, reviewing the company handbook, taking a tour of the new surroundings, meeting co-workers, and getting the workstation ready. All of these activities are important, but the best way to cultivate a positive, committed, high-performance employee is through an introduction to the values, culture, and expected work ethic. With the high cost of hiring a new employee and the substantial cost of turnover, companies can no longer afford to treat the employee orientation process casually.

Creating an efficient and successful orientation process takes time and effort. It can be helpful to ask those who have recently joined your company their opinions about the orientation process. Or you may wish to set up a committee to review the orientation process, inviting both new hires and veterans to participate. Next are some guidelines and suggestions for topics and activities to include in orientation discussions.

Planning for Orientation.
1. What information will employees need to feel comfortable in their new surroundings?
2. What impressions should be made on the first day? (What impressions would I like to receive if I were the new employee?)
3. What key policies and procedures must the employee be made aware of the first day so that mistakes will not be made on the second day? (Stick to vital issues.)
4. What can I do to ensure that the person will begin to know his or her fellow employees without feeling overwhelmed?
5. What can I do to make the person feel physically comfortable, welcome, and secure (desk, work area, etc.)?

6. What tasks can I teach the person to do on the first day to provide a sense of accomplishment?

7. What positive experience can I provide for the new employee that he or she can talk about at home?

8. How can I ensure that I will be available on the new employee's first day to convey a clear message that he or she is an important addition to the team?

The First Week.

1. Review the organization's structure.

2. Explain, in general terms, the organization's objectives and values. Provide a written statement of both.

3. Conduct a general item-by-item review of key policies and procedures.

4. Explain the fringe benefits that will affect the employee, and provide any written material on those benefits.

5. Present general information on career growth and training opportunities available through the organization and information on promotional opportunities.

6. Provide details on work safety, and schedule training if safety is an issue in your organization.

7. Specify the general parameters of the new employee's job, especially as it relates to other people and their jobs.

8. Review the new employee's job description, including the scope of authority and how this can be increased.

9. Introduce special policies and procedures of the department or supervisor.

10. Explain evaluation standards and procedures.

11. Explain probationary and disciplinary procedures.

12. Provide information on special forms, reference materials, and other details the employee needs to know.

30-Day Checkpoints. As the first month progresses, new employees should settle into a productive pattern of job performance and should begin to focus on their long-term relationship with the organization. If planning and training have been adequate, new employees should be generating enough work that their performance can be evaluated. Objective feedback at this stage can have a considerable impact on new employees' perceptions of themselves and of the job.

FAQs

Are there legal risks involved with the use of social media for recruitment?

Mary Glaeser:

Absolutely, but there are always legal risks in recruitment with or without the use of social media.

Generally, legal risks of recruitment and hiring have to do with whether the actions used could predict the success of a candidate in the position and, as a result, whether the action discriminates against a protected class of candidates who could be successful in the position. Remember that there are lots of different types of protected classes — gender, race, age, sexual orientation (in some places), disability, religious affiliation, etc.

There are two ways I can imagine using social media in recruitment. One is as a method of attracting/locating candidates, and the other is as a mechanism to learn information about a candidate.

In the first of these — attracting candidates — the issue is whether the pool of candidates attracted represents the general population or whether it represents a particular subset that might lead you to not attract from a particular protected class. For example, do you only attract 20- to 40-year-olds using social media? Then are you potentially discriminating against the protected class of those older than 40? So, if you use only social media as a recruiting tool, do you discriminate? If social media is one of many tools, it is probably different than if it is the only tool used to attract candidates.

For the second issue of using social media to learn more about a candidate, there are some rather complicated legal cases that have led to the general theory that the selection process should predict the success of a candidate in the position, which makes sense since you want to hire a candidate who can succeed. If you used random/unproven methods to determine the best candidate, you might discriminate against those in a protected class. This legal theory originally comes from the practice of giving something like a math test when there is no solid evidence that the test predicts success at a job; instead, the test may weed out people based on unrelated criteria and end up discriminating.

So, the question in using social media is "Why would something be a predictor of future success?" There might be some cases where it would be a predictor, particularly if the job is in the social media marketplace, but lots of times it might not be.

Employee retention is one of the most talked-about and critical issues in American business today. Why?

Sharon Jordan-Evans and Beverly Kaye:

Retention is a matter of survival. As companies become more and more technologically equal, talent will increasingly become the key differentiator. A company can build a new plant or replace a piece of equipment, but watching star talent walk out the front door is like handing the competition an ace in a poker game. Technology cannot replace the intellectual capital of key employees. And even in an economic downturn, the war for talent is fierce. Those stars always have choices.

What does hiring have to do with retention?

Sharon Jordan-Evans and Beverly Kaye:

Get the right people in the door in the first place to increase the odds of keeping them. When someone is being hired, think about how they will mesh with the team that is already there. Bringing in somebody who is going to kick up dust with the team may not work well.

Another link takes place at the recruiting interview. That is when managers should ask what would keep the prospective employee and what would entice the employee away.

Why do new recruits leave? How can we keep them?

Sharon Jordan-Evans and Beverly Kaye:

Companies need to pay much more attention to the first six months or the first year. One reason companies lose new recruits is because the picture that the recruiter and manager painted in the interviews is not borne out when the employee arrives — and then he or she leaves disillusioned.

A particular problem can be lack of communication between managers and recruits. Many times, at the exit interview, a recruit says, "I am leaving for a better opportunity." The managers say, "My gosh, that better opportunity was right here, but I didn't know she wanted it; she didn't ask me." Communication is a two-way street, and it is too bad that the truth is coming out at the exit interviews and not beforehand.

We are thinking about implementing an internal job-posting system. What should we consider?

William G. Bliss:

Internal job-posting systems have three main uses:

1. Posting jobs is a way of implementing a philosophy of promoting employees from within the organization. For an internal job-posting program to be effective, management must support this philosophy. Otherwise, employees will consider the process a farce. If your practice or plans are to hire the vast majority of people from the outside, you must examine your intention of having an internal job-posting program at all.

2. Job-posting can enhance an employee referral program, whether formal or informal. Many organizations offer a monetary or other reward to existing employees who refer candidates not currently employed by the organization. Posting is a way for employees to know about staffing needs throughout the organization, not just in their own departments.

3. Job-posting is a way to communicate to employees information such as job content, reporting relationships, and position qualifications. Some companies include grade level and salary range information, if such elements are part of their compensation program. Job postings also may explain the steps employees must take to apply for positions, including the procedure for notifying their current manager of their interest in another position.

Policies and procedures for a job-posting program should be clear and well thought-out. Items to consider include these:

- How long each job should be posted before the position can be filled. There should be enough time for interested internal candidates to actually apply and be considered before outside recruiting begins. Most organizations post jobs internally for a week or two.

- The amount of time an employee must be in his or her current position before being permitted to apply for another internal position. The current department has made an investment in the employee in the form of the learning process for the job, and the company needs to protect that investment. Depending on the level of the position, many organizations have a 6- to 12-month waiting period.

- A clear definition of the application procedure. What does the internal applicant have to do to apply? Does he or she have to notify the current manager? When?

- What existing personnel file information (job application, performance appraisals, etc.) the hiring manager will have access to in evaluating the qualifications of the internal applicant.

- The time, format, and location of posting positions, as well as who is authorized to post a position.
- The policy on stating in the actual posting whether an internal candidate already has been identified.
- Any positions that do not have to be included in the posting program. For example, some companies exclude officer-level positions. Ensure consistency in level and in department in applying any of these exclusions.

Can we use credit reports as part of our selection process?

Wendy Bliss:

Credit checks can provide information about credit standing, creditworthiness, and credit capacity. And they can give details about financial history, credit limits, current balances, payment habits, bankruptcies, and tax liens. Credit checks are available from firms offering preemployment screening services and from credit bureaus, often online.

Credit checks frequently are done on candidates applying for positions that involve financial responsibility or access to cash or other valuables. The report can help ascertain whether the potential employee's financial status might present a risk in a position that involves handling money or exercising financial discretion. However, credit checks tend to have an adverse impact on women and minorities and may be viewed by applicants as an invasion of privacy. Consequently, credit checks should not be conducted during the selection process unless they are job related and there is a business necessity to do so.

Employers that obtain credit reports or other consumer reports from third-party agencies must comply with the federal Fair Credit Reporting Act, discussed in this chapter, and with applicable state credit-check laws.

Are psychological tests a good idea when hiring? Are there risks?

Wendy Bliss:

Many employers have found psychological tests to be valuable staffing tools. In addition, such tests may minimize the risk of negligent-hiring claims. Commonly used psychological exams include those testing personality, integrity, and cognitive ability. Testing methods range from traditional paper-and-pencil instruments to computerized and web-based tests.

However, psychological assessments must be appropriate for the job in question, and they must be used properly. There are several legal issues related to the use of psychological tests.

- Title VII of the Civil Rights Act of 1964 does not forbid employers to use psychological tests, but such tests cannot be used to discriminate intentionally against members of protected classes. The tests cannot be used if they have an adverse impact on protected classes or if they are not job related and consistent with business necessity.
- Psychological tests that give information that could lead to the identification of a mental impairment or disorder are considered "medical examinations" under the Americans with Disabilities Act. That law prohibits the use of medical examinations in the employee selection process.
- Psychological tests that include questions on private matters that are not job related (such as beliefs or practices that are religious, political, or sexual) may give rise to invasion of privacy claims.
- Some states regulate or prohibit the use of certain types of preemployment tests.

Employers that use a psychological test as a selection tool should make sure that

- The test is job related and does not contain questions that are potentially discriminatory or personally intrusive or that could reveal mental illness.
- There is a correlation between test scores and job performance. This can be determined by validation studies done in consultation with an industrial-organizational psychologist or by the test publisher.
- The test is administered to all applicants for a particular job at the same stage of the hiring process, under the same conditions.
- Reasonable accommodations are made when testing applicants with disabilities.
- The test is not used as the sole or primary basis for the hiring decision.
- Test results and documentation are kept confidential. Results of medical examinations must be retained in a file separate from the general employment file.

Sample 1

Application for Employment

(This sample is based on one provided by the law firm of Ray & Isler PC, Vienna, Virginia.)
[Your company logo and address]

[Company] is an equal opportunity employer and does not discriminate against otherwise qualified applicants on the basis of any characteristic protected by law, including race, color, religion, age, sex, national origin, or disability.

PERSONAL:

Name _____ Date _____

              Last   First   Middle

Address _____

           Number & Street   City   State   Zip Code

Position Sought _____ Full Time _____ Part Time_____

Date Available _____ Salary Desired _____ Phone Number _____

Social Security Number _____ Are you over 18 years old? ❑ Yes ❑ No

Are you legally eligible for employment in the United States? ❑ Yes ❑ No

(If offered employment, you will be required to provide documentation to verify eligibility.)

EDUCATION: Please indicate education or training that you believe qualifies you for the position you are seeking.

High School: Number of Years Completed (circle one) 1 2 3 4

Diploma: ❑ Yes ❑ No G.E.D.: ❑ Yes ❑ No

Name _____ City/State_____

College and/or Vocational School:

Number of Years Completed (circle one) 1 2 3 4

Name _____ City/State_____

Major_____ Degrees Earned _____

Other Training or Degrees:

Name _____ City/State_____

Major_____ Degree or Certificate Earned_____

PROFESSIONAL LICENSE OR MEMBERSHIP:

Type of License(s) Held _____

State of [Virginia] License Number _____

License Expiration Date _____

Other Professional Memberships _____

(You need not disclose membership in professional organizations that may reveal information about race, color, sex, religion, national origin, age, disability, or any other protected status.)

Sample 1, continued

SKILLS:

❏ Data Entry   ❏ Spreadsheet or Typewriter _____ wpm
❏ Word Processing   ❏ MS Word

Other _____

Other Software Skills _____

Have you ever been employed in any facility of [Company]? ❏ Yes ❏ No
If so, please state facility name and location and dates of employment.

_____

RECORD OF CONVICTION:

During the last 10 years, have you ever been convicted of a crime other than a minor traffic offense?
❏ Yes ❏ No
If yes, explain: _____

(A conviction will not necessarily automatically disqualify you for employment. Rather, such factors as your age and the date of conviction, seriousness and nature of the crime, and rehabilitation will be considered.)

EMPLOYMENT: List last employer first, including U.S. Military Service.
May we contact your present employer? ❏ Yes ❏ No
If any employment was under a different name, indicate name _____

1) Employer _____ Address _____
    Telephone _____ Position _____
    Dates of Employment: From _____ To _____
    Salary _____ Supervisor _____ Department _____
    Duties _____ ❏ FT ❏ PT No. of Hrs. _____
    Reason for Leaving _____

2) Employer _____ Address _____
    Telephone _____ Position _____
    Dates of Employment: From _____ To _____
    Salary _____ Supervisor _____ Department _____
    Duties _____ ❏ FT ❏ PT No. of Hrs. _____
    Reason for Leaving _____

3) Employer _____ Address _____
    Telephone _____ Position _____
    Dates of Employment: From _____ To _____
    Salary _____ Supervisor _____ Department _____
    Duties _____ ❏ FT ❏ PT No. of Hrs. _____
    Reason for Leaving _____

If you wish to describe additional work experience, attach the above information for each position on a separate piece of paper.

Sample 1, continued

Explain any gaps in work history: _____

Have you ever been discharged or asked to resign from a job? _____ Yes _____ No

If yes, explain: _____

REFERENCES:

PROFESSIONAL:

Name: _____
Address: _____
Phone: (_____) _____

Name: _____
Address: _____
Phone: (_____) _____

Name: _____
Address: _____
Phone: (_____) _____

PERSONAL:

Name: _____
Address: _____
Phone: (_____) _____

Name: _____
Address: _____
Phone: (_____) _____

APPLICANT'S CERTIFICATION AND AGREEMENT

I hereby certify that the facts set forth in the above employment application are true and complete to the best of my knowledge and authorize [Company] to verify their accuracy and to obtain reference information on my work performance. I hereby release [Company] from any/all liability of whatever kind and nature which, at any time, could result from obtaining and having an employment decision based on such information.

I understand that, if I am employed by [Company], falsified statements of any kind or omissions of facts called for on this application shall be considered sufficient basis for dismissal.

I authorize [Company] to make a thorough investigation of all statements contained in this application about my past employment, education, and other activities. I release from liability all persons and organizations supplying such information.

I understand that should an employment offer be extended to me and accepted I will fully adhere to the policies, rules, and regulations of employment of the Employer. However, I further understand that neither the policies, rules, regulations of employment, nor anything said during the interview process shall be deemed to constitute the terms of an implied employment contract. I understand that any employment offered is for an indefinite duration and at will and that either I or the Employer may terminate my employment at any time with or without notice or cause.

Signature of Applicant: _____ Date: _____

This application for employment is good for 30 days only.
Consideration for employment after 30 days requires a new application.

Sample 2

Applicant Evaluation Form

Position: Public Relations Coordinator

Criteria—rate on a scale of 1 to 5 (5 being the highest):	Candidate #1	Candidate #2	Candidate #3	Candidate #4	Candidate #5
B.A. degree (journalism)	5	4	5	4	3
Three years' experience in media relations position	3	5	2	3	3
Experience with use of Internet	5	3	3	3	3
Experience with use of e-mail	5	4	3	3	3
Indication of ability to generate publicity for organizational efforts	4	5	4	3	3
Indication of strong writing skills	4	5	4	3	3
TOTAL:	26	26	22	20	20

Sample 3

Reference-Checking Form

From *Legal, Effective References: How to Give and Get Them,* by Wendy Bliss.
© 2001, Society for Human Resource Management

Applicant: _____

Reference: _____

Job Sought: _____

Employer: _____

Title: _____

Address: _____

Checked by: _____

Title: _____

Telephone: _____

Date/Time: _____

Relationship to Applicant: _____

Contact Method: _____

Basic Facts

1. When did _____ start working for your company?

   _____

2. What was _____'s last day working for your company?

   _____

3. What was _____'s position?

   _____

4. How was _____ paid by your company—salary, hourly, commission?

   _____

5. What was the gross pay of _____ the last month/year of employment?

   _____

6. Did that include overtime, bonuses, or incentive pay?

   _____

Sample 3, continued

Employment History

1. What were _____'s duties?

   _____

   _____

   _____

2. From your perspective, what is the most challenging aspect of that job?

   _____

   _____

   _____

3. How many other employees hold the same position?

   _____

4. How large is your company?

   _____

5. How large is the department _____ worked in?

   _____

6. Was there anything unique about your company or _____ 's job
   that you think would be important for a potential employer of _____
   to know?

   _____

   _____

   _____

7. Are there any particular customers or clients _____ worked with
   closely and regularly?

   _____

   _____

8. Who else at your company would be familiar with _____'s job
   performance?

   _____

   _____

Sample 3, continued

Employability

1. What would you say were _____'s strengths in this position?

   _____

   _____

   _____

2. What would you say were _____'s areas of weakness in this position?

   _____

   _____

   _____

3. How did _____'s performance compare to the performance of the person now/previously performing the job?

   _____

   _____

   _____

4. What would you say is _____'s most significant accomplishment with your company?

   _____

   _____

   _____

5. On a scale of 1 to 10 (with 10 being the best performance possible), how would you rate the overall quality of _____'s job performance?

   _____

6. Did you find _____ to be a dependable employee?

   _____

7. Approximately how often was _____ absent/tardy?

   _____

8. Did you find _____ to be a person of high integrity?

   _____

9. Was _____ well-liked by co-workers?

   _____

Sample 3, continued

10. How would you describe _____ in terms of professionalism?

11. What characteristics do you find the most admirable in _____?

12. What characteristics do you find the least admirable in _____?

13. What changes, if any, have you observed in _____ during the time you worked together?

14. Would you recommend _____ for a position as a _____? If not, why not?

15. What is your assessment as to how well-suited _____ is to a career in _____?

   _____
   _____
   _____

Problems

1. Why did _____ leave your company?

Sample 3, continued

2. Would _____ be eligible for rehire by your company? If not, is that because of a general policy or something about _____ in particular?

_____

_____

_____

3. Are you aware of any problems with _____'s job performance? If so, how were the problems addressed?

_____

_____

_____

4. To your knowledge, was _____ ever investigated or disciplined for serious misconduct such as violence, theft, drug or alcohol use, sexual harassment, or violations of company policy? If so, what where the alleged circumstances and what was the outcome?

_____

_____

_____

_____

_____

5. To your knowledge, did _____ ever engage in any unsafe or violent behavior on the job? If so, how were the problems addressed?

_____

_____

_____

_____

_____

CHECKER'S COMMENTS:

_____

_____

_____

_____

_____

_____

_____

_____

_____

_____

_____

Lessons from the Trenches

Making Hiring Connections Through Social Media

"We three are the HR and Training department at Verity Credit Union. Tina, Justin, and Daryl want you to tri_Verity!" That is the message visitors to the http://twitter. com/tri_verity page receive. It is an account focused specifically on hiring and recruiting, says Daryl Rother, one of the HR consultants with Verity Credit Union in Seattle. And it's working. Verity uses Facebook, LinkedIn, and — most recently — Twitter to promote its job openings and to establish connections with members of these online communities that may lead to both applicants and referrals.

Social media and social networking are all the rage these days. But beyond the purely "social" aspects of sites like Twitter, Facebook, and LinkedIn, does social media represent any legitimate business value? In the area of recruitment, it seems, it definitely does.

The viral nature of social media is a key benefit, says Rother. "Maybe the people who are reading the message aren't actually looking for a job themselves — that's not our expectation — but they might have a friend or a family member who is."

Rother admits that there are still a lot of people who are "somewhat apprehensive of social media — they don't see the business value of it." But, he adds, "I myself started out as a skeptic. Now you can consider me one of the converted!"

"Verity has been doing things that involve social media for several years now," says Rother. "We've been recognized as one of the first financial institutions to start a corporate blog, which really helped set the stage for what our culture is."

It may not be the right solution for all companies, of course.

In Seattle, says Rother, it makes sense because the competition for staff is high and it is a very technologically-savvy environment. In early July 2009, jobs mentioned on Verity's Twitter page included a manager of internal audit, call center representative, call center assistant manager, and director of consumer lending.

Rother suggests starting out by considering the overall objective. "People can easily get sucked into social media," he admits. "You have to limit yourself and focus. I probably spend no more than 10 minutes per day on Twitter. You have to be very conscious about what you will do versus what you won't do."

Making the "right" choice, he notes, will depend on a company's employees and demographics. "You really have to analyze that," he says.

Another important point: Even if you are not currently recruiting or not currently sure that social media holds value for you in terms of recruitment, it does not hurt to start "dabbling" in the social media environment.

As Rother stresses, it is all about building community — a community that can help spread the word and help serve as ambassadors. Just getting out there is an important starting point — from both a marketing and a recruitment perspective.

Performance Management and Ending Employment

Ensuring that the organization's human resources function as effectively as possible is a critical HR responsibility. Performance appraisals are a tool that many organizations use to measure and evaluate the performance of individual employees. Developing a performance management process for a workforce made up of employees with different personalities, attitudes, and aptitudes is not an easy task. However, the most important responsibility of managers is to evaluate effectiveness, reward performance that meets expectations, and correct performance that does not.

Managers frequently balk at the prospect of performing employee evaluations. This can occur for a variety of reasons, including the managers' own hesitance to criticize employees. Or it may be the result of inadequate knowledge of how to evaluate performance objectively. The HR professional has an important role to play in ensuring that the company's employees are evaluated appropriately and consistently.

In September 2005, SHRM conducted a Talent Management Survey, which asked HR professionals about their organizations' talent management initiatives and specific information about their recruitment, employee development, and employee retention practices. The survey was distributed to 2,415 HR practitioners and generated 384 responses.

Over one-half of the respondents indicated that their organizations had specific talent management initiatives in place. Among respondents who reported that their organizations had such initiatives, over three-quarters indicated that those initiatives were a top priority for their organizations.

According to HR professionals, the top four areas of improvement for their organizations' talent management programs were
- Building a deeper reservoir of successors at every level.
- Creating a culture that made employees want to stay with the organization.
- Identifying gaps in current employee and candidate competency levels.
- Creating policies that encouraged career growth and development opportunities.

The areas in the least need of improvement included
- Creating a culture that valued employees' work.
- Creating a culture that made individuals want to join the organization.
- Creating an environment where employees' ideas were listened to and valued.

Among respondents whose organizations had specific talent management strategies in place, over three-quarters indicated that HR worked directly with employees or managers on talent management initiatives. Those with such programs in place were asked to indicate the top areas needing improvement. These included
- Building a deeper reservoir of successors at every level.
- Creating a culture that made employees want to stay with the organization.
- Identifying gaps in current employee and candidate competency levels.
- Creating policies that encouraged career growth and development opportunities.

The areas least likely to need improvement included
- Creating a culture that valued employees' work.
- Creating a culture that made individuals want to join the organization.
- Creating an environment where employees' ideas were listened to and valued.

Overall, the majority of HR professionals felt there was no need for major improvements in these areas because they believed they were doing well in each of them.

By working closely with your company's top management and developing and communicating a process that managers can feel comfortable with, the HR professional serves both organizational and individual needs. The organization is concerned with identifying and rewarding behaviors that contribute to the success of the organization — and identifying and eliminating behaviors that do not. Employees want to know how they are doing, to be recognized for good performance, and to learn and grow on the job.

Managers who correct poor performance objectively and fire employees when necessary are more likely to avoid costly discrimination charges and employee relations lawsuits for the organization. But even more important, an effective performance appraisal process can help create a more committed and dedicated workforce and can lead to greater employee stability and less turnover.

This chapter is divided into two parts. First, it discusses performance appraisals, both informal and formal, including setting performance goals, conducting appraisals, agreeing on corrective action, and documenting the conversation. Second, it gives suggestions for changing behaviors through formal corrective action and discipline and for terminating employment effectively.

Performance Appraisals

Laying the Groundwork

Performance appraisals are among the most valuable and important tools available to management. Successful companies require measurement to value profitability, manage costs, ensure safety and accident prevention, staff the company correctly, conserve resources, improve marketing and sales, conduct research, and develop products. In most companies, the performance appraisal is the main strategy for motivating and retaining valued employees and the primary vehicle for awarding compensation and pay increases.

Most employees have experienced the highs and lows of good and not-so-good ratings. If performance appraisals are so valuable, why are there so many obstacles? Is too much emphasis placed on the process? Is the process used to accomplish the wrong objective? Are companies using unfair, highly subjective standards? Do employees believe that each has to be number one and that being average or being rated satisfactory is not acceptable? Do managers really understand the process? Has HR done an effective job of *communicating* the process?

Not surprisingly, lack of understanding of the evaluation process and how it should be applied can create numerous problems within an organization — large or small.

An engineer at a major utility company shares the following experience:

> "Each employee was given a rating at their performance review ranging from 90 (poor) to 200 (walks on water). I continually asked what I had to do to get closer to 200. At the beginning of the year, I wrote my annual work plan around specific goals such as 'sell three new technologies for a rating of 160, four new technologies for a rating of 170, etc.' My supervisor would not sign off on this work plan. He later told me that it was not possible to achieve those types of ratings on that project, because it did not have enough 'impact' on the company. I then asked him if a secretary could ever achieve a 200 rating, and he said it was impossible. We obviously had two different philosophies on the rating system. I saw it as how the individual performs with his or her goals being written around the company's overall objectives. I felt that if the employee did a superior job in achieving those goals, he or she should be rewarded. The ideas that my supervisor had about the rating system created artificial ceilings. No matter how hard I worked, I could *never* achieve a top rating. That was very defeating."

In reality, in this organization, the employee's perception of the way the process was supposed to work was correct — the manager's perception was flawed. How could it be, though, that the HR department had failed to adequately communicate something so critical as the philosophy of the performance evaluation rating system?

It happens all too frequently for a variety of reasons. The challenge for HR professionals is to ensure, first, that an effective performance evaluation process exists and, second, that managers understand the process and how it should be applied. These issues can be communicated to management in a variety of ways.

- When a manager is initially hired, part of his or her orientation process should be an overview of the performance evaluation system and its application, including the role of HR in the process, the forms and rating system, timelines, and company philosophy.
- On a regular basis, perhaps annually, HR can hold "in-service" sessions for managers to review the evaluation process (similar sessions may be held for the hiring process, constructive discipline, etc.). It is an opportunity to review and reinforce the process.
- When an employee's performance is due to be reviewed, HR can generate a reminder to the manager, reiterating the information covered during orientation and annual in-service sessions, providing the appropriate forms and guidelines, and reinforcing the important things to do and not to do in the process.
- HR can make evaluation materials and information readily available to managers — in procedure manuals, on the company intranet, or in the HR office.

By all means, do not assume that every manager knows how to conduct an employee evaluation or that, once trained in your company's procedures, the manager will forever remember the intricacies of the process. Performance evaluation is a critical function, and it is worth the effort to use multiple opportunities to reinforce how the process works and to ensure that managers clearly understand their role, the rating system, and the organization's expectations.

In addition, be sure to emphasize to managers the importance of the appraisal process to the organization in ensuring a fully functional, skilled, and well-trained workforce as well as in employee development. While some managers may balk at the review process, when fully aware of *why* employee appraisal is so important, and armed with the proper tools and education to perform their role effectively, they will be more likely to embrace the process. But they need support from HR.

The manager of a small customer service information team says, "I actually like to conduct the evaluations, but HR could make it more consistent. HR offers training for managing the performance evaluation process, but managers don't apply it consistently. Some managers stick to the goal-setting process and properly score work of their team members. Others are lax about the process; some employees don't have individual goals. They apparently receive a rating based on the department's or business unit's success. How does that show the employee that individual contributions count? There's no real linkage."

Another manager, a woman who manages a graphic design operation for a large print production company, says she loves doing the "good" reviews but dreads the "bad ones." "Confrontation is always difficult," she admits. "People tend to dwell on the negative comments made about them and tune out the positive. And if there's a restriction on raises, that can be difficult to explain as well."

Is there anything HR could do to make the process more effective? "In a perfect world," she says, "we would have some type of criteria that would be measurable, rather than going on our perceptions as managers. If an organization developed specific criteria for performing certain jobs, it would be easier to measure whether or not someone was meeting the expectations for that particular job.

"Doing reviews more frequently would also help," she adds. "The once-a-year approach is nice in that you only have to deal with the stress involved once. But I think more often would serve everyone better, as progress toward goals can be checked and employees can be steered back on track if need be — before it's too late."

With laws prohibiting discrimination in all personnel processes, promotions, pay increases, and performance must be based on job performance measurements. Maintaining valid records of employees' performance is crucial.

The Appraisal Process

The employee appraisal process should be ongoing — not a once-a-year event. It should be designed to measure the employee's contributions to the organization — both in terms of ability to do the specific tasks and work processes of the job and in terms of how well the employee exemplifies critical cultural elements valued by the organization (teamwork, customer service, etc.).

Sample performance evaluation forms for both exempt and nonexempt positions are included at the end of this chapter.

A critical first step in the evaluation process is ensuring that employees understand what is expected of them. This seems obvious, but it may be overlooked or it may be covered in a general way, not in specific terms that the employee fully understands. Employees should be involved in the establishment of goals. In addition, both manager and employee should understand how the employee's performance contributes to the goals of the organization.

Once objectives are clear, the employee should be evaluated on an ongoing basis — not just once a year. While the formal evaluation may occur annually, managers should provide continuous feedback to employees, reward behavior that is on track and contributing to the goals of the organization, and identify and correct behavior that is not contributing to those goals.

Just as in the recruitment process, the job analysis and job description should provide the basis for the evaluation. The set of criteria used when hiring employees provide a benchmark against which to judge their performance. If the job changes or evolves — as many do — both the evaluation process and the hiring criteria should be changed correspondingly.

This is a continual process. Employees who are performing according to their goals and objectives will be rewarded — through praise, compensation, and so on. These employees will also be provided with new challenges and growth opportunities. Employees who need course correction will require a corrective action plan, perhaps a review and some revision of their responsibilities (with training and coaching provided as needed), and continued evaluation of progress. If an employee is not able to perform to the requirements of the job, disciplinary action and eventual termination may be necessary.

Sources of Feedback

While traditionally managers have been the primary source of feedback on an employee's performance, there is value in obtaining feedback from a wider range of sources including other managers, the employee's peers, customers, and vendors. When using any of these sources, it is important to retain the focus on objective work performance issues. Peer evaluation should not deteriorate into personal attack or become a popularity contest.

Evaluations involving multiple raters are often referred to as 360-degree feedback because a wide range of individuals may be involved in the process. This type of review is particularly useful in today's team-based work environments where the employee interacts with many individuals who rely on him or her for quality output, effective communication, and cooperation. Because 360-degree feedback may also involve feedback from the employee's customers, it is widely used in organizations that have a strong focus on customer service.

When considering a 360-degree feedback program, HR should encourage managers to select raters based on those raters' interaction and involvement with the employee and their knowledge of the employee's performance. About five to 10 raters is a good number. In choosing raters, it is important not to stack the deck too heavily with either friends or detractors of the employee. The goal is to achieve a valid and objective view of the employee's performance. Depending on the culture of your organization and the comfort level of employees with sharing constructive feedback with their peers, you may want to offer the option of submitting comments anonymously.

When using 360-degree feedback, keep in mind the following points:

- Employees should be involved in the selection of raters.
- The focus should be on generating valid, work-related feedback from peers who work with or receive services from the employee being evaluated. Avoid feedback that is more personality-based than work-based.
- The feedback received from peers should not be used in determining salary increases or promotions, but should be viewed as general information to help aid in employee development.

One of the drawbacks of 360-degree feedback can be the time it takes. It is important for HR to communicate the value of this feedback process and, as practical, to assist in the administration of the process. For example, having forms available for managers to use, detailing the steps that managers should take in implementing the process, or even automating the data-gathering and analysis process can help reduce the time commitment involved.

Benefits of a Well-Planned Appraisal

When managers see the appraisal process as an ongoing management responsibility, it becomes possible to help employees develop the skills they lack. When feedback is given consistently, problems can be solved more easily as they arise. A good performance appraisal system has the characteristics listed in Figure 4.1.

The Setting

Performance appraisal should be a joint effort between employee and supervisor. Input and involvement from both is essential for a successful outcome. When handled well, the performance appraisal process can provide both the appraiser and the employee with a sense of accomplishment, direction in priorities, and commitment to a specific career path.

Employees need to know how they have been rated. They need a clear understanding of how they fared in the eyes of their appraiser and their organization. The evaluation session gives the appraiser an opportunity to discuss the rating, the rationale, and future development. It also provides an opportunity for the employee to share his or her perspectives, to respond to the manager's feedback, and, in turn, to give feedback on the manager's performance.

FIGURE 4.1. Characteristics of a Good Performance Appraisal System

A good performance appraisal system

- *Identifies performance goals.* Employees should know, specifically, what their goals and objectives are. Further, they should understand how their performance is being evaluated.

Aids in selection and recruiting. The performance appraisal process is integrally tied to the selection and recruiting process. Just as potential hires are evaluated against criteria based on the expectations of the job (job description) and the cultural values of the organization, so are incumbents measured against these criteria.

- *Provides feedback.* Employees crave feedback. They want to know how they are doing. Effective managers provide feedback continually. HR can play an important role here by ensuring that managers have the communication skills necessary to perform this function and that they understand the organizational benefit of feedback.

- *Includes training and development.* Whether employee performance is being corrected, or the employee is being offered an opportunity for growth and development, training is an important part of the process. Employees should be provided with the information, tools, and education they need to be successful in their positions.

- *Facilitates promotion and, if appropriate, transfer.* The value of an effective performance appraisal system lies in its ability to identify good performance and reward it and to identify substandard performance and correct it. Ultimately, in both cases, the purpose is to ensure that the organization's human resources are being effectively deployed. Sometimes this means a talented employee should be promoted or a challenged employee may be more successful in another position.

- *Rewards and recognizes achievement.* Employees deserve to be rewarded and recognized for their achievements. The performance appraisal process helps facilitate this recognition and reward because, in most companies, the process is tied to compensation.

- *Formalizes and documents goals and specific activities.* The performance evaluation process provides written documentation of the goals and performance expectations that the employee is expected to achieve.

- *Identifies areas where performance is good and where it can be improve*d. Employees will neither succeed nor fail at all aspects of their jobs. Some tasks will be performed more efficiently than others. The performance evaluation provides a tool that can be useful in identifying those areas where the employee excels and those where corrective action – or job redesign – may be necessary.

- *Identifies specific areas of improvement and the process required.* A corrective action plan may be part of the evaluation process. More than telling an employee that improvement is needed, the process must include a prescribed plan, created by the manager and the employee with assistance from HR as needed.

- *Documents broader opportunities and career development.* Again, employee development is one of the benefits of formal employee evaluation. Identifying opportunities for employees to grow and advance benefits not only the employee but also the organization.

Encourage managers to hold formal evaluation meetings in a private, comfortable setting where there will be no distractions or interruptions.

The Form

No part of the performance appraisal process has received more attention than the design of the rating instrument. Over the years, a variety of forms and instruments have been designed to help managers rate and document employee performance. The Civil Rights Act of 1964 characterized performance appraisal forms as a test of disparate impact. Thus, these forms may be considered to determine whether an employer's practices have the effect of excluding a disproportionate number of members of a protected class.

Courts have found that some performance standards were arbitrary and not job related, and that some commonly used forms seemed to discriminate. While companies try to focus on performance measurements and the communication process, the forms themselves continue to be as important as guidelines to managers. In addition, the forms serve as important documentation.

Most appraisal forms today include a narrative descriptive review, a checklist of job-related responsibilities and duties, performance dimensions and rating scales, and a section for goal-setting and results achieved. No matter how valid and accurate a form may be, though, the test of an effective system still lies in the ability of the manager to use the form effectively.

The evaluation instrument itself may take a variety of forms. The most simple instrument uses a set of scales on which to rate any measurements or characteristics of expected performance. Other forms commonly used include forced-choice and mixed-standard rating systems. Some performance appraisal instruments include a management by objectives (MBO) approach or a combination of MBO and forced choice. Several companies use a process of identifying key objectives and then describing the performance in narrative form.

Some model instruments are included at the end of this chapter to provide a foundation for discussing the essential components of any appraisal form. They are not intended to be used without modification for your specific company. Keep in mind that the specific points of evaluation for any employee should be derived from your organization's culture and values as well as from the specific tasks required of an employee as identified in the job description.

When designing an appraisal form, it can be helpful to involve some managers and employees in the process. The following questions serve as a good starting point:
- What information does the company need from the appraisal process?
- What does the company want to measure?
- What degree of validity and reliability does the company need?
- What degree of validity and reliability is possible considering the skill and performance of management in the organization?
- Should specific procedures and instruments be designed for specific work units and levels (e.g., exempt versus nonexempt) within the company?
- What adverse or undesired effect may occur because of the use of the specific rating procedure or form?
- Should the performance appraisal instrument be developed in-house or should outside consultants be used?
- What kinds of checks and balances should be used to ensure the reliability of raters?
- Is the benefit worth the cost?

Simple Ranking

A simple performance appraisal process is to have managers rank individual employees against specified job-related performance standards. Although some participants would object to the subjective nature of this process, it can be accurate and valid, especially in small companies where the raters know each member of the workgroup well, know the job requirements, and can suppress personal biases. However, a major problem with this type of ranking is usually the inability to justify the ratings, especially to those ranked in the lower half of the group. This problem can be minimized by encouraging managers to explain to employees, before the formal evaluation, the criteria used to justify ratings at various levels and, to the extent possible, to ensure that these subjective ratings are tied to objective criteria.

Narrative Descriptive Review Procedures

These procedures include the essay method and the critical incident technique, each of which requires the manager to write a description of the employee's performance. Ordinarily, some specific rating is included that the manager must assign to the performance. These techniques are often used efficiently and productively in smaller companies. The following are brief descriptions:

Essay Method. The manager describes the employee within broad categories. These might include an overall impression of the employee's performance, the jobs the employee currently can and cannot do, the strengths and weaknesses of the employee, and the employee's readiness for promotion. This method can be extremely useful in describing performance that managers cannot identify in the more structured checklist format.

Critical Incident Technique. The manager maintains a log containing observations of successful and unsuccessful performance. Although this method requires close supervision and observation, documentation is easy. The technique is often used in companies where an employee may work for many supervisors, such as shift workers in manufacturing. A serious weakness is the elapsed time between the incident and the formal appraisal. The competence of the manager also influences whether the descriptions are straightforward, honest, and accurate.

The Checklist. A checklist uses a list of job requirements, behaviors, and traits. The manager reviews the checklist and values the performance of the employee as to the particular behavior or trait. Some checklists assign a weight to each item to permit a more accurate score. Some companies use a more sophisticated checklist to reduce bias and the ability of the manager to inflate the evaluation of the performance.

Rating Scales. Although many managers would like to use the performance appraisal instrument as a definitive measure of an employee's performance and value to the organization, there are limits to describing and appraising human performance. Performance appraisals will never be completely objective. In trying to develop useful measures, a rating scale is often the best device. Rating scales are easy to administer, they transfer to quantitative terms, they permit standardization, and they relate to levels of performance dimensions.

There are problems, however, in defining the various descriptions and applying them to the employee's behavior. Although it is relatively easy to differentiate between the top 20 percent and the bottom 20 percent of the workforce, it is difficult to differentiate among the middle 60 percent.

A simple adjective rating scale is common in many companies, using descriptors such as *unsatisfactory, marginal, satisfactory, commendable,* and *superior.* Some companies try to get away from the "satisfactory" category by using such descriptors as *does not meet expectations, meets expectations,* and *exceeds expectations.*

Behaviorally anchored rating scales (BARS) are descriptions of various degrees of behavior with regard to a specific performance level. BARS are usually constructed by identifying the behaviors normally present in a particular job and then separating those required to be successful from those that would result in unsatisfactory or unacceptable performance.

Be cautious about making your ratings too limited and, again, involve management in the process of developing or revising rating forms. In addition, make sure management staff understands how the HR department views the meaning of each description.

A utility manager, managing a small professional staff, says he does not mind doing evaluations because "it forces you to take time to do the things you know you should do as a supervisor." He does not like, however, that his organization's evaluation form allows only four choices. "Practically speaking," he says, "you have only two rating choices for most, if not all, employees. I would prefer five grades similar to the academic system — it gives the manager more discretion, and everyone understands it. My perception is my employees view 'consistently meets expectations' as an average rating, and 'partially meets' as a bad rating. Therefore, if they aren't rated 'consistently exceeds,' they're disappointed. In my experience, 'unacceptable' is only used once, right before you go down the positive discipline road."

Choosing the Best Approach

A company starting a performance appraisal process should look for the simplest tool possible. A complicated process will take too much time and effort and may be misused or resisted by managers.

There are many possible combinations of methods and techniques for performance appraisal. It is important, though, that you develop a form that is specific to your organization. Use caution when considering the use of preprinted forms from the office supply store or forms used by another company, no matter how well designed.

The forms at the end of this chapter are examples of what some companies use. While they may serve as a good starting point as you consider the development of an evaluation tool, the forms should not be adopted as is. Take the time to analyze your company's needs and develop an appraisal form and process that will meet those needs.

Although most appraisal forms and instruments can be used for all levels of employees, companies may use different forms for hourly, nonexempt, and exempt employees. The hourly and nonexempt appraisal forms are less sophisticated and easier to complete. The exempt appraisal forms are usually a little more extensive and precise because the employees have broader responsibilities and accountability. Top executives are seldom appraised using standard instruments. If a formal process is used at all, it is usually a written narrative.

The sample nonexempt performance appraisal form included at the end of this chapter (Sample 4) is a checklist combined with a brief narrative. The form forces the manager to rate the employee on five aspects of performance that the company has identified as contributing to employee success. The number of aspects evaluated can be increased or decreased. This form does not quantify the five aspects, and the overall rating may or may not be the sum of the five ratings.

Sample 5 is a performance appraisal form for exempt employees that can be adapted for use with nonexempt employees (especially those in technical jobs) if a detailed form is necessary. This form uses a checklist, a brief narrative, and goal-setting to provide a detailed view of an employee's performance. The seven aspects of performance include descriptive phrases that provide direction to the manager and limit the opportunity for inflating the performance rating. At the end of the form, the manager and the employee review objectives from the previous 12 months and set objectives for the next year. The form does not use numerical scores for performance. An overall rating is given, which may or may not be the sum of all ratings and success in meeting objectives. Again, managers should focus more on obtaining mutual agreement on performance and less on the ratings per se.

Sample 6 is also a performance appraisal form for exempt employees, but it focuses primarily on a narrative description of performance. This form provides much more space for the manager to describe performance. It requires the manager to answer several questions about continuous improvement and also provides an opportunity for employee comments.

The Annual Performance Expectations form (Sample 7) was designed for a company that wanted to incorporate a brief Management by Objectives form into its performance appraisal process. This form allowed the company to document objectives without complicating the performance appraisal process.

Guidelines for Useful Feedback

Feedback is a way of helping people consider changing their behavior. It tells a person how his or her actions affect others, based on overall company objectives. Feedback helps individuals keep their behavior on target and thus better achieve their goals. It is a key tool in the performance appraisal process. The HR professional can help managers improve their ability to give and receive feedback. Some tips on giving effective feedback are provided in Figure 4.2.

FIGURE 4.2. Tips on Giving Feedback

Feedback should

- *Be descriptive rather than evaluative.* For example, instead of saying, "This memo is poorly written," offer specific examples of areas for improvement and tell how your suggestions will make the memo better. Avoiding evaluative language reduces the need for the individual to respond defensively.

- *Be specific rather than general.* To be told that one is "domineering" probably will not be as useful as being told, "I felt forced to accept your arguments or face attack because it seemed as though you didn't listen to what others said."

- *Take into account the needs of both the receiver and the giver.* Feedback can be destructive when it serves only the manager's needs.

- *Be directed toward behavior that the receiver can do something about.*

- *Be solicited rather than imposed.* Feedback is useful when the receiver has asked for it and less so if it is not asked for.

- *Be well timed,* and offered as soon as possible after the event.

- *Be checked to ensure that the communication was clear* and was received the way it was meant. Use active listening skills (repetition, paraphrasing, etc.).

Motivating Managers to Conduct Effective Performance Appraisals

There are a number of things that HR departments can do to improve managers' compliance with the organization's performance evaluation process.

Ensure Meaning

The performance appraisal process should be viewed as a *process*, not a task. HR can help managers understand this process by ensuring that it is clearly tied to organizational goals, individual goals, the hiring process, and education and training efforts. These are not separate functions. They are all part of the process of ensuring that the company's human resources are used effectively.

Performance evaluation should also be viewed as a developmental process, and, again, HR can help reinforce this message. Rather than looking back at what the individual did or did not accomplish, the manager and the employee would look *for-*

ward to develop a training and mentoring plan based on the employee's performance and what is needed to move ahead.

Offer Involvement

HR should not attempt to develop or implement a performance evaluation process in a vacuum. Involvement from managers, supervisors, and employees is critical. Systems that are developed in a vacuum — or behind the doors of the HR department — are not likely to be accepted by managers. Work with the managers in your organization to develop a process that meets their needs as well as yours. Many managers complain about the complexity and length of performance evaluation forms. Through their experience in working with the forms, they may have excellent insights and suggestions on how this administrative part of the evaluation process can be improved.

Keep It Simple, Stupid

Do not overcomplicate the process. If your goal is to ensure that managers in your organization conduct performance evaluations *effectively*, the more you can follow the "keep it simple, stupid" (KISS) approach, the more likely you are to achieve compliance. If you can make performance evaluation a process that is easy to work with, managers will be more likely to comply. Consider, as well, how technology can be used to help simplify overly complex performance appraisal systems.

Provide Training and Ongoing Coaching

Training managers to conduct effective performance evaluations is an important part of the process. Use multiple opportunities to keep managers aware of the evaluation process and to ensure that they understand how the process works. Share tips and techniques with managers to help make their role in the process easier. Training should also incorporate the big picture. Why is performance evaluation valued by the organization? How does an individual's performance benefit the organization? How can that performance be measured objectively? What forms and tools does the organization make available to expedite this process?

Serve as a Role Model

It should go without saying that HR personnel should serve as role models for the performance appraisal process — if you are responsible for employees, make sure you are following the same guidelines and procedures you require from other managers in your organization!

Corrective Action

Few organizations escape the need to correct the behavior of employees, yet managers in most organizations avoid disciplining employees rather than confronting them. Experience does not prepare most supervisors to administer discipline. When faced with the need to discipline an employee, they are at a loss. The principal elements of a good employee corrective action program include the following:

- *Standards.* Standards for performance and appropriate behavior should be established and clearly communicated to all employees.
- *Facts.* The burden is on the supervisor to establish the facts on which the decision was based.
- *Consistency.* When managers discipline consistently, they gain the support and respect of their employees.
- *Timeliness.* Discipline should follow as soon as possible after the specific behavior that warrants correction.
- *Appropriate discipline.* The discipline imposed should be appropriate for the circumstances and the employee's behavior.
- *Positive action.* If discipline is corrective and positive, a change of behavior is more likely to result.
- *Realistic expectations.* If discipline will not produce or has not produced a change in behavior, the employee should be removed for the benefit of all.

Application of these basic principles will benefit both the employee and the supervisor. The employee will be clear on the standard of behavior required and the consequences that will follow from not meeting that standard. The supervisor will be clear on how to proceed when an employee does not perform satisfactorily and behave appropriately.

Dealing with Problem Employees

There are many sources of inappropriate employee behavior. Supervisors are responsible for eliminating these behaviors regardless of the source. When the cause of the inappropriate behavior is the employee's personal life, the supervisor can help the employee recognize his or her responsibility to change the behavior and the need to confront and work through the problems.

Employees can solve their own problems and change their inappropriate behavior, but they may need help in distinguishing among behaviors, feelings, and opinions. The supervisor can be a sounding board for ideas, encourage straight thinking, give assurance that improvement is possible, and help by following a problem through to a successful solution. While the employee ultimately must correct his or her own actions, the supervisor can be a powerful factor in that process.

The following questions can be helpful to the supervisor involved with an employee whose performance or behavior is inappropriate:

- Have I fully explained to the employee exactly what he or she is supposed to do? Have I pointed out how work is to be done? Can I say for sure that there is no misunderstanding on these two points between the employee and me?
- Are my requirements for the employee the same as those for employees in similar jobs in my unit? Do these requirements compare favorably with those established by other supervisors for similar tasks? Are my requirements reasonable under the conditions? Am I consistent?
- Can I show clearly that I have seriously attempted to train the employee in the skills and knowledge needed to meet my requirements? Have I given enough time to develop the skills?
- Have I discussed the performance with the employee? Does the employee know that the performance is below that required for the job? Have I told the employee exactly what improvements must be made to meet the requirements?
- Have I followed administrative procedures? Have I notified the employee in writing of unsatisfactory performance and discussed what needs to be done to bring the work up to a satisfactory level?
- Am I prepared to defend my actions before my superiors, top management, and perhaps a hearing officer?

Corrective Discipline Policy

Disciplinary practices should be consistent throughout the organization and should be based on an established corrective discipline policy that is communicated to and understood by employees. Employees should fully understand the types of behaviors or level of performance that can lead to discipline and the consequences — up to termination — that may be involved. A documented corrective discipline policy, consistently applied, is critical in defending employment decisions.

When dealing with problem employees, or employee disciplinary issues, clear documentation is extremely important. Some companies use forms to provide a guideline to ensure that all points are covered. Two sample forms are included at the end of this chapter, an Employee Counseling Form (Sample 8) and a Corrective Action Form (Sample 9).

Employee Assistance Programs

Employee assistance programs (EAPs) provide professional services to employees whose job performance is affected by substance abuse, emotional problems, family difficulties, legal issues, health issues, and so forth. An EAP allows managers to provide a valuable resource for employees while maintaining appropriate boundaries.

As companies increasingly focus on work-life issues, it is more common for managers to acknowledge the impact of an employee's personal life on performance. In addition, strong relationships frequently develop between managers and subordinates; those relationships can be a positive and motivating force. However, even though managers are human and often feel compassion for employees who are facing difficult issues, it is not appropriate for a manager to become personally involved in helping an employee work through these issues.

It is important for HR to advise managers to focus on employee *performance*. That focus on performance is key. The problem is not that Joan's husband has a terminal illness. The problem is that Joan's performance has been declining. While managers can, and should, express compassion for their employees, their focus must remain on performance issues.

While managers can and should encourage employees to take advantage of EAP services, when available, the use of these services should be voluntary. An employee may exercise his or her right to not use these services, but the employee must be prepared to face the consequences of continued poor performance or inappropriate behavior triggered by whatever personal issues that employee is facing, up to and including termination.

Again, the focus of the supervisor or manager should be on performance and not on the personal issues that may be affecting performance. A uniform policy on EAP referrals — routinely referring all employees to an EAP as part of the final step in a corrective counseling process, for instance — can help protect the employer from Americans with Disabilities Act-related claims and maintain the focus of disciplinary actions on performance-related, and not personal, issues.

The Termination Decision

Companies cannot afford to keep marginal or poor performers on their payroll. Too frequently, managers may be hesitant to terminate an employee, either out of sympathy for the employee or out of distaste for confrontation or because of concerns for potential legal liability.

No company needs to feel coerced into retaining an employee whose performance is inadequate. But there is one guiding principle that should always be followed — a termination should never come as a surprise. Employees should know, long before they are actually terminated, that their performance is not satisfactory and that, therefore, their jobs are in jeopardy. Giving fair warning, and an opportunity for the employee to improve his or her performance, has several important advantages.

- The employee may improve significantly, sparing everyone the unpleasantness of a termination.
- The employee may decide to leave the company voluntarily.
- The employee is less likely to make a scene if he or she is terminated.
- The employee is less likely to bring a suit against the company for wrongful discharge.
- If your company is sued, you will have documentation of the performance issue.

Managers should be advised to follow the company's progressive discipline system as outlined in the company's policies and procedures. Before a termination decision is made, an effort should be made to coach and counsel the employee to improve his or her performance. A typical progressive discipline procedure might include an oral warning for a first offense, a written warning for a second offense or lack of improvement, a suspension for a third offense or lack of improvement, and discharge for a fourth offense or lack of improvement.

The role of the HR professional is to educate your company's managers about progressive discipline and to support managers in using the process. HR may also assist managers in meeting with and counseling employees.

When a manager determines that one of his or her subordinates is not performing effectively, steps must be taken immediately to correct the problem. Doing nothing is never a wise idea — employees will not know that they are supposed to improve, and they may wonder why the boss comes down on them later when the issue has never been raised. Train your company's managers to do the following:

- *Handle disciplinary matters privately.* The manager should set up time to get together one-on-one with the employee to discuss the problem. An employee should never be chastised in public.
- *Focus on objective behaviors, never on subjective feelings or vague complaints.* The manager should keep the discussion centered on the undesirable behavior. He or she should quantify what is being said and provide as many actual examples as possible. For instance, instead of saying, "You're always making mistakes," the manager should say, "Last Tuesday you ... On Friday ..."
- *Keep it brief.* A prolonged "attack" will only make an employee feel defensive. The manager should cover a single problem concisely.
- *Give the employee an opportunity to respond.* The manager needs to take the time

to listen to the employee's perspective. It is possible that a situation has been misinterpreted or that there is a good reason for the performance problem or difficulty.

- *Decide what will be done to correct the problem.* The manager and the employee should agree on a plan of action. At this stage, the HR professional can help develop specific goals and a time frame for improved performance — and assist the manager with documentation and follow-up.

Additional points to remember:

- Job discipline is essential. Employees need course correction from time to time, and the supervisor is in the best position to provide this correction. The role of HR is to make sure the supervisor has the training and the tools to provide effective feedback to employees and to serve as a consultant to management in dealing with problem employees. HR professionals may also be called upon to mediate in situations where conflict arises between employees and management.

- Correcting an employee's behavior is more important than fixing blame for it. The goal of the manager should be to improve behavior or performance so the department can function efficiently. There is little benefit in attempting to fix blame for a problem. Instead, managers should focus on positive corrective action.

- Problems affect employee performance both on and off the job. No longer do companies expect employees to leave their personal lives at home. Today, there is widespread recognition that an employee's personal life affects the workplace — and vice versa.

- Sudden or abrupt changes in behavior can be indications of important employee problems. In smaller companies, it may be easier for supervisors to know their employees and to recognize behavioral changes. In all companies, though, it is important for supervisors to be alert to behavioral and performance changes and to take action immediately to correct behavior as necessary.

- Problems should be dealt with as soon as possible after they have been identified. Do not let an issue languish in hopes that it will improve. While confrontation can be difficult, it is easier when done at the outset of an issue rather than after the issue has developed into a much bigger problem.

- A supervisor should resort to disciplining an employee only after the supervisor is sure that training or counseling will not be helpful. Managers should approach employee performance and behavior problems from the standpoint that the employee wants to be successful in the job. From this standpoint, training and counseling is effective in most situations. There are exceptions, however, and in these cases disciplinary action may be advised.

- All interactions — whether training, counseling, or discipline — should be documented.
- The disciplinary action should be based on facts rather than on personal feelings. The manager, with the help of HR, should focus on specific, documentable behaviors. "The employee has a bad attitude" is a personal opinion, not a fact. "The employee was disrespectful to a customer on (date) — responding in anger to a simple request" is more objective.

Voluntary Terminations

Losing good employees happens to even the best employers. When it does, it pays to have a good process in place for helping the employee make the transition as smoothly as possible.

Each situation will be different, but assuming the employee is leaving the organization on good terms, you will have an opportunity to make the departure a positive one, to gain valuable information about the company and its management practices, and to send the employee off with a positive impression of the company.

When an employee announces his or her decision to leave the company, the information should be shared with other staff members as soon as possible; you can allow the departing employee the opportunity to do this personally, if appropriate. Encourage the manager to publicly thank the employee for his or her contributions and to wish the employee well in his or her new responsibilities.

Work with the manager and the departing employee to develop an exit plan. This is a plan that the employee develops detailing all of the outstanding issues the employee was working on and including recommendations about how those issues should be resolved and who should handle them until a replacement is found. This involvement provides closure for the departing employee and an opportunity for comment. It also eases the burden on the manager, who will be involved in recruitment activities to find a replacement for the departing employee. An action plan is developed for each item on the exit plan, and the employee then spends his or her last two weeks finalizing as much as possible.

When an employee leaves your organization, you should take the time to gather information about the employee's decision. This information can be invaluable in improving your retention efforts. Commonly, these parting conversations are called exit interviews. The exit interview can be a good way to gather valuable information from the departing employee — information that can help you examine your operations and provide the basis for making improvements. To ensure that your exit interviews are effective, try the following:

- Have someone outside the employee's department conduct the exit interview. This will generate more open and truthful answers from the employee than, for instance, an interview with his or her immediate supervisor. The HR department is a good place to centralize responsibility for conducting exit interviews. If your organization has high turnover and your HR staff is small, you may wish to consider outsourcing this function.
- Focus the exit interview from a positive perspective by telling the employee you are interested in ways to continuously improve the organization.
- Know what you want to know. Do not go into an exit interview without preparing. Have a prepared set of questions designed to elicit constructive feedback from the employee on the company's operations and atmosphere.
- Maintain control. You do not have to be rude or abrupt to keep the interview on track. Do not be too timid to interrupt when an employee strays off on a tangent. Say something like, "Let's get back to ..." or "You've answered my question about ...; now let's go on to ..."
- Ask open-ended questions — questions that require more than a simple yes or no answer. Open-ended questions allow you to gather more information.
- Thank the employee for his or her candor, even if some of the feedback was difficult to hear. End the interview on a positive note.

These are some useful questions to use in an exit interview:
- What did you enjoy about your work for our company?
- What parts of your job did you not find enjoyable? Why?
- How would you describe the atmosphere at our company? Was the environment here compatible with your needs? If not, why not?
- How would you describe your supervisor's management style? Was this style compatible with your needs? Why or why not?
- What might we have done to prevent you from leaving?
- What suggestions for improvement would you like to share with us?

While there are occasions where quickly severing the relationship with a departing employee is a good idea, more often it is possible for the company to maintain a positive relationship with the departing employee. You never know when or how you may interact with a departing employee in the future. Maintaining a positive relationship can be a benefit for all involved.

Giving References

Reference-givers walk a legal tightrope. On the one hand, providing inaccurate or inappropriate information may provide grounds for discrimination, defamation, or invasion of privacy lawsuits. It is improper to share information about any characteristic protected by federal or state law (including age, race, religion, national origin, or disability), false statements that are damaging to a former employee's reputation, or embarrassing personal facts.

On the other hand, failing to disclose information about a former worker's harmful tendencies can create a misleading positive impression about a potentially dangerous individual. A misleading impression can provide the basis for misrepresentation claims by persons in the new company who are harmed by the employee.

The fear of lawsuits has resulted in the widespread adoption of name, rank, and serial number policies that limit the content of references to verification of basic factual information about dates of employment, title, and earnings. This tight-lipped approach penalizes good former employees and makes it difficult for prospective employers to obtain essential information about applicants. It also may lead to increased unemployment taxes and outplacement costs for the former employer.

Employers can significantly limit potential legal liability while providing useful, in-depth information to reference-checkers by taking the following steps:

- Develop and enforce a written reference policy that clearly specifies who may give references and what information may (and may not) be provided, to whom, and under what conditions. Limit the people in your company who are authorized to give references to individuals who have been trained to do so.
- Obtain the former employee's written consent to provide a reference based, if applicable, on his or her last performance appraisal. Obtain a written release of liability before you give a reference.
- Provide only truthful, job-related information, based on documented facts.
- Provide references in good faith, without malice; never make comments about a past employee's character.
- Give a job reference only when it has been specifically requested by a party who has a legitimate need to know.
- Train those who give references on how to do this legally and effectively.
- Document reference requests and what information was provided.

Reference-givers definitely need to be careful when responding to inquiries. But they should also be aware that truth and the consent of the employee are solid legal defenses to claims of wrongful references. Moreover, in many situations the doctrine of "qualified privilege" protects former employers that give defamatory references. In addition, most states have enacted reference-checking laws that give employers immunity from civil liability for good-faith references.

FAQs

What is employment-at-will, and what does it mean to the HR department?

Mary Glaeser:

For an HR department, employment-at-will is a double-edged sword. It means that, in theory, you can end an employee's employment at any time. In practice, however, you must make sure there is no discrimination when you end the employment. Generally, this means making sure there is a good business reason for ending someone's employment; frequently, it means writing that up in a clear and concise way. If the employee is not in a protected class, HR probably can get by with less due diligence. But if the employee is in a protected class, HR needs to do more due diligence and have more documentation in case a claim is brought against the company for illegal discrimination. In the case of a large layoff, this due diligence gets even more complicated. The number of age discrimination claims has been on the rise with the number of layoffs in the last year or two.

The other piece of this for HR is that an employee can quit with no notice, and the company not only must be prepared to do all the administrative tasks to end the employment but also must deal with the lack of notice, get the former employee's work done, and/or replace the employee.

What is the difference between a termination and a layoff? Does it matter?

Kevin Doherty:

A termination is the general term for any type of situation where an employee's employment is ended involuntarily. Most people believe the term applies to a cessation of employment that is performance based, but that does not necessarily need to be the case. A termination simply means that an employer has decided to end the employment of an employee for some reason.

A layoff is a type of termination. A layoff most often refers to a termination decision that is based on economic conditions, lack of work, corporate restructuring, or similar issues that usually apply to a broader group of workers, as opposed to the performance or other characteristics of a specific individual employee. Layoffs can be either temporary or permanent.

Demont Daniel:

It absolutely matters. A layoff involves eliminating positions, not people. Termination would typically be the inverse.

Remember that the term "layoff" is often a misnomer for "reduction in force." A reduction in force is defined as a permanent elimination of a position that results from a lack of work; in comparison, a layoff has been historically viewed as a temporary employer action that removes workers from the payroll for limited periods of time. In the entertainment business, for example, production employees may be laid off when one production ends, only to be reemployed once a new production opportunity surfaces.

Employers more commonly use the term "layoff," but you are better off using the terms "reduction in force" or "position elimination" in your written records when referring to the permanent elimination of a position.

Sample 4

Performance Appraisal Form—Nonexempt

Name: _____ Job Title: _____ Grade: _____ Date: _____

Location: _____ Department: _____

❏ Annual   ❏ Midyear   ❏ New employee

PERFORMANCE STANDARDS

KNOWLEDGE OF JOB: *A clear understanding of the facts or the factors required in the job.*

Outstanding
Above standard
Meets standard
Below standard

QUALITY OF WORK: *Accuracy and completeness of work.*

Outstanding
Above standard
Meets standard
Below standard

PRODUCTIVITY: *Number of accomplishments, volume, and value.*

Outstanding
Above standard
Meets standard
Below standard

DEPENDABILITY: *Conscientious, responsible, reliable: work completed on time.*

Outstanding
Above standard
Meets standard
Below standard

COOPERATION: *Ability and willingness to work with associates, supervisors, and others.*

Outstanding
Above standard
Meets standard
Below standard

OVERALL RATING ❏ Outstanding ❏ Above Standard ❏ Meets Standard ❏ Below Standard

Comments: _____

Position ready for now: _____ Position ready for in 12 months: _____

Mutual development plan: _____

Manager: _____ Employee: _____

Date: _____ Date: _____

Sample 5

Performance Appraisal Form (A)—Exempt

Name: Job Title: Grade: Date:

Location: Department:

❏ Annual   ❏ Midyear   ❏ New employee

PERFORMANCE EVALUATION

KNOWLEDGE: *Comprehension of basic principles, techniques—has know-how. Excellent comprehension in*

❏ All areas   ❏ Comprehension in most areas   ❏ Satisfactory comprehension   ❏ Not well-informed

Describe:

_____

_____

_____

_____

ANALYTICAL ABILITY AND JUDGMENT: *Obtains adequate facts; appraises and applies good judgment to the solution of problems.*

❏ Has keen insights   ❏ Good problem-solver   ❏ Satisfactory decisions   ❏ Makes decisions without
—makes right   —has facts and uses   —sound judgment   preparation or adequate
decisions   judgment   info

Describe:

_____

_____

_____

_____

PLANNING AND ORGANIZATION: *Ability to plan own work to ensure efficient use of time— establishes goals and priorities. Gets things done on time.*

❏ Organized—   ❏ Meets most deadlines   ❏ Meets schedules and   ❏ Poorly organized
makes use of time   —good use of time   objectives satisfactorily

Describe:

_____

_____

_____

_____

_____

Sample 5, continued

QUALITY OF WORK: *Performs assignments creatively, conscientiously, and accurately with high standards of quality and overall effectiveness.*

❏ Highest quality ❏ Quality work ❏ Satisfactory ❏ Poor quality
—error-free work —can be relied on —turns out accurate —work needs inspection
  to be error-free work

Describe:

_____

_____

_____

_____

_____

HUMAN RELATIONS SKILLS: *Gets along with others extremely well—uses tact and diplomacy. Maintains respect and confidence without trying to control.*

❏ Excellent ❏ Very good ❏ Satisfactory ❏ Lacks tact
—respected, —seldom has —maintains positive —controls rather
not feared criticisms or grievances work environment than supports

Describe:

_____

_____

_____

_____

_____

SUPERVISORY ABILITY: *Organizes, coordinates, motivates, and develops through responsibility, authority, and recognition. Gets work done through others.*

❏ Excellent ❏ Capable and ❏ Satisfactory ❏ Lacks leadership
—leader and competent —works well with —has frequent
manager, people problems
not controller

Describe:

_____

_____

_____

_____

_____

Sample 5, continued

BUDGET AND COST CONTROL: *Uses all resources economically. Looks for ways to eliminate non-valued activity and offers cost-reduction ideas.*

❏ Excellent use of   ❏ Good use of assets   ❏ Satisfactory   ❏ Routinely exceeds budget resources   —stays within budget   —does not control costs
—reduces
unneeded work

Describe:

_____
_____
_____
_____
_____

PERFORMANCE OBJECTIVES FROM PREVIOUS 12 MONTHS	Met Expectations	
	Yes	No

PERFORMANCE OBJECTIVES FOR NEXT 12 MONTHS	Completion Date

OVERALL RATING   ❏ Outstanding ❏ Above Standard ❏ Meets Standard ❏ Below Standard

Comments:
_____

Position ready for now: Position ready for in 12 months:

_____

Mutual development plan:

_____

Manager: _____   Employee: _____

Date: _____   Date: _____

Sample 6

Performance Appraisal Form (B)—Exempt

Name: Job Title: Grade: Date:

Location: Department:

❑ Annual   ❑ Midyear   ❑ New employee

PERFORMANCE EVALUATION

LIST BELOW THE MAJOR OR MAIN DUTIES OF THE JOB IN ORDER OF PRIORITY. AFTER EACH MAIN DUTY, APPRAISE THE PERFORMANCE OF THE EMPLOYEE—BE SPECIFIC.

Duty:
Appraisal:

Duty:
Appraisal:

Duty:
Appraisal:

LIST BELOW THE MAJOR OR MAIN OBJECTIVES OF THE JOB IN ORDER OF PRIORITY. AFTER EACH MAIN OBJECTIVE, APPRAISE THE PERFORMANCE OF THE EMPLOYEE—BE SPECIFIC.

Key Objective:
Appraisal:

Key Objective:
Appraisal:

Sample 6, continued

HOW COULD IMPROVEMENT BE ACHIEVED IN ACCOMPLISHMENT OF DUTIES AND COMPLETION OF OBJECTIVES?

_____
_____
_____
_____
_____
_____
_____
_____

WHAT FURTHER INFORMATION, TRAINING, OR EDUCATION IS NEEDED TO FILL THE REQUIREMENTS OF THIS JOB?

_____
_____
_____
_____
_____
_____
_____
_____

WHAT EXPECTATIONS FOR PROMOTION DOES THE EMPLOYEE HAVE, AND HOW CAN THESE BE ATTAINED?

_____
_____
_____
_____
_____
_____
_____
_____

WHAT COMMENTS DO YOU HAVE ABOUT THE WORK PERFORMANCE OF THE EMPLOYEE OR THE QUALITY OF THE WORK?

_____
_____
_____
_____
_____
_____
_____
_____

Sample 6, continued

EMPLOYEE COMMENTS—DIFFERENCES OF OPINION OR PERFORMANCE
MISUNDERSTANDINGS.

_____
_____
_____
_____
_____
_____
_____
_____

DETAIL MUTUALLY AGREED-UPON PERFORMANCE IMPROVEMENT PLAN.

_____
_____
_____
_____
_____
_____
_____
_____

FURTHER COMMENTS AND REMARKS.

_____
_____
_____
_____
_____
_____

OVERALL RATING ❑ Outstanding ❑ Above Standard ❑ Meets Standard ❑ Below Standard

Comments:

Position ready for now: Position ready for in 12 months:

Mutual development plan:

Manager: _____   Employee: _____

Date: _____   Date: _____

Sample 7

Annual Performance Expectations

Position: _____ Department: _____

Name: _____ Title: _____

Supervisor: _____

Priority	Key responsibilities/accomplishments/ objectives	How Measured	Completion Date
1.			
2.			
3.			
4.			
5.			
6.			
7.			

Supervisor's Signature
_____

Employee's Signature
_____

Date

Sample 8

Employee Counseling Form

NAME: _____

JOB TITLE: _____

DATE OF INCIDENT: _____

DESCRIBE INCIDENT: _____
_____
_____
_____
_____

EMPLOYEE COMMENTS: _____
_____
_____
_____

ACTION TAKEN

❑ First warning   ❑ Second warning   ❑ Final warning

You are given this notice so that you may have an opportunity to correct the problem. If the situation is repeated or if you engage in any other breach of our expectations, you will be subject to other appropriate corrective action.

Supervisor's signature: _____ Date: _____

I have received a copy of this notice. I have read this notice and have had an opportunity to discuss it with my supervisor. I understand the rules and requirements.

Employee's signature: _____ Date: _____

Sample 9

Corrective Action Form

NAME: _____

JOB TITLE: _____

DEPARTMENT: _____

DATE OF INCIDENT: _____

State the nature of the problem and the solution sought exactly as discussed with the employee.

_____
_____
_____
_____
_____
_____
_____
_____
_____
_____
_____
_____
_____
_____
_____
_____
_____
_____
_____
_____
_____

Describe the activities required for improvement and the benchmarks.

_____
_____
_____
_____
_____
_____
_____
_____
_____
_____
_____
_____
_____

Training and Development

Employee development involves anything that prepares employees to do their jobs better. This includes improving their skill levels and encouraging them to work toward common and mutually agreed-upon objectives. Company development focuses all of the company resources, including employee activities, on working well together in a productive and motivational work environment; it is an ongoing effort to enhance the problem-solving, decision-making, and renewal process.

SHRM's 2000 Performance Management Survey indicated the following:

- Classroom training was the most popular method for professional development. Eighty-six percent of respondents' organizations conducted in-house classroom training, and 84 percent had employees participate in external classroom training.
- On-the-job training and in-house classroom training were rated as the most effective professional development methods. Independent study — both traditional and online — was viewed as the least effective development method.
- Respondents reported that a lower percentage of executives at their organizations — compared with exempt and nonexempt employees — participated in most development activities.

Even though classroom training was preferred, exempt employees spent 2.6 days a year, on average, in classroom training, compared with 2.3 days for executives and 2.1 days for nonexempt employees. In addition, over the past several years, advances in Internet technology have made online training applications more visually appealing through the use of video, and more interactive through the use of real-time Q&As, forums, etc.

Smaller organizations had the lowest usage level for several forms of training, including in-house classroom training (83 percent), traditional independent study (53 percent), online independent study (34 percent), and externally hired coaches (17 percent).

It is important for any training effort to be tied to the organization's overall strategic goals and culture. If it is not, employees may be given tools they cannot use. For example, communication and people skills are popular topics of training. However, those skills have less impact in the face of organizational barriers such as lack of rewards and recognition, lack of information, or autocratic management.

Training takes time. It can be costly to administer. Employees and managers may be resistant. Results may not be readily apparent. For all of these reasons, HR professionals who are committed to providing training and development opportunities to employees should be prepared to deal with this resistance, provide training that is meaningful and tied to organizational objectives, and search for ways of demonstrating training effectiveness.

Training of any kind requires some form of change on the part of the individual being trained, whether a change in knowledge, a change in how a process is performed, or a change in attitude or behavior. While there is often a natural resistance to change, employees do not resist all change. Employees do, however, resist changes that they do not understand, that they do not feel involved in, or that they cannot see the need for or the benefit of. Employers that want to make workplace changes must find ways to involve employees in decisions that affect their jobs, must develop open communications, and must build trust between workers and management.

There are certain types of training needs in any organization: job skills training to ensure that employees understand the work processes involved in performing their assigned duties, compliance training to ensure that employees and managers understand the legal issues affecting their performance on the job (e.g., sexual harassment training, diversity training), and developmental training designed to prepare employees for higher-level positions and responsibilities.

Succession planning is an important part of organizational development and a critical component of a successful training and development effort.

Training can be delivered in a variety of formats — direct one-on-one training, coaching and counseling provided by managers and peers, traditional classroom training, and computer-based training.

As a final and important step in any training initiative, HR professionals need to be prepared to evaluate the effectiveness of the training provided to ensure that it is furthering the needs of the organization.

Job Skills Training

It is the company's responsibility to get employees from performing at entry level to performing at a level that meets or exceeds minimum standards. It does not matter if the new hires are Harvard MBAs, experienced employees hired from competitors, recent college graduates, or high-potential professionals enticed away from another industry. New hires are not fully able to perform their job duties until they understand the company's policies, procedures, systems, and culture. Only when the employee is up to speed on these basic issues is he or she able to move on to more formal training.

Some employers assume that employees have all the skills they need when they join the company, but this is seldom the case. Because managers often do not have the knowledge or the skills to provide the level of training that new employees need, this is an area that is often overlooked. Consequently, employees are left to fend for themselves, learning from their peers or learning through the school of hard knocks. Successful companies take this responsibility seriously; it is a responsibility that is frequently handled through the HR department.

For employees who need additional skills, an ongoing training process can improve individual employee productivity, but the process must augment activities required in the employer's strategic plan and must be based on employees' assessment of their own needs.

Compliance Training

Certain types of training are either required or extremely well advised to assist companies in managing or minimizing the risk of employees or managers acting in opposition to federal and state laws. Training in the next areas is either mandated or highly recommended.

Civil Rights Act of 1964

While the Civil Rights Act does not specifically require training, it does hold the company and its managers responsible for acts of discrimination. Because of the potential for liability, most employers offer training to managers and supervisors to make them aware of the issues involved, and consequently to reduce the company's exposure to charges of discrimination and employee lawsuits.

Title VII of the Civil Rights Act

Title VII prohibits sexual and other forms of harassment in the workplace. While the Act does not specifically require training, the U.S. Supreme Court decision has held that an employer would be strictly liable for any harassment engaged in by a supervisor. However, the decisions also held that if an employer could show that it had done everything possible to prevent and correct any harassing conduct, it would not be held liable for the harassment. Thus, training supervisors in what constitutes prohibited harassment and how to deal with the issue lessens the potential for liability. In addition, all employees must be told of the employer's policy against harassment and how to use company procedures to file a complaint or grievance.

Affirmative Action Compliance

Executive Order 11246 requires federal contractors and subcontractors and federally assisted construction contractors and subcontractors that generally have contracts that exceed $10,000 to take affirmative steps to ensure that equal opportunity is provided in all aspects of their employment. This could include regularly communicating the company's policy in staff meetings and in company publications.

National Labor Relations Act

Most employers provide managers and supervisors with some training on employee relations. In unionized companies, most supervisors are trained in the administration of the union contract. In union-free companies, managers and supervisors are usually given significant training in human relations skills. Many union-free companies also provide specialized education in how to deal with organizing attempts.

OSHA-Mandated Training

Safety training is discussed in detail in Chapter 8. The federal Occupational Safety and Health Administration (OSHA) has mandated general safety practices, hazard communication education, and employee training in the use and storage of potentially dangerous materials such as blood-borne pathogens.

Employee Development

Employee development focuses on self-awareness, motivation, and job skills. Companies typically seek to improve employee attitudes, behaviors, and accomplishments using the following processes:

- *Career development programs.* These programs help employees become more aware of their own interests and abilities. By helping employees think about a career rather than just a job, the employer can help them see their current jobs as learning experiences.
- *Personal assessment programs.* These programs are designed to help employees understand their strengths and the areas in which they need to improve. If employees accurately assess themselves and compare that assessment with the needs of the job, they have a better chance of doing well. These programs should be tied to the performance evaluation process.
- *Job skills programs.* These programs are oriented toward improving the technical skills of employees. On-the-job training (OJT) is the primary vehicle for initial

job training. Formal OJT programs can make a significant impact on both the profitability of the employer and its ability to maintain a positive work environment. But much training is informal, with few guidelines or measurements of achievement. Informal processes seldom do more than get new employees up to a low level of achievement and may allow them to develop bad habits. Formal training processes are more effective. Employees participate in the planning, development, implementation, and, in many cases, administration of training. The involvement of both employees and supervisors usually means the program is more effective and accepted.

Employee development is a matter of deciding where the employee is in terms of knowledge and skill, where you want the employee to be, and what techniques you can use to close the gap. A number of techniques can be used to provide development opportunities for employees. These include

- *Job assignments.* Employees can be assigned to special tasks or limited-term projects that will provide them with hands-on, practical experience in a given area. This kind of development is similar to an apprenticeship program; employees are actually learning as they are performing.
- *Mentoring programs.* Many companies assign mentors or sponsors to new employees to aid in their development. These mentors are chosen from the ranks of experienced employees and are available to lend a hand with assignments, provide counsel, and serve as role models for new, inexperienced employees.
- *Reading assignments.* Reading assignments can be a good way to introduce employees to new concepts, to encourage them to stay abreast of new developments, and to help them understand the nuances of the business or industry you are in. The key to effectiveness is follow-up. After an assignment is given, make sure an opportunity is built in to follow up with a discussion of how the content relates to the job.
- *Task force or committee assignments.* Task force assignments allow employees not only to learn more about their own jobs but also to learn about the functioning of the company as a whole. Task forces help develop independence and initiative and allow employees to interact with other company representatives and learn how parts of the whole fit together.

Effective training is tied to the needs of the individual as well as the needs of the organization. Use the following criteria when determining what type of training is most appropriate for employees:

- What skills does the employee already have that are appropriate and required for the job?
- What skills are lacking or need to be improved?

- How can these skills be measured?
- How will improved performance or skill development be exhibited?
- What development options can be put in place to move employees from where they are now to where you want them to be?

Succession Planning

The demand for skilled middle managers, executives, and professionals continues to be high. As the population ages, companies are at risk of losing a substantial number of their seasoned executives.

Whether your organization's employee replacement needs are the result of tragedy, transition, or trial and error, considering the issue of succession now can help you accomplish these staffing changes smoothly, with minimal disruption to your internal processes and with a seamless transition for internal and external customers.

In the not-so-distant past, organizations were eager to find new talent from outside; today, many recognize the value of growing talent from within. Unfortunately, the talent pool in many organizations is shallow, forcing employers to look outside to fill key positions. HR can play a critical role in grooming existing employees to move into more challenging roles, benefiting both the company and its employees. There are several important steps to implementing an effective succession planning process.

1. Identify the skills and competencies you need. Competencies might include delegating responsibility, establishing strategic direction, making operational decisions, building trust, communicating, or demonstrating financial acumen. The process of identifying competencies can be time-consuming, but it is an important first step.

2. Make sure the direction comes from the top. The impetus for succession planning efforts needs to come from the very top of the organization. Do not be surprised if you have a difficult time getting your existing managers to support the effort. While managers certainly play an important role in developing employees, they are concerned about their own career progression, and those self-interests can get in the way of total commitment to ensuring the career progression of others. Adding a section on career pathing to the employee evaluation process, so that succession planning is considered part of every manager's job and managers at every level are evaluated on their participation in it, and initiating discussions between employees and their supervisors can be important steps in developing a culture that supports succession planning. Keep in mind, though, that managers may be resistant

both because of their own feelings of competitiveness with staff and because of their resistance to losing good employees to other areas of the company when they have invested a great deal of time and effort in training and developing those employees.

3. Develop an acceleration pool. How can you identify the employees who are likely to have potential for growth? While keeping your eyes open for natural talent is a good idea, you should also consciously look for employees who exhibit the competencies you have identified as critical to the success of the organization. Every organization has hidden talent — employees who quietly and consistently do their jobs but have the potential to do much more. The challenge is to find — and develop — these employees. Once employees with potential (and interest) have been identified, they can be provided with both training and job experiences to help prepare them to move into more advanced positions. Focus on competencies, not specific positions. Seek to develop employees who exhibit the competencies you have identified as critical to the success of the organization. Keep in mind, too, that not everybody wants more responsibility. A certain percentage of your staff will be happy to remain in their current positions.

4. Identify skill and knowledge gaps, and work to fill those gaps. Determine what you need to do to get the individuals you have identified to the next level of performance. What kinds of skills need to be developed? What developmental opportunities need to be provided? Provide employees with a series of training and operational experiences to help prepare them for higher-level contributions.

5. Encourage employees to self-identify. Who is, ultimately, responsible for an employee's career? Not the HR department. Not the manager. The employee. While there are direct benefits to taking a proactive approach to identifying employees with the skills and capabilities your organization will need in the future, you should also expect employees to play an integral role in their own career management.

Effective succession planning assumes that you are prepared to be honest with employees about their potential. Some employees may simply not be management material. They need to know that. There are a limited number of opportunities in any organization. You do not want chance to decide who gets into those positions.

Also keep in mind that just because there are a limited number of advancement opportunities does not mean that there aren't other developmental opportunities for employees. There may be opportunities to participate in special projects, to lead teams or task forces, or to learn a new skill. These opportunities can be available to any employee who expresses an interest. And just because an employee is not identified as a candidate for advancement now does not mean he or she won't be identified as such in the future. Employees will still have opportunities for training. They will still have opportunities to develop their skills.

Figure 5.1 lists some topics typically included in management and supervisor training programs.

FIGURE 5.1. Management and Supervisor Training Topics

- Transition to supervisor–Change focus from "doing" to "getting things done through others."

- Role of supervisor–Learn what supervisors really do.

- Administration of employer policies–Lessen misunderstanding of policies and reduce employee complaints and problems.

- Interviewing/selection–Hire better, more productive employees while reducing exposure to discrimination complaints.

- Conducting performance appraisals–Improve communication and coaching skills to develop better, more committed employees.

- Discipline and documentation–Correct unacceptable behavior fairly and efficiently.

- Team building–Build cooperation by teaching techniques of working together.

- Productivity improvement–Get more accomplished with less.

- Effective communications–Learn conversation and listening skills.

- Time management–Get things done on time.

- Effective decision-making–Learn techniques for making the right decision at the right time.

- Supervisor as a trainer–Learn methods of instructing others to do things the right way.

- Evaluating performance–Institute effective ways to evaluate employees.

- Motivating employees–Learn practical patterns of employee behavior and how to get employees to do their best.

Computer-Based Training

Training costs and training demand are increasing exponentially. As employers compete for an ever-shrinking number of skilled workers, and as free time becomes increasingly precious, alternatives to traditional training and education have become more necessity than luxury. Luckily, as bandwidth becomes a less scarce resource and more companies become networked, the move to training using Internet, intranet, or extranet technology is a growing option.

The benefits of online learning to employers include these:
- Saving money on traditional training (reduced travel costs and employee time away from the office).
- More convenient access to just-in-time training and information.
- The ability to update information easily and inexpensively so that it is immediately accessible to any number of employees in any number of locations.

- The opportunity to track, test, and report users' progress and scores to verify learning results.
- The ability to have instant access to information for additional learning reinforcement.

Benefits for employees include these:
- The ability to view enjoyable, interactive business learning presentations at their desktops, in full-color and full-motion video, audio, text, and slides.
- The ability to work at their own pace.
- The ability to navigate or search topics, slides, or text at any time in the program.

Employees can be in a virtual classroom environment at their convenience. They can be participating with a group, yet doing so independently. Computer- or Internet-based training can be especially useful when you only have one employee to train. You do not need to wait until you have a sufficient number of employees to justify a training session.

CD-ROM technology allowed many companies an easy entry point for online training, but it does have some drawbacks. Internet- or computer-based training expands on this technology, providing even greater flexibility and options. For example, computer-based training can be delivered to employees who do not have CD-ROM drives, and there is no need to have a training CD on-site; courses can be accessed through a computer network or via the Internet. If the training you will be providing contains information that changes frequently, Internet- or computer-based training provides greater flexibility for updating information. Another major advantage of Internet-based training, and one that offers endless opportunity, is its ability to allow interaction between learner and instructor.

The benefits of computer-based training are obvious, but there are certain issues that must be addressed before you move in this direction.
- *Computer systems.* The primary barrier to instituting an Internet-based training process is your existing computer system and system support. You will need to work with your information systems staff to determine whether your existing systems are sufficient or whether you need additional hardware to accommodate computer-based training. Another issue will be employee access. If all employees do not have ready access to a computer, the benefits of computer-based training will be minimized.
- *Learning transition.* Another barrier to the successful implementation of a computer-based training environment involves the transition from face-to-face learning to learning in an electronic environment. Experts and those who have participated in these activities claim the transition is relatively easy to make and

that the new environment offers its own benefits.

- *Management commitment.* As with any other initiative, the success of your computer-based training efforts will depend largely on the commitment of top management.
- *Content.* Some topics are simply not suitable for online learning. Customer service training, for example, may be best delivered in an environment that allows for interaction and role-playing. However, as videoconferencing technologies become more sophisticated, even some of these barriers can be removed.

Computer-based training should not be viewed as a replacement for traditional training — it is an enhancement and a complement, as is providing training to employees via the Internet.

Evaluating Training Effectiveness

Training efforts need to be evaluated for both quality and usefulness. Although many employers use simple appraisal instruments, there are more efficient ways of showing a return on the investment.

Training is an important investment in the human resources of a company. It requires considerable expense and time commitment. HR professionals need to develop and conduct relevant, reliable, and practical training programs. Evaluating and documenting improvements is just as important as conducting the training.

FAQs

What are the key points HR professionals should know about training?

Hilarie Frank:

HR professionals should be an important part of an organization's performance management system. Thus, HR should assist in developing, implementing, and executing a performance management system.

HR should assist management with setting specific, measurable, realistic goals and a time frame for reaching such goals. Furthermore, managers must be held accountable for assisting their staff in reaching their goals.

The performance management system will identify performance gaps. HR should be responsible for implementing training and development programs to address those gaps. HR should also implement training and development programs to assist employees in enhancing the skills that align with the employees' career path goals (growth opportunities).

Jim Sutton, SPHR:

The most important idea to know about training is that many "problems" do not go away when only training is applied. Some managers turn to training to hide from bigger issues or when they simply need to show they are doing something.

- Many performance issues are simply not training problems because the person could perform the task if his or her life depended on it. The person chooses not to, and that is a management problem.
- Many times, the system prevents or punishes the behavior we would like to see. Again, a management problem.
- Many times, managers expect a 10-year-old habit to change instantly with no follow-up coaching after a one-day class. This will not happen, and it is not the fault of the trainer. Expect to need follow-up after training to help get the new habits in place.
- Think of "problems" as part of a larger picture because they really are. Systems thinking is a great place to start sorting out what is really a training problem and what is a management problem.

Many times, there may be a training component of the problem but another solution must also be implemented at the same time to get the desired result. An example is a car that needs a new battery and gas. Both solutions are needed for the car to run, and *both* will fail without the other.

Should our company set up a mentoring program?

William G. Bliss:

Mentoring programs can be valuable, but, like other tools, they must be clearly understood and have a clear purpose. Mentoring programs may be used as tools for

- Retention.
- Recruiting.
- Developing high-potential employees.
- Recognizing and rewarding both mentors and protégés.
- Passing on critical information about company practices.
- Developing mentors.

There should be clear definitions as to who qualifies to be a mentor or a protégé. The program should outline how the mentoring relationship will be established, how long it will last, and what specific measures will be used to gauge its success or effectiveness.

The process of matching mentors to protégés must be carefully considered and communicated. For example, the best mentors must not be so overloaded that they cannot perform their regular responsibilities effectively. And the protégés must not receive any intangible benefits, such as preferential treatment, because they have been assigned to a well-connected mentor.

A mentor's qualifications must relate to the overall purpose of the program. He or she should

- Be an effective communicator who can be direct without seeming to be giving a performance appraisal. Listening skills are of paramount importance.
- Use a coaching approach, helping the protégés discover the answer to an issue on their own rather than taking a directive approach and providing the answer.
- Be a trusted, respected executive or high-level manager.
- Have empathy and a strong ability to understand the needs and motivations of other people.
- Have a strong desire to give back some of the expertise learned over the years, purely for the satisfaction of giving.
- Be willing and able to devote the necessary time to the relationship.

Lessons from the Trenches

A Learning Experience

In the early 1990s, Marian Hall started an HR function in a wholesale-distribution organization with 95 employees. When she left six years later, the company had 125 employees and some solid HR systems and processes that she had put into place. "Starting up an HR function was incredibly valuable for me," says Hall, "and the fact that I was successful at it gave me a lot of confidence in my abilities when I looked at opportunities in larger organizations." During her entire time with the company, Hall remained a one-person department.

The company had never had an HR department before, and the owners were at the point where they needed someone professional to guide the process. While they had a few things in place — performance appraisals, benefits programs, and a sales incentive plan — they did not feel comfortable moving forward with their limited level of expertise.

At the time, Hall's background was primarily as an HR administrator. "Although I had held manager titles before," she says, "I was primarily administering HR programs designed by a corporate HR staff. I knew this was an opportunity to take my knowledge and apply it to the creation of programs, rather than just to implementation and administration."

Taking Stock

Hall's first step was to review the programs that were already in place. "I looked at forms, at database systems, at benefits designs, and so on." Then, based on discussions with her boss and input from sales and corporate management, she developed a list of project priorities and got started.

Hall relied on a variety of resources as she moved forward. "In some cases, I purchased software packages or bought books. I purchased an HR research series. When I started working on compensation, I called on a friend who was a compensation analyst. I attended every seminar I could on employment law, benefits, employee relations, and law updates. I joined all the HR groups and attended several workshops on compensation program design and, later on, sales compensation design. I networked with my HR friends and borrowed from materials I had used other places," she says.

Facing Challenges Head-On

The greatest challenge that Hall faced initially was that she had really never designed any of these programs before. "I had convinced my boss that I had resources to do it. Now I had to deliver. The fact that the company was generous in providing resources helped. Whenever I was faced with something new, like designing the base pay program, it paid for me to get the education I needed. As time went on and I learned more and networked more, the company benefited from the improvements."

Another challenge was implementing changes in the face of a certain amount of resistance from managers. "If we were doing something we'd never done before, like a base-pay plan or results-based performance appraisals," Hall remembers, "there was initial resistance. This reluctance usually was due to a lack of knowledge, and I used these situations to educate. The base-pay program is a particular example. I worked primarily with the senior management team, none of whom had any knowledge about base-pay design — but all of them certainly had lots of opinions. As I designed the program, I took the approach of 'Here's what we're doing, here are the options, here's what I've selected and why.' Over the course of the five years that we did this, they learned an incredible amount about base-pay design and became great supporters."

Relying on Others

Hall found that advice and support was readily available and much appreciated as she felt her way along in her new role. "In starting up an HR function," she advises, "especially if you are like me and don't have a lot of design expertise, create your own little advisory board of HR professionals that do have that expertise. Then you have ready resources.

"Another piece of advice is to be sure to spend time with your customers and find out what their needs are and their attitudes toward HR. Again, I was lucky in that most managers welcomed the support, but they did have their own quirks about content on certain projects. Understanding their needs and learning how to help them helped me be more successful."

Compensation and Benefits

The cost of compensation and benefits for employees is the most substantial cost most employers face. While the cost of benefits alone is very high, often representing up to 50 percent of the company's payroll, few employees truly understand the value of the benefits they receive. There is a role for HR here in ensuring that both management staff and employees understand not only the company's compensation philosophy but also the full extent and value of benefits provided.

The development of a compensation and benefits plan has increasingly become a major strategic initiative for most companies. To attract and retain qualified employees, companies feel pressure to ensure that their pay and benefits are competitive. In addition, there is a growing awareness of the importance of communicating the compensation philosophy to employees.

In the past, when companies needed to develop a formal compensation structure, they often copied one used by another company or hired a consultant to develop one specific to them. When they needed to revise their pay schedules, they surveyed similar companies in the area and established pay rates and salaries based on those in the market. When inflation and the rising cost of living devalued real earnings, companies initiated automatic pay increases based on the Consumer Price Index. These increases became institutionalized as cost-of-living adjustments (COLAs).

As companies began to feel more pressure to meet business and sales objectives, they developed methods of compensating employees based on their contributions to the organization — linking individual pay to individual or departmental objectives. Pay for performance became a rallying cry for both employees and managers.

Today, many companies compensate employees using some form of base pay with additional monetary incentives. Successful incentive plans reward employees based on mutually accepted standards. One problem with this type of compensation system is that management is rewarded for achieving short-term financial goals rather than long-term viability. In addition, large executive bonuses and stock options have generated considerable criticism because they often are not linked to the company's performance. The dot-com industry, in particular, demonstrated that the result of these kinds of incentive systems can be poor performance leading to dramatic downsizing and the closing of facilities to achieve profitability targets.

Clearly, the ability to attract and retain employees through competitive compensation and benefits plans is important to any company's success (see Figure 6.1).

Employee turnover is disruptive as well as expensive. While turnover rates vary dramatically by geography, industry, and position, companies everywhere aim to minimize turnover to avoid incurring the costs associated with recruitment, orientation, and training — and to maintain their intellectual capital.HR consulting firm Caliper in Princeton, New Jersey, offers an online turnover calculator, available at www.caliperonline.com/cost-of-turnover.asp, that companies can use to calculate the cost of their turnover.

This chapter will discuss the development of a compensation plan based on internal equity, external equity, and employee characteristics and contributions; thorough job analysis; and consideration of how benefits — monetary and nonmonetary — can contribute to the overall compensation package for employees.

FIGURE 6.1. Perceived Effectiveness of Employee Retention Strategies

	Employees (n = 450)	HR Professionals (n = 357)
Career development opportunities	52%	46%
Competitive salary	50%	59%
Flexible work schedules	29%	47%
Promotion of qualified employees	28%	38%
Bonuses	27%	15%
Competitive merit increases	20%	19%
Competitive vacation and holiday benefits	16%	19%
Increased health care benefits	14%	25%
Telecommuting	12%	6%
Stock options	7%	4%
Child care (paid for, subsidized, or provided by employer)	4%	4%
Early eligibility for benefits	4%	4%

Note: Employees were asked which items would be most effective in encouraging them to stay with an employer or with their current employer. HR professionals were asked which retention efforts they believed to be most effective, regardless of whether the strategy was used at their organizations. Employee data were gathered from a convenience sample of CareerJournal.com web site visitors through a pop-up window directing them to the online survey. Readers should proceed with caution when generalizing these results. Percentages do not total 100 percent, as respondents were allowed up to three choices. Data are sorted in descending order by employee column.

Source: SHRM/CareerJournal.com 2006 U.S. Job Retention Poll Findings. Available at www.shrm.org/Research/SurveyFindings.

Forms of Compensation

Figure 6.2 outlines the various forms of compensation that companies might offer to employees. Compensation can be indirect, in the form of benefits, or direct, in the form of cash.

The compensation and benefits process is one of the first areas that HR should address. Without HR direction, compensation decisions are likely to be based more on expediency than on strategy, and inequities may well exist. Management may already be aware of concerns through feedback from employees in the form of high turnover, formal complaints, responses to employee surveys, or the office grapevine. Or the company may be having a difficult time recruiting skilled employees.

SHRM's 2005 Reward Programs Survey provides an overview of the types of reward programs most commonly used by HR professionals and the use of incentive compensation programs in organizations. Most HR professionals report that their organizations offer some form of monetary or nonmonetary reward programs for employees. The most commonly offered monetary reward programs are incentive compensation programs or variable bonuses based on company and/or individual performance, with more than two-thirds of those responding indicating that their organizations offer these types of monetary reward programs. Most HR professionals rate monetary reward programs as more effective than nonmonetary programs overall. However, nonmonetary rewards cost less and are still seen as effective.

It is important to note, though, that a large number of HR professionals felt that these programs are not at all effective in motivating underperforming employees to improve their levels of performance.

Coordination of all aspects of the company's reward and recognition strategy is essential to achieving the outcomes the company hopes for — low turnover, ease of recruiting new employees, and high levels of employee satisfaction and productivity. Given the expense of this area and its importance to the company's overall success, appropriate study, planning, communication, and analysis is critical.

FIGURE 6.2. Compensation and Benefits

Indirect (Benefits)			Direct (Cash)			
Protection Programs	Pay for time not worked	Employee services and perquisites	Base Pay	Merit Pay	Incentives	Cost-of-living adjustments

Compensation Philosophy

Most companies adopt some combination of the three types of compensation policies or philosophies outlined in Figure 6.3. These philosophies serve as the foundation for designing and administering pay systems.

Regardless of the philosophy adopted, the overall objectives should be the same — efficiency and equity. How do companies develop pay processes that meet these objectives? The three parts to a pay model are these:

1. The objectives.
2. The policies that form the foundation of the system.
3. The techniques that make up the specific operations.

The following compensation objectives are applicable in practically every company:

- Identify prevailing market wages and salaries.
- Pay competitive wages and salaries, taking into consideration the company's profitability.
- Increase employee satisfaction with the company's reward strategy.
- Maintain a strict relationship between the value of the work performed and employees' value to the organization.
- Identify the best methods and techniques for awarding pay increases while restraining the ability of managers to grant unwarranted increases.
- Reward levels and types of performance that add to the profitability of the company.

External Competitiveness

External competitiveness or equity refers to how an employer pays compared with what similar — or competitive — companies are paying. Based on its goals and objectives as well as the resources available, a company may decide to pay compensation at, below, or above the market. Some companies may want to set their pay levels higher than those of their competitors, hoping to remain union-free or to attract better employees. Some may offer lower base pay but a greater opportunity to get overtime pay, better benefits, or a better incentive plan. Or pay and benefits may be lower in a company that instead offers job security or excellent supervision.

As Figure 6.3 indicates, market surveys and pay levels are two techniques used by companies to achieve external competitiveness in compensation.

FIGURE 6.3. Compensation Philosophies

Philosophy	Techniques	Objectives
External competitiveness	Market surveys Pay levels	Efficiency
Internal equity	Job analysis	Pay structure
Employee characteristics and contributions	Seniority Performance increase guidelines Incentives	Equity

Market Surveys

Market surveys reveal what other employers are paying for positions requiring similar experience and skills. In considering market surveys, companies generally try to find organizations in their own area for comparison. If there are few or no competitors or companies with similar jobs in the area, the HR professional may choose to go outside the local market for survey data. The three attributes to look for when selecting companies for a market survey are similar jobs, similar size, and similar geographic location.

Companies use several techniques for conducting salary surveys. Personal interviews usually garner the most accurate responses, but they are usually the most expensive technique. Mailed surveys are probably the most frequently used and the cheapest; however, the jobs must be clearly defined or the results may not be accurate. Many companies validate mail responses with telephone follow-up inquiries.

Companies usually do not seek market data for all jobs, but only for benchmark positions that can be easily compared across company lines. Benchmarking is a process of identifying comparable positions, gathering information on pay ranges, and using the data as a point of reference to compare rates of pay. These key jobs typically are chosen for particular reasons — because work content is stable over time, many employees are clustered in these positions, concentrations of minorities and females are unlikely, and similar positions are commonly found in the broad employment community. Once the market data have been received and summarized, the results can be used to modify actual pay practices.

Pay Level Decisions

Pay level decisions start with determining the relationship between the company's compensation philosophy and its pay objectives. The company decides if it wants to pay above the market (lead), with the market (match), or below the market (lag).

If the company wants to attract experienced employees with high potential, it may have to pay above the market. Many compensation professionals believe that leading the market in pay allows the company to attract and retain the best applicants and that these higher-quality employees will be more productive. However, research does not support these beliefs. Anecdotal evidence from HR and quality consultants suggests that higher pay does not necessarily result in increased productivity.

If the compensation objective is to reduce turnover, retain valued employees, or reduce dissatisfaction with pay, the company should either match or lead the market.

If the compensation objective is to contain labor costs, paying below the market has traditionally been the technique used. However, paying below the market may cause serious employee relations and compensation problems that typically cost much more than the company can save in wages.

The decision to lead, match, or lag can be made specific to individual jobs. For example, the company can decide to lead in information technology jobs and match in secretarial or office support jobs.

Figure 6.4 gives an example of how market survey data can be used to benchmark positions to determine pay levels.

In this example, weighted averages are used as points of comparison against the company's midpoint. In the first three examples, each data source is assigned an equal weight; to determine a market midpoint, the final example shows how different weights can be assigned to each data source. The resulting number is used as the new market midpoint for that job grade.

The first position (account coordinator/market research) is found to be paid at a higher level than indicated by the market analysis, and the other positions are near or below market. Although the market analysis is based on data, judgment must be exercised in determining how to adjust internal pay grades as well as individual compensation levels to maintain internal as well as external consistency and to take into account the impact decisions will have on morale and job satisfaction.

FIGURE 6.4. Benchmarking/Market Survey Analysis

ACCOUNT COORDINATOR/MARKET RESEARCH:

Demographic	Weighted Average	Weight Assigned	Weight Per Hour
Companies in state with more than 1,000 employees	16.34	50%	8.17
Health care organizations with more than 1,000 employees	19.97	50%	9.99
Market midpoint			18.16
Current Grade:	41	(min) 16.25 (mid) 19.50 (max) 22.75	
Recommended:	37	(min) 15.25 (mid) 18.30 (max) 21.35	

PUBLICATIONS SPECIALIST:

Demographic	Weighted Average	Weight Assigned	Weight Per Hour
Companies in state with more than 1,000 employees	19.59	50%	9.80
Health care organizations with more than 1,000 employees	17.88	50%	8.94
Market midpoint			18.74
Current Grade:	30	(min) 13.50 (mid) 16.20 (max) 18.90	
Recommended:	38	(min) 15.50 (mid) 18.60 (max) 21.70	

PUBLIC RELATIONS COORDINATOR:

Demographic	Weighted Average	Weight Assigned	Weight Per Hour
Companies in state with more than 1,000 employees	20.11	50%	10.06
Health care organizations with more than 1,000 employees	19.87	50%	9.94
Market midpoint			20.00
Current Grade:	41	(min) 16.25 (mid) 19.50 (max) 22.75	
Recommended:	42	(min) 16.50 (mid) 19.80 (max) 23.10	

COMMUNITY RELATIONS COORDINATOR:

Demographic	Weighted Average	Weight Assigned	Weight Per Hour
Public relations specialists in health care firms with more than 1,000 employees	19.87	10%	1.99
Writers/editors within state in companies with more than 1,000 employees	17.83	30%	5.35
Communications specialists in health care firms with more than 1,000 employees	17.88	20%	3.58
Technical writers within state	15.97	40%	6.39
Market midpoint			17.31
Current Grade:	20	(min) 11.00 (mid) 13.20 (max) 15.40	
Recommended:	33	(min) 14.25 (mid) 17.10 (max) 19.95	

Internal Equity

Internal equity refers to comparisons among jobs or skill levels inside the company. Pay relationships that are internally consistent are based on the content of the work, the skills required, and the relative contribution of the work to the company's overall objectives. How does the work of an executive secretary compare with the work of an accounting clerk, a computer operator, or a supervisor? Which jobs require more skill, experience, human relations expertise, or ability to communicate effectively? Does the output from one job add more value to the company's bottom line than that from another?

Internal consistency is hard to achieve in determining pay, both for those doing similar work and for those performing different tasks. Internal equity issues cause more dissatisfaction than any other approach to compensation, including external equity.

As Figure 6.3 indicates, the techniques companies can use to achieve internal equity include job analysis and pay structure. Job analysis and job descriptions are discussed in more detail later in this chapter.

Pay structure focuses attention on the link between employee perceptions and their work behaviors. Pay differences induce employees to join a company, undertake training, progress through jobs, meet performance expectations, and continue (or not continue) employment with the company. Traditionally, pay structures have been based on steep hierarchical progressions, with unskilled laborers receiving the lowest pay.

Pay structure drives movement within the organization and should be carefully thought through. Consider, for example, what can happen in a company where employees who have responsibility for supervising others are paid at a considerably higher rate than peers with comparable skills, experience, and responsibility who are not supervising other workers. If the way to improve pay is to assume responsibility for others, the organization may soon find itself top-heavy with managerial staff.

Employee Characteristics and Contributions

Under this compensation philosophy, emphasis is placed on individual performance or seniority. Should all employees doing the same work receive the same base pay? Should one employee be paid more than another based on seniority or superior individual performance? Should managers and supervisors be paid based on the performance of the department they supervise or based on the performance of the company overall? Should they be paid based on achieving short-term goals?

As Figure 6.3 shows, the techniques companies can use to implement this philosophy include seniority, performance increase guidelines, and incentives.

Two basic factors go into determining pay for individual employees based on this philosophy. Should different employees holding the same job be paid the same? What factors should be used to recognize differences between employees?

Seniority

When employers do not wish to differentiate between individuals' performance, or where there is a collective bargaining unit, often one flat rate is paid for a particular job or class of jobs. The existence of a flat rate does not mean that performance or experience differences among employees do not exist, but that the employer chooses not to consider these variations. However, even in these companies, seniority or tenure is often used as a pay differential.

Performance

Most employees have come to expect annual pay increases, even when the business has not been profitable. The tradition of basing pay increases on performance is well established. But companies often disguise annual pay increases by calling them performance-based or merit increases. The idea is that lower performance ratings are tied to lower pay increases, while higher ratings result in larger increases.

Annual Guidelines

The *general increase* is typically found in unionized companies. A contract is negotiated that specifies some equal percentage increase across all job classifications for each year of the agreement. A *cost-of-living adjustment* is most often triggered by an increase in the Consumer Price Index; the same percentage increase applies to all covered positions. *Performance-based* and *merit increases* are discussed above. *Lump-sum payments* are often used by companies to reward employees who have reached the top of their salary range. The benefit to the company is that high-performing employees can be rewarded without inflating the salary range.

Incentives

Incentives are different from annual increases because they are usually distributed irregularly and do not form a basis for future increases. The two varieties are group incentives and individual incentives. A group incentive might be structured to provide a bonus to a product development team, for example, for meeting a product introduction deadline. An individual incentive might be designed to reward a salesperson for meeting certain sales targets.

Piecework Rates. Piecework rates guarantee employees an hourly rate for producing at a minimum level of production. The employee is paid more according to how much faster he or she works. Many companies still use piecework rates as an alternative to a formal appraisal process or as a motivational device. For example, retail sales associates are often paid a guaranteed hourly rate, with a certain dollar volume of sales required to keep the position. Even professional firms (accounting, engineering, and law) may have a minimum volume of sales required for continued employment. The employee receives a salary based on that minimum; if individual sales do not reach the minimum, the employee might be terminated.

Commissions. Commissions are commonly found in sales jobs. Straight commission is typically a percentage of the price of the item sold. A variation is for a company to pay a small salary and also a commission or bonus when a minimum sales goal is achieved. With commission sales, there is usually a small draw against earnings or very limited base pay. Commission sales are more prevalent in some industries than others.

Job Analysis, Job Description, and Job Evaluation

Job analysis is a technique used by companies to achieve internal equity among positions. It is a systematic process through which information about jobs is collected, often through the use of a questionnaire that is filled out by employees and supervisors. The questionnaire asks for information on the essential functions of the job, the frequency of the activities performed, and the priority for each job *function.*

Once the basic job analysis has been completed, the resulting data are summarized into a standard format called the *job description.*

Not only is the job description an important tool in the development of a compensation and benefits plan, as we have already seen it is also a document that companies rely heavily on for employee recruitment and performance evaluation. While not legally required under either federal or state laws, job descriptions can help companies avoid a number of legal problems, including the following:

- *Discriminatory hiring.* Job descriptions provide an objective, written source documenting the requirements of a position and the qualifications required to perform effectively in that position.
- *Americans with Disabilities Act violations.* Job descriptions should separate out the essential and nonessential functions of the job. Essential functions are those that must be performed by the person holding that job. If an individual with a disability cannot perform the essential functions of the position, with or without a reasonable accommodation, he or she is not qualified for the job and need not be hired or retained. Any job descriptions that separate essential from nonessential functions must be reviewed and updated regularly to ensure that they reflect accurately the actual job being performed.

- *Discriminatory termination.* When job descriptions include the core competencies required for the position, and employees are evaluated against those requirements, expectations are clearly established and documented.

The job description typically contains the following three sections that identify, define, and describe the job:

1. The job title, the number of people holding the job, whether the job is exempt or nonexempt from the overtime provisions of the Fair Labor Standards Act, and the supervisor of the position.
2. The purpose of the job, the criteria for satisfactory performance, and how this job fits in with other jobs and company objectives.
3. The content of the job, including the major duties of the job holder, the specific work to be done, the supervision required, and the discretion allowed. Content should also include the training and experience required for the job.

Since the Americans with Disabilities Act was implemented in 1990, only essential job requirements may be used to decide qualifications for positions. Requirements for physical activity should be included only if they are essential job functions.

There are job description software packages and books of sample job descriptions on the market that can provide a good starting point for developing your own job descriptions, as can a review of job descriptions for similar positions available from other businesses or your professional HR contacts. While these sources can be a good starting point, do not rely too heavily on these templates. Your job descriptions should be an accurate reflection of the unique requirements for each position within your own company.

The job description can be used as the basis for *job evaluation*, a systematic process that helps maintain pay structures by comparing the similarities and differences in the content and value of jobs. When properly designed and administered, job evaluation can also help ensure that pay structures are internally equitable and acceptable to both employer and employee. Job evaluation can have the following four functions, depending on how the process is designed and administered:

1. To classify or group jobs based on similarities and differences in their work content.
2. To establish a job hierarchy based on the relative value of jobs.
3. To link internal job content with external market rates.
4. To serve as a tool for measurement and negotiation of pay rates.

The four fundamental methods of job evaluation — ranking, classification, factor comparison, and the point method — are outlined in Figure 6.5.

Objectivity is extremely important in the job evaluation process — but it can be difficult to achieve. Managers may find it hard to remain focused on the requirements of the *job* versus the skills and capabilities of the *job holder*. Consequently, the value of positions may be inflated based on the positive characteristics of the job's incumbent. HR professionals can help bring objectivity to this process, or they may decide that outside assistance is warranted.

Why not just pay market rates? Although certain key jobs might be comparable across several companies, not all jobs are alike. Setting pay rates for dissimilar jobs using market data is difficult. The solution is to set pay rates for key jobs and slot other jobs around them. This slotting is accomplished through job evaluation.

FIGURE 6.5. Job Evaluation Methods

Method	Description	Disadvantages/Challenges
Ranking	Ranks jobs according to their relative value. The simplest, fastest, easiest-to-understand, and least expensive method.	Simple definitions result in subjective opinions, which can be difficult to explain or justify. Requires users to be knowledgeable about every job
Classification	Involves slotting jobs into a series of classes and grades covering all jobs in the company. Widely used in the public sector and in engineering, technical, and scientific jobs in the private sector.	Each class must be described generally enough to slot several jobs, yet specifically enough to have meaning.
Factor comparison	Involves evaluating jobs on the basis of two criteria: 1) a set of compensable factors and 2) market wages or points for a selected set of jobs.	Very complex. Limited usefulness.
Point method	Assigns points for three features: 1) compensable factors, 2) a scale of factors, and 3) weights reflecting the importance of each factor. Total points for all jobs are calculated and a hierarchy is established. Once implemented, it is easy to administer.	Very complex. Must be communicated clearly to managers and supervisors.

Administration

Even a well-designed compensation system — one that integrates external equity, internal equity, and employee characteristics — may not meet its objectives if it is not administered properly. Administration involves planning the elements that should be included (short-term versus long-term incentives), talking with employees, evaluating the system, assessing the competency and validity of supervisors' actions involving pay, and changing the system when it needs improvement.

Do employees see the system as fair? Do they understand which factors will be considered in setting pay? Do they have channels for raising questions and voicing complaints about pay? How do better-performing companies pay their employees? Such information is necessary to evaluate and redesign a system, to adjust to changes, and to highlight potential problem areas.

Planning

Properly designed and administered compensation processes help managers achieve their objectives. A properly planned compensation process will assist managers in achieving consistency in pay practices. It will improve employees' perception that individuals are rewarded for their performance. It will allow the employer to control compensation costs. It supports a culture in which employees perceive the company as a good place to work. In the planning process, the top salary should be paid for activities that produce the most value for the company. It is work output that is valued and paid for.

Budgeting

Instructing managers in the use of the compensation system — its objectives, policies, and techniques — is crucial. It is not uncommon for managers to believe that their employees deserve more than is available for pay increases. When budgeting for personnel expenses, managers need to understand that properly developed budgets offer many benefits and contributions to the company's profitability. Budgeting enables managers to foresee the financial impact of pay increases on profitability.

Communication

A positive approach to talking about the compensation process can be beneficial to the organization. A well-designed pay process can positively influence behaviors and attitudes. Pay differentials can influence employees to seek better positions within the company, obtain additional training, and gain experience. If, on the other hand, employees do not perceive the system as based on work-related and logical processes, they will be dissatisfied. Effectively communicating the philosophy and process minimizes this problem.

Evaluation

Employee dissatisfaction with pay is costly. It erodes commitment to work, and it can lead to absenteeism, high turnover, low productivity, increased numbers of grievances, and other management problems. While more pay is seldom the solution to these problems, regularly evaluating the effectiveness of the process is important.

Compliance with Laws on Compensation

The Fair Labor Standards Act (FLSA) is a federal law that defines the employment relationship, regulates child labor and hours of work, and sets the minimum wage and requirements for paying overtime. The federal minimum wage was raised to $7.25 on July 24, 2009. All employees covered by the FLSA (nonexempt employees) must be paid at least one-and-a-half times their regular rate for any hours worked over 40 in a work week. (State law may be even more generous.) Executive, professional, and administrative employees who are not covered by the FLSA (exempt employees) do not have to be paid overtime. There is a substantial body of law and administrative ruling covering the payment of overtime, exempt status, and minimum wage, placing it far beyond the scope of this book.

Employee Benefits

Direct compensation is only one part of the compensation package. An equally important part is benefits. A 2004 U.S. Chamber of Commerce benefits survey found that the average cost of employee benefits is about 40.2 percent of payroll. Benefits include those that are required by law (e.g., Social Security), those that are so commonly provided by employers that a company would be at a competitive disadvantage without them (e.g., paid time off), and those that are unique and may serve to set an employer apart from its competitors (e.g., an on-site health club or a day care facility).

Many employees look beyond direct compensation when evaluating satisfaction with their jobs. A common misconception among managers is that money drives employee loyalty. This is not necessarily true. Consider, for example, the employees of a company like Microsoft — many became millionaires because of their equity ownership in the company. Yet those millionaires stay on the job, even though they do not need salaries. Why do they stay?

The needs of employees have changed dramatically over the past 30 years. Fueled by a rapid increase in the number of women entering the workforce, more employees are expecting — and demanding — a balance between the expectations of work and the demands of personal life. Workers are most likely to be satisfied with their jobs, committed to their employers, and productive at work when they have jobs that offer autonomy, meaning, learning opportunities, support from supervisors, and flexible work arrangements that are responsive to individual needs. The benefits offered by your organization can help address these employee needs.

Typically, benefits are expected to accomplish these four objectives:
1. To foster external competitiveness.
2. To increase cost-effectiveness.
3. To meet employees' needs and preferences.
4. To comply with federal and state laws.

If offering some benefits is good, is offering more benefits better? Executives and HR professionals often express concern about the belief that the more benefits offered, the more productive and satisfied employees will be. Although failing to offer commonly provided benefits such as paid time off can result in employee dissatisfaction, more benefits do not necessarily result in more productive employees.

Figure 6.6 outlines the results of SHRM's 2009 Employee Benefits Survey covering health benefits. SHRM asked 2,710 randomly selected SHRM members about the benefits their organizations offered or planned to offer within the next year. Responses from 522 HR professionals provided some interesting insights into trends in benefits.

FIGURE 6.6. Types of Health Benefits Offered by Employers
[Percentage offering each benefit, overall and by number of employees]

	Overall (n = 500)	Small (1–99 Employees)	Medium (100–499 Employees)	Large (500 or More Employees)
Prescription drug program coverage	96	94	97	97
Dental insurance	96	91	98	98
Mail-order prescription program	91	83	87	90
Preferred provider organization (PPO) plan	81	77	80	88
Chiropractic coverage	80	74	84	80
Mental health coverage	80	72	83	84
Accidental death and dismemberment insurance (AD&D)	78	76	77	80
Long-term disability insurance	77	77	72	82
Vision insurance	76	63	74	91
Employee assistance program (EAP)	75	66	75	88
Medical flexible spending account	71	64	69	81
Dependent care flexible spending account	70	60	69	80
Short-term disability insurance	70	67	70	72
Contraceptive coverage	66	67	62	71
Life insurance for dependents	58	44	57	73
Health care premium flexible spending account	43	38	46	53
Supplemental accident insurance	40	37	41	42
Long-term-care insurance	39	32	39	46
Health care coverage for dependent grandchildren	37	30	35	45
Domestic partner health care coverage (opposite-sex)	37	34	38	36
Rehabilitation assistance	37	42	32	39
Domestic partner health care coverage (same-sex)	36	29	34	42
HMO (health maintenance organization) plan	35	32	33	40
Health care coverage for part-time workers	35	31	27	53
Intensive care insurance	35	39	34	34
Critical illness insurance	34	40	33	29
Cancer insurance	33	27	38	32

CONTINUED ON NEXT PAGE

FIGURE 6.6. Types of Health Benefits Offered by Employers, continued
[Percentage offering each benefit, overall and by number of employees]

	Overall (n = 500)	Small (1–99 Employees)	Medium (100–499 Employees)	Large (500 or More Employees)
Health savings account (HSA)	32	27	30	39
Surcharges for spousal health care coverage	32	31	30	38
Health care coverage for foster children	31	26	27	41
Infertility treatment coverage (other than in-vitro fertilization)	30	23	28	36
Bariatric coverage for weight loss	29	18	33	35
Acupressure/acupuncture medical coverage	28	28	29	27
Health reimbursement account (HRA)	26	23	26	26
Point of service (POS) plan	26	23	29	26
Retiree health care coverage	26	15	25	39
In-vitro fertilization coverage	23	19	21	31
Hospital indemnity insurance	23	22	24	21
Laser-based vision correction coverage	19	13	20	23
Pharmacy management program	18	13	17	22
Wholesale generic drug program for injectable drugs	17	17	18	17
Alternative/complementary medical coverage	16	18	13	16
Employer-matched contributions to a health savings account (HSA)	15	15	15	15
Grief recovery program	15	18	13	14
Consumer-directed health care plan (CDHP)	12	8	10	18
Support groups	12	12	13	11
Exclusive provider organization (EPO) plan	8	5	7	14
Indemnity plan (fee-for-service)	7	3	8	9
Elective procedures coverage (other than laser-based vision correction coverage)	5	2	5	9
Experimental/elective drug coverage	3	3	2	5
Subsidized cost of elder care	3	2	3	4
Gender reassignment surgery coverage	1	1	1	2

Source: 2009 Employee Benefits: A Survey Report by SHRM. Available at www.shrm.org/Research/SurveyFindings.

Respondents indicated that the decline in the national economy had had an impact on their benefits decisions, with 60 percent reporting that their benefits offerings had been impacted. Respondents indicated that their organizations spent, on average, 20 percent of an employee's annual salary on mandatory benefits, 19 percent on voluntary benefits and 11 percent on pay-for-time-not-worked benefits. Most organizations (81 percent) review benefits annually; 12 percent do so even more frequently. Despite challenges resulting from the economy and tightening budgets, respondents acknowledged that employees continue to rate benefits as one of the key factors in job satisfaction.

Employers are faced with a wide range of options — and corresponding costs — when considering the mix of compensation and benefits to offer to employees. As they weigh these options, HR professionals need to consider issues related to the following:

- *Competitiveness:* How should benefits compare with those of competitors?
- *Coverage:* Which benefits should the company offer? Which benefits are mandatory?
- *Communication:* How can the company inform employees about their benefits?
- *Choice:* What degree of choice or flexibility should be included?

Just as with direct compensation, companies need to position their total compensation package, including benefits, in the marketplace, striving for both internal and external equity. Most large companies compare their benefits with those of similar companies. Assessing competitors' benefits programs is valuable, but a company's own program should not exceed its ability to pay. The four comparisons to make are total cost of benefits, cost per employee, cost as a percentage of the company's payroll costs, and cost per employee per hour.

Four kinds of benefits typically are provided to employees: paid time away from work, life and health insurance, employee services, and retirement income. Some benefits are legally mandated, such as unemployment insurance, workers' compensation, and Social Security. Companies often do not consider these costs as benefits, mistakenly believing that the cost is small compared with other labor costs. However, in many large companies the cost of all benefits exceeds 40 percent of payroll. To maximize value while meeting employees' needs for flexibility and choice, many companies offer a "cafeteria plan" providing employees choices among the benefits offered.

Optional Benefits

Paid Time Away from Work

Employers usually offer pay for holidays and vacations; sometimes they pay for sick leave. Often, neither managers nor employees see the real cost of providing these benefits — it is more than the out-of-pocket cost of paying the employee for time away from work. The cost also involves the lost opportunity or value of the work the employee *would have been doing* if on the job. If the position is really needed, any time away from work means something is not getting completed or someone else has been assigned to do the work.

Insurance

Three major forms of insurance are common: health, disability or accident, and life. *Health insurance* is extremely costly, but it is also extremely popular with employees. In addition to basic medical care, coverage may include prescription drugs, specialized mental health services, and dental care. In spite of cost-containment efforts by both employers and the government, health care costs continue to escalate dramatically. *Group life insurance* is generally very inexpensive, but for most employees, life insurance is a low priority. *Long-term* and *short-term care insurance* and *accident or disability insurance* protect employees who have accidents or injuries off the job, or illnesses or medical problems, that leave them temporarily or permanently unable to work.

It remains to be seen what the full effects of the Patient Protection and Affordable Care Act (PPACA) — more commonly referred to as "health care reform" — will have on all of us. One thing that is clear, however, is that confusion and concern reign.

Mercer recently analyzed data collected through its *2009 National Survey of Employer-Sponsored Health* Plans to qualify the extent to which employers will be affected by certain key reform provisions. Some of their key findings include:

- One of the more challenging provisions to interpret and apply may be the rule that employers provide "affordable" coverage — meaning that full-time employees must generally be asked to pay no more than 9.5 percent of their household income for coverage.
- Reform may have the biggest impact on employers with large part-time populations that don't provide coverage to any part-time employees or that require them to work more than 30 hours/week for coverage eligibility.
- The majority of employers can anticipate making some plan changes.

What does all of this mean? Unfortunately, it means a certain amount of confusion and uncertainty; the need to review and potentially update/change benefit plans; the need to communicate soon, often, and effectively with employees — and, potentially, an increase in the cost of health care benefit coverage.

Jonathan Braddock is president/CEO of ISG Advisors in Madison, Wisconsin. "I think in the short-term employers may see some potential increases to the premiums that they're currently paying," says Braddock. Many of the good things in the act are likely to impact costs, he says. For instance, "there will no longer be any lifetime limits allowed by insurance companies that have historically had limits of from $1-2 million," he says. "All insurance policies as they renew after September 23 will no longer have a cap — so that's going to test the actuarial departments of insurance companies," he says.

Another change that will impact costs is dependent coverage for adult children up to the age of 26 — regardless of whether or not they're in school, independent, married, or living with their parents. In addition, he notes:

- Insurance companies can no longer exclude those under the age of 19 with pre-existing conditions. (And, beginning in 2014, this will extend to new enrollees of all ages.)
- Insurance companies can no longer rescind coverage unless for fraud or blatant misrepresentation.
- Preventive services must now be covered with no cost-sharing. So, if a health plan had a $30 co-pay for routine annual exams, this co-pay will no longer apply.
- Insurance companies must cover emergency services at in-network costs even if received out of network.

Each of these changes benefit certain segments of the population without a doubt and can generally be considered "good things" — but they are good things that come with a cost, Braddock points out.

"Initially people were all excited because we have health care reform, but as the dust has settled and people have actually read the 2,000-page bill, they're finding some interesting things in there."

Pamela Wolf is an attorney and employment law analyst who tracks and analyzes employment law issues, court decisions, and trends. She is a principal analyst for CCH's *Law, Explanation and Analysis of the Patient Protection and Affordable Care Act*, a comprehensive analysis of the 2010 health reform law. Her analysis indicates that there are additional elements of the PPACA that may be of interest to employers (see Appendix C for timeline):

- **Automatic enrollment.** Effective on March 23, 2010, employers with more than 200 full-time employees and that have one or more health benefit plans are required to automatically enroll new employees in a plan. Automatically enrolled employees must have the opportunity to opt out of the coverage.
- **W-2 reporting.** Starting with amounts paid in 2011, employers must disclose the aggregate cost of employer-sponsored health insurance coverage provided to their employees on the employee's Form W-2. Contributions to any health savings account of the employee or the employee's spouse, or salary reduction contributions to a flexible spending arrangement under a cafeteria plan, will not be included.
- **Dependent coverage**. Effective for plan years beginning on or after September 23, 2010, group health plans and health insurers offering group or individual

health insurance with dependent child coverage must make available coverage for the enrollee's adult children who are younger than age 26, regardless of whether or not the dependent is a full-time student, disabled, or married.

Communicating the Impact of Health Care Reform

Health care reform is raising a myriad of questions for organizations and individuals across the country. For employers the questions involve not only what health care reform will mean to them, but also how health care reform will impact employees and how they can best communicate the changes to employees. At the outset, it can be helpful to understand what employees are most concerned about. These concerns are basic and personal: "How will this affect me in terms of coverage and cost?" Those are the foundational questions that any employee will have — unfortunately, there are no clear answers yet. Still, there are steps that employers and managers can and should be taking now to communicate with employees about the implications of health care reform.

With any Communication Issue, the Same Basic Rules Apply

- Tell employees what you know when you know it. Too often employers and managers are hesitant to say "I don't know," or "I don't know right now." But that is often the reality. Waiting to tell employees *anything* before you have definitive information simply creates a vacuum. Remember that employees are media consumers and are getting information from other sources as well. They know that issues related to health care reform are still unclear. Be upfront with employees about what you know, when you know it, and work to establish a relationship of trust so they feel confident that you will share information with them as soon as it becomes available.

- Provide a mechanism for two-way communication so you can stay on top of questions they may have. This provides benefits to both employees and employers. For employees it allows an outlet for their questions and concerns (assuming that these questions and concerns will be responded to). For employers it provides a way to assess the types of questions and concerns — and the level of concern — that exist among employees. Technology allows for many options to provide a forum for this type of feedback through polling/surveying, chat rooms, private forums, etc. When using forums and chat rooms make sure that somebody has been tasked with the responsibility to monitor input and to respond quickly to questions raised. Again, sometimes the answer will be: "We don't know yet." That's OK — as long as you've developed a culture of trust so that employees are confident that when you *do* know you'll get them up to date.

- Cascade communication down through management ranks so that each layer of management is charged with communicating down to the next level. Studies continue to suggest that an employee's most trusted source of information is his or her immediate supervisor. Companies can leverage this knowledge by cascading information throughout the organization using leaders, managers, supervisors, etc., as the messengers. Armed with key messages and information (and training, as necessary) they can help to significantly impact the effectiveness and credibility of these messages.

- Augment that cascaded information with organization-wide information. Don't rely only on the leadership structure, though. Not all leaders are created equal — some will share information, some won't — some will augment the information they receive with their own perspectives. Some will inadvertently convey misinformation. For these reasons it is always a good idea to augment information shared through the management structure with company-wide information that may be disseminated through intranet sites and other standard communication tools.
- Take advantage of credible third-party sources. Health care reform is a complex issue and difficult for even experts in the area to fully understand. Take advantage of third-party resources that are available through your health care benefit providers as well as through government sites such as the Department of Health and Human Services. The issues are complex and the impacts on the organization and various employee segments are different and raise different sorts of issues, questions, and concerns.

Have a Plan

Don't leave communication about the impacts of health care reform on employees to chance. Keep in mind that health care coverage is a very important benefit for most employees and they will be understandably concerned about how these changes will impact coverage for them and their families and, of course, about how their costs will be impacted.

Now is the time to begin planning your communication efforts. You can begin this process by taking the following steps:

Laying the Foundation

- Identify the various segments of your employee population you will need to communicate with (identify segments by considering those groups who have different concerns and will need different types of information.)
- Identify the key issues they are concerned about and questions they have (this can be done through polls/surveys and other interactive methods discussed above.)
- Identify sources of information (benefits providers, etc.)

- Identify spokespeople (this could be anyone from the CEO to the VP of HR to the benefits manager.)
- Identify the communication mechanisms that currently exist in your organization that can be used to convey messages related to health care reform.

Establishing a communication process — the ability to get messages out quickly — is critical. Don't hinder the process with excessive bureaucracy and approval processes. Develop a process including accountable people who can approve and quickly disseminate messages now. Make sure the process is flexible enough to provide back-up for when key people may be out of the office. Keep in mind that we are in an era where there is an expectation of immediacy in communications. Put a plan in place so that you can literally get information to employees as quickly as you receive it.

Creating a "go-to" place for information can readily be done on your intranet site. Establish a page specifically related to health care reform issues. This can be a link from your home page, the HR page, and other pertinent areas of your site. Make it easily accessible and communicate its existence to employees. Again, establish accountability/ responsibility for the messaging that will appear here and ensure the process is efficient and flexible. Begin populating this site now with the information you do know to establish it as the place where employees can go to get up-to-date information on how health care reform will affect them.

Employee Services

"Employee services" is a catchall category for a variety of voluntary benefits such as education assistance, cafeterias, saunas and gyms, health club memberships, commuter vans, discounts on company products, and child care services.

Educational Programs. Many organizations provide education assistance for employees. The coverage varies considerably, from job-related training to degree and advanced degree programs. Educational support is often part of the employee development program.

Social and Recreational Programs. Companies have found that wellness and recreational programs increase productivity and reduce health care costs. Some — such as smoking cessation and employee assistance programs — have significant, proven cost-cutting benefits; others — such as in-house gyms — may not provide the same return on the investment but may nonetheless be positively perceived by employees.

Child Care. Some employers support child care centers on the premises, but it is more common for companies that offer a child care benefit to subsidize the cost without actually operating the center. Many companies opt to offer referral programs, assisting employees in finding suitable child care arrangements.

Retirement Income

Employees' retirement income comes from four sources that are directly related to their employment and benefits: Social Security, retirement plans, investment income, and earnings.

Retirement (Pension) Plans. The Employee Retirement Income Security Act (ERISA) of 1974 and subsequent federal tax legislation have subjected qualified pension and other benefits plans to comprehensive government control. Although employers are not required to offer benefits plans to their employees, once such plans are established, they must conform to the requirements of ERISA. The purpose of these laws is to ensure that employees who put money into retirement plans and depend on the plans for retirement funds actually will receive the money when they retire.

Qualified Plans. Qualified plans must be in writing and communicated to employees; be established for the exclusive benefit of employees or their beneficiaries; satisfy rules on eligibility, vesting, and funding; and not discriminate in terms of contributions or benefits in favor of officers, shareholders, or highly compensated employees. Qualified plans offer tax-favored benefits to both employers and employees.

- *Defined benefit plans.* The employer agrees to provide the employee with a retirement benefit amount based on a formula. The employer funds the plan and bears the responsibility for ensuring that sufficient funds will be available in the plan when they are required. The employee receives a predetermined amount upon retirement.

- *Defined contribution plans.* The employer pays a specific amount into the pension fund for each participant. This contribution may be a percentage of salary or a percentage of profits. Once the employer has made the contribution, there is no further financial requirement. The amount of the benefit received by the employee upon retirement is determined by how the investment funds perform and is not guaranteed.

- *Deferred compensation.* Many companies offer deferred compensation programs such as 401(k) plans. These plans permit employees to postpone income taxes on part of their pay, if that portion is contributed by the employer to a qualified plan. Larger companies typically match part of the employees' contributions. Smaller companies and many professional firms do not. Ongoing tax law revisions affect the attractiveness of these plans.

- *Employee stock ownership plans (ESOPs).* In stock ownership plans, employers contribute to a trust that purchases company stock for employees. Employers get a tax deduction for the contributions, and employees get equity in the company.

- *Profit-sharing programs.* Profit-sharing is the payment of a regular share of the company profits to employees as a supplement to normal compensation. Such programs may be perceived as a group incentive process rather than an employee retirement strategy. The plans usually require that the employee's share be added to a company-controlled investment pool. Some plans are more flexible; however, since most plans have a maximum vesting period, employees commonly view profit-sharing as a retirement strategy. The assumption (as with ESOPs) is that employees who have a direct interest in the profitability of the company will reduce waste and increase productivity. Some of these programs are successful, but many do not meet expectations (for instance, if there is no cash payment but the profits must be invested, employees may become discouraged). In closely held and small companies, profit-sharing is touted by financial planners and public accountants as a tax-avoidance strategy. When this is the true objective, employees often sense the insincerity and recognize the program for what it is. Companies that are considering profit-sharing should carefully assess their objectives and plan accordingly.

Nonqualified Plans. Federal law has made it difficult to use company benefits to compensate highly paid executives. One way for companies to provide additional benefits to key executives is to offer nonqualified deferred compensation plans. These plans are a promise by the employer to pay a given amount at a later date. Nonqualified plans are not deductible to the employer, nor are the benefits guaranteed to the individual.

Mandated Benefits

Employers are legally required to fund the provision of certain benefits to employees through employer-paid taxes; these include Social Security and unemployment insurance. In addition, employers must provide employees with workers' compensation and with family medical leave as provided by the Family and Medical Leave Act. The employee and the employer have little or no discretion over these benefits.

Social Security

The Social Security Act of 1935 created a system designed to prevent the severe financial hardship that many elderly people suffer on retirement. Covered employees are compelled to pay a certain percentage of their annual income to the system throughout their working careers, and employers must match this amount. At retirement age, the contributors become eligible to receive payments from the general Social Security fund. When people refer to "Social Security," they normally are referring to Old-Age, Survivors and Disability Insurance (OASDI). OASDI is the compulsory retirement program; all but a very few working Americans contribute to and are covered by OASDI. Taxes paid into the Social Security fund are governed by the provisions of the Federal Insurance Contribution Act.

Eligibility for benefits is based on the number of quarters of coverage an individual has been credited with during employment. There are three categories.

1. *Fully insured status* grants eligibility for all types of old-age and survivor benefits. For an individual to achieve fully insured status, quarters of coverage must equal or exceed the number of years since 1950 or since age 21.

2. *Insured status* grants eligibility for some survivor benefits. It requires at least six quarters of coverage in the 13-quarter period ending with death, disability, or the attainment of age 62.

3. *Disability status* grants eligibility for benefits. It requires at least 20 quarters of coverage in the 40 quarters preceding disablement.

Benefit amounts are calculated by means of a complicated formula that is modified annually to account for cost-of-living increases. The benefit formulas are heavily weighted in favor of lower-income contributors.

HR professionals should have a general understanding of Social Security to answer employee questions about to whom and under what circumstances benefits are payable, and to encourage employees to plan for their retirement.

Unemployment Compensation Insurance

Unemployment insurance is established by state statutes prompted by a federal tax. All covered employers pay federal unemployment tax. Employers that contribute to a federally approved state system are relieved of paying to the federal government an amount equal to their state contributions, up to 90 percent of the state tax. Thus, if a state did not enact an approved plan, employers in the state would pay the same tax, but employed workers would get no benefits. For this reason, all states have unemployment insurance systems.

The premium paid by employers is based on each company's experience rating (claims filed divided by number of employees). An employer with a good record can substantially reduce its tax, while a company with a high turnover rate will pay more. This system encourages employers to keep turnover low and to oppose unemployment compensation claims. Eligible employees must have worked a specified amount of time and must be available and actively seeking work. Employees may be disqualified if they refuse to accept suitable employment.

HR professionals sometimes may take the unemployment compensation process lightly and not contest benefits claims. Keep in mind that if the employer can prove that the employee quit without good cause or was dismissed because of job-related misconduct, unemployment benefits can be reduced or denied. Such action not only reduces the company's experience rating but also sends a powerful message to employees who might be considering quitting and filing for unemployment compensation.

Workers' Compensation Insurance

Workers' compensation insurance statutes establish a process through which employees who are injured or who contract a work-related illness on the company's premises or while performing duties within the scope of employment are covered for medical costs and for their disability. Employees are entitled to benefits regardless of fault or the employer's liability. The benefit for employers is that liability is limited by the schedule set by state regulations.

Workers' compensation insurance is a state system, and benefits vary considerably from state to state. Payments for hospital and medical expenses and rehabilitation service are normally included. Injured employees may also receive compensation for lost wages and for permanent partial disability. The system is generally funded through private insurance, self-insurance, or payment into a state fund. The amount paid by each employer is determined by various factors, including type of industry, type of work performed, and previous accident rate. All states require that every company with employees be covered. If an employee is injured or contracts a work-related illness and the company does not have workers' compensation insurance, the company may be subject to general personal injury liability without limits and may be assessed severe penalties by the state.

The Family and Medical Leave Act

The Family and Medical Leave Act (FMLA) allows employees who have met minimum service requirements (12 months employed by the company, with 1,250 hours of service in the preceding 12 months) and worksite requirements (employed at a worksite with at least 50 employees within a 75-mile radius) to take up to 12 weeks of unpaid leave for

1. A serious health condition;
2. Caring for a family member (parent, child, or spouse) with a serious health condition;
3. The birth of a child and to care for the child after birth; or
4. The adoption of a child or acceptance of a child for foster care and the subsequent care of the child.

Although there is no complete list of medical conditions that are considered serious health conditions, there are six general criteria that must be evaluated to determine whether an employee (or his or her family member) has a serious health condition. These criteria include hospital care, absence plus treatment, pregnancy, chronic conditions requiring treatments, permanent/long-term conditions requiring supervision, and multiple treatments (non-chronic conditions).

The FMLA requires employers to

1. Allow their eligible employees to take up to 12 work weeks of unpaid leave in

a 12-month period for the above circumstances;

2. Provide continued health benefits during leave;

3. Restore employees to the same position when they return from leave (or to an equivalent position with the same pay, benefits, and terms and conditions of employment); and

4. Appropriately notify employees of their rights and responsibilities under the Act.

Employees may recover back pay and benefits with interest, as well as reinstatement and/or promotion for noncompliance. Attorneys' fees and costs may also be awarded.

Flexible Benefits

Traditionally, employees were involved in their benefits program only to the extent of being asked to choose among options offered by the employer. Today, employees may be involved in choosing not only the types of benefits offered but also the components for which they will pay. Surveys have shown that with increased employee participation and involvement, benefits programs are more responsive to employees' needs and employees are more satisfied with them.

With a flexible benefits program, companies generally mandate a certain level of health and life insurance and some minimal level of retirement contribution. The company generally pays the full costs of these benefits. The company then offers a cash contribution from which the employee may choose additional health, life, or retirement benefits. Some companies require that the contribution be used within specific guidelines; others allow employees to use this amount for benefits with no restriction. Employees may choose, for example, more life insurance, dependent health care, long-term disability insurance, or dental coverage. Some companies allow employees to use the cash for child care services, add it to their retirement investments, or even buy additional vacation time or days off.

The advantage of flexible benefits is that employees can choose those benefits that fit their individual needs. Someone with a family might choose additional health care coverage, while a single person might want to invest in more days off. The disadvantage of flexible benefits is that the tax treatment of these plans is subject to the whims of Congress and to changing Internal Revenue Service regulations. A flexible benefits plan also requires a significant amount of administrative time, although the administration may be outsourced to a plan administrator or third-party administrator. Another disadvantage, because of the wide choice of benefits offered, is that the cost of individual components of the plan may increase dramatically. For example, if employees with many medical expenses are the only ones to choose an enhanced health plan, the cost of that plan is likely to rise.

Many companies, even very large ones, are beginning to rethink their benefits contribution process. Rather than increasing their contribution as the costs of benefits increase, more companies are allocating a small cash contribution at a set amount and supplementing it with additional cash bonuses based on profitability. This eliminates the need to meet all of the increases in benefits costs.

Whatever option the company chooses, it is important to keep employees informed and to ensure that they understand the total compensation process and the value they receive through both direct and indirect compensation.

FAQs

How can we determine what employees really want?

Beverly Kaye and Sharon Jordan-Evans:

Many companies guess what their employees want or they bring together task forces to guess what people want.

But these guesses are not checked. There is nothing like looking at another individual face-to-face and saying, "What is it that keeps you here?" A manager should take an employee aside for five minutes and say, "You matter. I notice you. You count. We depend on you. Tell me some things I can do to keep you here." Managers are afraid to ask. They are afraid the answer will be "Double my salary." What if the answer is "I want a 20 percent raise" and the manager can't give it? Then he or she says, "I would love to give you what you want salary-wise, but frankly my hands are tied right now. Tell me what else you want."

If managers can get their employees to name five "what-elses," there will be one or two that they can do something about.

We have high turnover, and we think we have low morale. Should we consider fielding an employee attitude survey?

Tom Fitzpatrick:

Yes, fielding an employee attitude survey is a good idea; however, two critical outcomes must ensue.

1. Executive management must be willing to publicly share the results of the

survey with employees, and

2. Positive actions must result from the survey, and communication must occur that credit the survey for the actions.

Surveys without appropriate follow-up become an action of embarrassment. Surveys require accountability.

Tom Adam:

Absolutely! If you do not find out why these phenomena are present, you will never be able to resolve them. However, I highly recommend that you engage the services of a third party to get to the heart of the problem, and not conduct the survey, analysis, and recommended actions via internal resources. There are three reasons why I say this.

1. A third party has no vested interest in the findings and is therefore less likely to bias the data and the interpretation of that data. There are bound to be factors within the company — and by that I mean people or departments in key areas — that are contributing to the problems. A third party will be able to identify those factors, whereas conducting the analysis internally introduces the risk of it being run by the very people causing the difficulties. How likely are people in a company, particularly in upper management, to stand up at the end and say, "Guess what? It's my fault!" Not likely at all, I'd say.

2. A third party may also have access to external data that may not be readily available to the company. This data, whether in the form of salary surveys, best-practices reports, or whatnot, can be used to benchmark the troubled company's own situation and operations.

3. If existing employees are to be surveyed, they are far more likely to be candid with an external resource than with their own management. No matter who runs the survey internally and no matter how much assurance of confidentiality employees are given, there will always be fear in the back of their minds that whatever complaints they voice will be tagged to them and will result in repercussions later. That fear is greatly alleviated when it is not a company representative asking the questions.

Is compensation important?

Beverly Kaye and Sharon Jordan-Evans:

Compensation is important when it is not competitive. When salary is seen as competitive, it seems to go down in the list of factors that keep people. It rises higher on the list when it is not seen as fair. In two years of research, the top three or four factors in retention never were pay. They always were things such as the meaningfulness of the work, challenge of the work, professional growth, respect from the boss, and opportunities.

What is the manager's role in retention?

Beverly Kaye and Sharon Jordan-Evans:

Good management has a vital role to play in retention. To emphasize that role, companies should hold managers accountable — put retention on managers' performance appraisals, make it part of the calculation of the manager's bonus.

Measurement begets accountability, so companies can start by saying, "Whom have you lost and why?" and then consider the consequences of losing that talent. A key part of management is staff development, and retention and development go arm in arm. Employers, HR professionals, and managers all need to ask, "Are we growing people? Are we keeping them on their own cutting edge? Are we teaching them how to manage their careers? Are we making sure the structures we have in place support careers and learning?" If the company is not doing these things, it needs to start.

Rules, Communication, and Record-Keeping

In any society, rules develop as a natural outgrowth of a developing population. As the number of employees grows, so do the number and complexity of the interactions among the people. Rules are required to guide and govern the nature of those interactions. Those rules frequently start out informally — "we will come to work at 8:00 a.m. and leave at 5:00 p.m." — and this system works well for a while. As time elapses, however, and as the company grows or changes, the rules need to be formalized. They need to be written down.

The result is policies, procedures, employee handbooks, and personnel files.

Policies and Procedures

Other than the Family and Medical Leave Act (FMLA), federal law does not specifically require policies, although case law supports the creation of anti-harassment policies. State laws address requirements for workers' compensation insurance coverage, safety regulations (such as minimum age for operating hazardous equipment), and occasionally state minimum wage. Cities often have additional requirements, such as equal access to public accommodations, and sometimes even separate nondiscrimination requirements.

As an HR professional, you need to know all of the federal, state, and local requirements that affect your company. Your task is made somewhat easier, fortunately, if you start by identifying federal laws and general HR requirements.

Definitions

A *policy* is a broad guideline to be followed under a given set of circumstances — a policy addressing the use of the Internet, for example. Policies are written to allow managers to easily grasp the policy's intent and to take the necessary action to ensure compliance. When policies are based on sound judgment, good management practices, and common sense, they are perceived as fair and consistent. Policies are often included in employee handbooks to give general direction on management's expectations of employees.

A *procedure* is a sequence of steps for accomplishing an objective — the steps in processing payroll, for example. Procedures may further interpret or define how a policy should be carried out; they might be considered the rules for certain actions or nonactions.

The development and implementation of policies and procedures varies by company and is guided by the company's overall philosophies and culture. Some companies create comprehensive policies that cover every conceivable aspect of management activity, while others focus on basic areas and leave broad discretion to managers.

The Need for Policies

Policies govern the execution of various activities in an organization and provide guidance for making decisions and taking action on a variety of employee-related activities. Carefully developed policies are vital to the successful management of human resources. Inconsistency in making decisions and taking action can quickly destroy employee productivity and morale. When management or organizational decisions are perceived as unfair and unequal, employees will become dissatisfied and disgruntled and may pursue employee relations lawsuits and discrimination charges.

Well-defined and appropriate policies serve to assure employees that the company will treat them fairly and objectively. Policies tell employees what is expected of them. Managers also benefit from clearly established and well-communicated policies. Well-developed policies help managers resolve problems with greater confidence by providing an objective basis for their decisions. In addition, policy statements can provide answers to employee questions that might otherwise have to be referred to supervisors.

There is a direct tie between HR policies and policies relating to the operation of the business. For example, the policy of providing a union-free stabilized employee environment cannot be accomplished without coordinating sales, production, and transportation policies. A policy of encouraging a pro-employee, pro-family workplace cannot be accomplished without considering scheduling, flexible hours, the philosophy of management, and even the recruitment policy. A marketing objective of expanding sales into foreign countries or a focus on expanding sales into a minority population also requires integration with HR policies.

Fair and Consistent Treatment

Employees should be treated fairly and consistently. Fair and consistent treatment of employees does not mean identical treatment. A certain degree of flexibility is necessary to allow management discretion based on the specific circumstances surrounding any decision. For example, an employee who has a firmly established work record with no disciplinary actions might not be treated as severely for violating a work rule as another employee who has a poor record. Policies should be designed to provide the limits within which some discretion is permitted.

From a risk management standpoint, the safest and least risky policy is also usually the strictest. For example, to reduce exposure to sexual and other forms of harassment charges, the most reliable policy would be to restrict fraternization in the workplace. Although some states restrict the ability of companies to control the personal relationships of their employees, a strict policy will significantly reduce hostile work environment and sexual harassment difficulties. On the other hand, companies that want to be family-friendly may not want to prohibit employees (other than supervisors) from engaging in personal relationships. Some companies prohibit employees from supervising relatives. Other companies do not impose any such regulations.

Clearly, the establishment of policies and procedures is unique to the organization and should be carefully considered. It is not possible to purchase an off-the-shelf book of policies and procedures and simply put them into practice within your organization. Regardless of the policies and procedures established, the key to effective implementation is ensuring that the company's managers and supervisors clearly understand the policies as well as the flexibility and limitations permitted by the organization.

What Policies and Procedures Are Needed

Certain policies and procedures should be incorporated by virtually any company. Sample 10 at the end of this chapter provides a sample table of contents from an employee handbook that can be used as a checklist of common policies and procedures. Federal law requires some of these policies and procedures; some are discretionary. It is always a good idea to work with an attorney when developing policies and procedures to ensure that legal issues are adequately addressed and that the policies and procedures established are appropriate.

There is no magical list of what should or should not be included. Your policies and procedures are a reflection of your corporate culture. Their contents will depend on the size, nature, and background of your company and your employees.

Developing Policies

The job of the HR professional is to coordinate the development of policies. Involvement from other managers — and employees — in the organization is an important part of the process. The HR professional serves various roles in this process. He or she may need to encourage management to develop pro-employee policies and procedures that may restrict managers' discretion to treat employees as they wish. Conversely, human resources may need to oppose policies favored by management when the result would be a discouraged or demoralized workforce. Policies that are incorrectly designed and developed can easily have a damaging impact on an otherwise productive and committed workforce.

Policies should not be developed in a vacuum. Do not develop policies and procedures from the top down — the result will be that employees view the policies as edicts coming down from above. Involve management and employees in the process, both to elicit their ideas and to generate their support for the final product.

A good way to do this is to create a committee or team that includes both managers and supervisors and their employees. Team members should be chosen based on their roles in the organization, their understanding of corporate issues, and their ability to contribute valuable insights.

At the outset, make clear to the group what their role in the process is, specifically related to final approval of the policies and procedures. As outlined below, the majority of the policies and procedures developed will be subject to the approval of the organization's top management. While the group you develop will play an important role in generating an outline of issues that should be addressed and in developing draft language to address these issues, the group should not be led to believe it has more than an advisory role.

How policies are developed is as important as which policies are set up. The following should be considered:

- A policy committee of representatives from all functional areas should be appointed. The committee does not have to consist entirely of managers; it may also have representatives of different levels of employees, including nonexempt and hourly employees. (This committee might fall under the National Labor Relations Board rulings on employee participation committees. For further discussion, see the section on the safety committee in Chapter 8.)
- The committee should have a clear charter that identifies its authority and responsibility and the process that will be used for approval of its recommendations.
- If a cross-functional, multilevel committee is used, three policy approval levels might be considered. The first level should be for policies over which the

committee has full responsibility and authority. Top management involvement would be limited to review for overall coordination and final approval. These policies might include starting and ending times, staffing and recruiting, training and education, and performance appraisal. The second level might include policies on which the committee has the power to recommend, but on which the final decision rests with top management. Most policies will fall into this group. Some policies — such as those for equal employment opportunity and anti-harassment — allow for little modification, but they might be made more pertinent if the policy committee develops the exact wording. Policies on alternate dispute resolution, grievance resolution, safety, and compliance with the Occupational Safety and Health Act might also fall into this group. The third level of approvals would be for those policies over which top management retains full discretion and authority. These include policies on pay and salary, what benefits to offer, and how to administer those benefits.

- The main objective of the policy committee is to review all current policies for validity, consistency, and legal compliance; to suggest additional policies that are essential for the operation of the company; and to decide which policies should be deleted or revised. Only policies that are required or absolutely necessary should be considered for inclusion.

- A policy statement should explain the reason for the policy, the date it becomes effective, and when it should be reviewed. Some policy requirements remain consistent; for example, nondiscrimination and anti-harassment policies, once developed and implemented, will remain very much the same. Other policies, such as those on compensation and benefits, should be reviewed more regularly. All policies should be reviewed annually.

Many management consultants and employment lawyers write policies and procedures for companies. Having professional assistance in this task is important. However, in developing and writing policies, two points are important: Policies must be focused on strategy and related to company operation, and they must be discussed with and understood by both employees and managers.

A company should not choose policies from a checklist. It should assess its actual needs and then decide what policies are necessary. The policies should be written in plain language, not in legalese. Certain phrases or words have legal meanings — they have been found by the courts to mean certain things. One of these phrases is "with just cause," which used to be common in policies on discharge and termination. The courts have interpreted this phrase as requiring a legally acceptable reason for the termination, which often is more than employers thought should be required. A company may want to have certain policies reviewed by legal counsel or written in legal terms. However, the HR professional should use caution when using consultants, lawyers, or personnel policy software to develop policies. Policies written in legalese are of no value if the employees and managers do not understand their intent, purposes, or guidelines.

Employee Handbooks

Companies often use the words "handbook" and "manual" interchangeably and continue to do so even though these materials are generally accessible electronically through the company intranet, rather than in hard-copy format. Generally, an employee handbook is a document containing the policies of the company. Manuals generally contain procedures and are written for managers. Employment lawyers, management consultants, and managers disagree on the value of and necessity for employee handbooks and procedure manuals, and some large companies do not use either.

While there are pros and cons to having handbooks, most companies find that when properly written and administered, the pros outweigh the cons. For instance,

- An employee handbook can increase employee morale. When employment practices are in writing, employees feel the rules are being equitably applied. There is less concern that managers might be arbitrary in their treatment of employees.
- A well-written handbook can save time for managers in responding to employee questions related to policies, procedures, benefits, and so on.
- Properly drafted employee handbooks can reserve important employer rights that, left implied, might not be enforceable.

The drawbacks should not be overlooked, however. For instance, many courts have found that employers have created a contract through a handbook. One common example is the establishment of disciplinary policies that do not leave some discretion to the employer. Policies that are too proscriptive may unnecessarily tie the hands of employers, who are subject to risk if they terminate an employee without following the exact steps outlined in the handbook.

Language in the handbook may also inadvertently guarantee job security and put your status as an at-will employer at risk. In almost every state, there is a presumption that, unless you have an employment contract with your employee, you are an at-will employer. This means that the company can terminate an employee — with or without cause — at any time, with or without notice. It also means that the employee can leave, with or without notice, at any time. But loose language in an employee manual can threaten your at-will status, and in some instances courts will find that the employee manual created a contract.

These drawbacks illustrate one important requirement for preparing an employee handbook. Make sure before you distribute the handbook to employees you have your legal counsel carefully review all the material you plan to include.

The Essentials of Preparing Your Employee Handbook

- Be sure to comply with all applicable laws. Federal, state, and local regulations are changing all the time. As an HR professional, you have to be proactive and make sure you are staying on top of the court decisions that can affect the development of your handbook. In some states, this task may be simplified through available software programs. A good source of information about the availability of these tools can be trade and professional associations. While keeping up with these laws is a monumental task, it is one that you cannot overlook. An out-of-date handbook is useless, and in fact it may create unnecessary risk for your company.
- Do not be a copycat. Even though it can be helpful to look at other handbooks to generate ideas, you need to make sure you include well-thought-out policies that conform to the realities of your particular situation. Do not just take someone else's handbook, change the name, and make it yours. A handbook that is appropriate for one employer may be totally inappropriate for another. In addition, make sure you only include policies in your handbook that you intend to follow and implement.
- Include adequate disclaimers. While recommended content for disclaimers varies from state to state, one thing is consistent — the disclaimer must be clear and conspicuous. Burying the statement in small print is not advisable.
- Do not be overly restrictive. Draft your handbook to allow the maximum flexibility to your company and its managers. You want to leave discretion to your management staff and your company to handle violations of policies that are included in the manual as they feel appropriate given the circumstances.
- Require signed employee acknowledgments. When you distribute your handbook — or any handbook updates — to employees, have all employees complete an acknowledgment form. This form should indicate that employees either will read or have read the handbook, that they have had an opportunity to ask questions, that they understand the handbook, and that they agree to abide by the handbook and the policies it contains. Each employee's signed acknowledgment form should be maintained in the employee's personnel file. You want to make sure you have evidence, if it ever comes to litigation, that the handbook was distributed and that the employee read and understood the information contained in the handbook. These acknowledgments should be completed and filed each time a change is made to the handbook.

Communication

Do not forget the importance of communication! The key to an effective employee handbook is communication.

Regardless of its length, or whether your handbook is printed or available through the company intranet, your job is far from over once the handbook is introduced. One of the common problems with employee handbooks is that they are not treated as living documents. The result is that employees are, or claim to be, unaware of the benefits available to them, the sanctions that apply to various aspects of their performance, and the opportunities that exist within the company.

Your best weapon for combating the "I didn't know that!" syndrome is to ensure that employees do know — through effective communication. In any company, there are a variety of communication opportunities available — staff meetings, newsletters, annual reports, and bulletin boards, just to name a few. Following are some communication ideas that can help you make your employee handbook a living document:

- *Employee orientation.* New employees should be quickly introduced to the employee handbook, policies, and procedures. They should be provided with a copy, asked to complete and sign an acknowledgment that they have read and understood the handbook, and given information about how to get the handbook in the future (through supervisors/managers, online, etc.).

- *Update meetings.* When the handbook is changed or modified, consider calling employees together for brief meetings to discuss the changes. Involve managers and supervisors in this process as well, asking them to share information with employees through regular staff meetings.

- *Bulletin boards.* Make use of your company bulletin boards to post specific items in the handbook. Consider developing posters that highlight the availability of the handbook or point to critical new bits of information.

- *Intranet.* The company intranet can be a great place for employees and managers to get information from the handbook. The intranet allows you to change information readily, ensuring that staff always have access to the most up-to-date policies and procedures. In addition, intranet technology allows employees to search the handbook for specific information.

- *General accessibility.* Make sure all employees have a copy of the handbook. While the intranet is a great tool, in many companies not all employees have ready access to the intranet, and hard copies may still be necessary.

Personnel Files

HR records have three major functions in a company: They provide a memory or recall aid to managers and employees, they offer documentation of events for use in resolving questions or HR problems, and they provide data for research, planning, problem-solving, and decision-making.

While federal, state, and local laws require that certain employee information be maintained, even without these requirements HR professionals would want to keep certain basic records to avoid errors of memory and to provide information for making management and HR decisions. In addition, the company's managers need basic information on employee tenure and performance for use in employee review and decision-making.

There are many benefits to keeping accurate and valid records. Good records permit managers to see how well the company is doing in terms of turnover, competency of staff, and so on. Employee accomplishments and other critical events are documented. When there are questions about pay, disciplinary action, qualification, or experience, good documentation is essential. If a company uses good management and HR practices, records are invaluable in defending against lawsuits and charges.

Employee files should be kept in a safe, secure, and locked location such as a locked, fireproof cabinet.

What Should Be in the Files

The contents of HR files vary by company size and industry, but some practices are accepted by most HR professionals. Figure 7.1 provides a checklist of items that may be included in HR files — and where to keep them.

What Should Not Be in the Files

There are some things that should not be kept in employees' personnel files. Thus, some companies have a policy on the items that should be included in the official file and those that should not be included. Unfortunately, it is not uncommon for many companies to pay little attention to the contents of HR files until a problem occurs and the files are used as evidence of unlawful activity or discrimination. Consultants conducting assessments of HR departments routinely find problems and deficiencies in the contents of HR files. These problems may include inappropriate documentation such as the following, which should not be included in individual employee files:

- Data identifying medical information, occupational injuries, and disabilities.
- Racial designations on self-identification documents for affirmative action purposes.
- Application forms that ask for and include non-job-related data.

- Subjective and inappropriate comments on performance appraisal forms.
- Immigration Control Form I-9.
- Poorly written and subjective documentation.
- Trivial, outdated, or nonessential performance comments.

FIGURE 7.1. Documents to Include in HR Files

MAIN EMPLOYEE FILE
- Offer/transfer letter
- Application form
- W-4 form
- Nondisclosure agreement
- Acknowledgment of handbook
- Acknowledgment of new policies
- Software copyright compliance agreement
- Orientation checklist
- Termination checklist
- Performance appraisals
- Salary review
- Official performance documentation (memos, letters, recognition, etc.)
- Payroll documentation (change of address, cost center change, leave of absence, etc.)
- Tuition aid requests
- Copies of certificates, licenses, diplomas, and so on

SEPARATE MEDICAL/INSURANCE FILE
- Group benefit enrollment forms
- Profit-sharing/401(k) enrollment, change forms, etc.
- Insurance claim forms
- Consolidated Omnibus Budget Reconciliation Act letter sent

SUBJECT FILES KEPT SEPARATE
(usually in one folder for all affected employees; information kept in chronological order or by quarter)
- Child support
- DSS requests (Medicaid, etc.)
- Equal employment opportunity charges
- Exit interview form
- Garnishments
- Immigration Control Form I-9 – lawful employment
- Investigation notes or reports
- Litigation documents
- Reference checks
- Requests for employment/payroll verification

Documents to Include in HR Files
- Wage assignments
- Workers' compensation claims

SEPARATE PAYROLL FILES
- Credit union deduction authorization
- Savings on authorization
- Miscellaneous deductions (401(k) loan repayment, company computer purchase program, etc.)

OTHER SEPARATE FILES
- Targeted jobs tax credit forms
- Minority status information

Any medical information or information about the employee's physical condition must be kept strictly confidential, in a separate filing system with access limited to those with a job-related need to know. Managers generally should not have access to any of this information unless a work accommodation is required.

The Immigration Reform and Control Act of 1986 requires employers to complete and have on file I-9 forms documenting employees' legal right to work in the United States. The I-9s should be filed separately from the official HR file for at least two reasons. First, in completing the form, many employers make copies of the required identification documents and attach them to the form. At least one ID must have a photograph. Information showing the race or gender of an employee should not be in the official HR file. Second, during a compliance audit or investigation, auditors are empowered to refer evidence found in their investigation to other agencies such as U.S. Citizenship and Immigration Services. Companies should avoid causing problems for themselves by making it easy to find violations.

I-9 forms must be retained at the site of employment, although many companies forward copies to corporate headquarters. Employers are not required to make copies of identification. However, the company's policy about copying must be applied consistently to all employee I-9 forms.

Unofficial Files

Many supervisors and managers keep rough notes, copies of formal documents, and informal performance evaluations in department files or their own private files. Two problems can arise from this practice. First, the company probably cannot monitor individual corrective action and informal discipline unless all documentation is filed in a single location. Second, a formal action might be revised or withdrawn; if there is a second, unofficial file, the company cannot be sure the copies have been destroyed. In resolving a charge or employee relations lawsuit, these informal files can be used as evidence.

Records Retention

Records retention requirements are normally set by federal, state, and local laws or regulations. The annual *Guide to Federal Records Retention* details records retention requirements set by the federal government. State and local requirements vary. Contact local professionals, consultants, or an employee relations lawyer for more detailed information.

Files should be scrutinized periodically so that you can expunge outdated or unnecessary information and documentation. Files of long-term employees may have information and data that were legal when prepared but that may be evidence of discrimination today. Many applications from 1950 through the late 1980s contain requests for information about race, marital status, parentage, children, spouses, and disabilities. The information required of current employees is limited to that which is job related.

From a practical point of view, most companies retain basic employee records for the life of the company. After a certain time, these records may be filed in dead storage or encoded on storage tape.

Requirements for retention of employment applications differ depending on whether they are solicited or unsolicited. Unsolicited resumes and applications do not have to be retained at all. Many companies refuse to accept applications except when there are open positions, returning unsolicited resumes to the sender. Solicited applications and resumes of applicants not hired should be maintained according to the requirements of state law. While many companies keep applications for at least a year, some states have requirements for more time. New York, for example, requires that applications be maintained for three years.

The Equal Employment Opportunity Commission has advised that all resumes from online databases should be considered solicited. They must be retained for at least the minimum time. The people who sent these resumes must also be considered candidates for purposes of calculating a company's applicant flow rate for minorities and females.

Employee Access to Records

The right of employees to access their own files presents a dilemma with respect to balancing an employee's interests with the right of the company to obtain, maintain, and use the employee's information. The HR file often contains sensitive information from the application and preemployment screening process. In addition, the company has probably added data on performance, corrective action, readiness for promotion, and salary. However, without access to their own files, employees cannot determine whether they have been treated fairly. Generally, most companies allow employees limited access to their own information.

The Privacy Act of 1974 guarantees federal employees the right to know the type of information collected on them, to review the information, to correct or delete any incorrect information, and to restrict access to their files. Although this law applies only to federal employees, some states have also adopted strict regulations on access.

Private employers have generally decided to allow employees to see their files. Procedures vary, but employees commonly have the right to view their files, to know what information is added, and to restrict the release of that information. They have access to preemployment documents, performance appraisals, salary records, and corrective action documentation. In addition, some employers allow employees to copy information from their files and to correct or reply to information with which they disagree.

There are some benefits to allowing employees to view their HR files. First, it allays their fears about what might be in their files, which is good for morale. Second, employers that know files may be viewed tend to be more careful about the type, format, and verification of the information; consequently, that information tends to be more objective.

Remember, having clear, well-written, objective documentation is essential when the information is used to defend a company against employee relations charges and discrimination lawsuits. The best source for this information should be the official HR file.

Human Resource Information Systems

An HR information system (HRIS) is a system that allows you to manage employee records. Information is entered into the system, and it can be retrieved online or through reports. An HRIS can dramatically reduce the time spent maintaining and updating employee information as well as handling record-keeping. The functionality of these systems also allows companies to review and analyze employee data much more efficiently.

It is easy to see the value that an HRIS could provide for your company. What may not be so easy is making the next step — selecting a system that is right for your needs. Unless you have been moving from one company to another helping to install HR information systems, you probably don't have much experience in this area. Such a system, once in place, should serve your company for a number of years.

If you are thinking of purchasing an HRIS, the following steps and guidelines can help you make an informed choice — a choice you can live with for years to come. The first step is to determine specifically what you want your HRIS to do. Clearly identifying the company's needs can help define the functions that are necessary. You should sit down preliminarily with your CEO and other top management to determine what information they need and to discuss what you want the system to do.

Next, take the time to improve your existing systems and methods of data collection before you automate. The old saying "garbage in, garbage out" is pertinent here. It is a waste of time and effort to convert outdated and inefficient systems. The way you have always done something may not be the best way. Think about how you could leverage the power of an HRIS to help improve your workflow as well as to help you gain access to data.

Involve the right people in the selection process. Identify a project leader and team members, and make sure you include all of the key members of your company who will be affected by the functionality and usability of your HRIS. Obviously, you will need to involve information systems (IS) staff. But do not overlook other areas of the company. Every manager in your organization will be a customer of the HRIS system. Management input will be critical to your process.

Know what you are looking for. Do a thorough needs assessment and clearly outline the features that you must have (not necessarily those that would be nice to have) to help you make an informed and cost-effective choice. In general, most HRIS products have similar functions — they keep track of employee information, including everything from name, address, and Social Security number to work history, benefits, educational/training history, and so forth. The difference between the low-end and high-end products is often a matter of increasing flexibility in the amount and type of information that can be stored and how that information can be accessed and reported.

There are a number of criteria you may wish to consider.

- *System compatibility.* Will the system you are considering be compatible with your existing hardware and software needs?
- *Value.* You can purchase a system at any range of the price spectrum — from very low cost to exorbitantly expensive. The challenge is to find the price/value point that most closely meets your company's needs and budget.
- *Ease of access.* Who will be entering and accessing information? How readily accessible will the HRIS be? What level of training will be required, and how long will it take to become proficient in the system? Can the HRIS run parallel with other commonly accessed systems?
- *Support.* Will the vendor provide you with ongoing support, regular updates, and training? Will there be additional charges for these services?
- *Reporting.* The types of reports available to your company's decision-makers are a key driver of your decision. What types of reports can be generated automatically? What ability will you have to modify reports — or to create new reports?
- *Personal compatibility.* An HRIS is a long-term commitment, and it will require a long-term relationship with a vendor. While your selection will be based, to a large degree, on the capabilities of the system, your personal relationship with the vendor will also be important.
- *Future needs.* Consider any potential organizational changes that may affect operations over the next three to five years.

Identifying your needs involves ensuring that the product you select will be compatible with your existing software and hardware — or making a conscious decision to invest in new software and hardware. You do not want to make a selection only to find out that compatibility will be a problem and that you will need to invest several thousand additional dollars to integrate the system. Also consider your future technology needs. You want to make sure you are making a product selection that will grow with your company.

Ultimately, you want to select a vendor that is going to stand the test of time. You want to know that this vendor is going to be around for a while and that you will be able to get the support you need. How to determine this? Look for a company that already has an established history. Talk to colleagues at other companies.

In conducting your evaluation, be sure to consider total costs. The cost of the software is just the beginning. You must also consider training time, support, and any customization you might need — as well as the cost of computer hardware and equipment that might be necessary as part of the HRIS installation. There are a number of uses for an HRIS, as outlined in Figure 7.2.

Converting from a manual information system to an HRIS is a significant undertaking. It requires careful planning, and the decision should be made by the operating managers as well as HR professionals. Management support is essential.

FIGURE 7.2. Uses of Human Resources Information Systems

Affirmative action/equal employment opportunity	Licensure and certification
Applicant tracking	Payroll
Attendance tracking	Pension administration
Attitude surveys	Productivity/work measurement
Benefits management	Project and event scheduling
Career planning and assessment	Reward and recognition program administration
Employee history and records	Safety and health
Human resource planning and forecasting	Salary planning and administration
Job analysis	Succession planning
Job evaluation	Tuition assistance
Labor relations	Turnover analysis

HR and the Corporate Intranet

Technology is making it easier than ever before to streamline HR operations. Consider the company intranet. The possibilities for improving efficiency are virtually endless. Surprisingly, though, many HR departments have yet to move beyond the use of the intranet for sharing information to realize its full potential as a work tool.

The company intranet has typically evolved as a communication tool — a method of sharing information with employees. The 2009 HR Technology Trends Survey, a Watson Wyatt study, indicated that U.S. companies' main goal in implementing an HR web application was to "enhance employee communications" (29 percent of respondents). Increasing productivity received a mention only 17 percent of the time. While communicating with employees is a worthwhile goal, organizations need to move beyond the view of the intranet as simply a communication tool to consider its ramifications as a process improvement tool.

Certainly, an HR intranet site can aid in providing information to employees, and providing information is a worthy goal. But just as Internet sites evolved beyond brochureware, so must HR intranet sites. HR professionals need to be creative in considering ways in which the corporate intranet can save time (which ultimately saves money) and improve service to employees. Here are some examples.

Employee Handbook Online

In the old days, keeping employee handbooks updated could be a tremendous administrative and logistical task. Changes would be made to the original, copies made and distributed, and fingers crossed in the hope that managers and employees would dutifully update their three-ring binders. Today, employee handbooks (along with policy manuals and other documents) can be easily maintained and updated online, ensuring that employees and managers have ready access at all times to the most accurate and up-to-date information. One caveat: If there are employees in your organization who do not have ready access to the company's intranet, some hard-copy distribution may still be necessary.

Questions Frequently Asked of HR

In many organizations, the HR department is the catchall for questions from employees. Many of those questions are repetitive. In large organizations, responding to the same question several hundred times can be a drain on resources. Tracking and categorizing those commonly asked questions, and putting them on the HR home page where they can be searchable by keywords or phrases, not only cuts down on calls to the HR department but also provides a great service to employees.

Employee Activity Calendars

The intranet makes it easy to maintain a calendar of company-related events that is viewable by all staff and easily updated by HR personnel. Events could range from employee social activities, to organizational meetings, to educational offerings and other company activities. For organizations that participate in various fundraising efforts, calendars can be a good way for employees to promote these events and ensure that they are not competing with too many other offerings.

Forms

First-generation intranet sites frequently contained forms online that employees could download and fill out. That's a step in the right direction. But taking those same forms and making them interactive goes one step further. Interfacing the data that employees enter into the form into other corporate systems goes further yet. Here are some examples:

Name/Address Change Forms. Instead of calling HR, or filling out a form and sending it to HR, what if employees could pull up a screen to make changes to their name, address, and so forth and then, with a click of a button, automatically update all internal databases that contain the information?

Personnel Requisitions. Are managers required to fill out forms to request replacement or additional personnel? Why not make those forms interactive?

Family and Medical Leave Act (FMLA) Requests. While it will take more than an online form to simplify the requirements of complying with the FMLA, making this form interactive can help cut down on the administrative burden.

Leave Requests. Funeral leave, jury duty, leaves of absence — all of these requests can be streamlined and simplified by giving employees and managers the ability to process them electronically.

Other Requests. Take a look at all of the forms that cross your desk each and every day. How many of these forms could be automated?

Employee Evaluation

Processing evaluation forms online streamlines the process not only for HR but also for managers. Another option would be to automate 360-degree feedback, with forms automatically sent to appropriate individuals, who fill in their ratings. The ratings are then compiled and reported back to the supervisor — electronically. And, of course, the data can be readily stored in that format for easy access and review later.

Job Postings

More companies are moving toward the online receipt and processing of applications for open positions. With some slight modifications, the same process that is used for processing external applications can be used with internal staff. Employees can be kept up-to-date on positions they may be interested in, and managers will have online access to information about the status of a job opening, the ability to view resumes and applications online, and the ability to work through — and document — the entire hiring process electronically.

Payroll

Is your payroll system automated yet? Consider a system whereby employees enter their time worked and time off and send the information electronically to managers for approval, and then the information is automatically uploaded to the payroll system, where payments are processed.

Online Benefits Enrollment

The annual benefits enrollment process can be a paper-pushing nightmare. But the intranet can automate this process. Combining both the information-sharing aspects of the intranet with the ability to process transactions, the chore of benefits enrollment can be greatly eased while staff receive enhanced access to information and illustrative examples about the benefits available to them. Online benefits calculators can help employees choose among various options or model the impact of various elections.

Education and Training

What if employees could review course offerings and availability and register online? What if they — and their managers — could log on at any time to view an up-to-date record of the courses they have taken and to ensure that they have completed any mandatory training?

Corporate Logo Goods Online

Does the HR department in your organization have responsibility for the sale and distribution of corporate logo items for use by employees or for distribution to various goodwill efforts? Wouldn't it be nice if these products could be ordered online?

Many companies have programs whereby employees earn points from managers and fellow employees in recognition of their efforts above and beyond the call of duty. They can then spend these points for movie tickets, corporate logo items, days off, and so on. This process could readily be automated, allowing managers to distribute points online as well as letting employees spend the points they have earned.

It is important for HR to move beyond considering the intranet as a way to convey information and to begin considering it as a way of streamlining the work that the department does. Take a critical look at all of the tasks you perform — particularly those of the pushing paper variety. Consider the major headaches for your department — the duties that take up a great deal of time but that don't seem to yield the commensurate value. How could these tasks be automated through the corporate intranet?

Some of these innovations may be quite simple to accomplish — like putting FAQs online. Others may be more complex and expensive, requiring close coordination with IT staff and external vendors — like online benefits enrollment. For each application you consider, you will need to do a cost-benefit analysis, considering out-of-pocket costs as well as administrative costs (e.g., employee time).

And just as you do in implementing any process change, you may encounter resistance from your staff. To minimize this resistance, make sure you involve them in the process of devising new and innovative ways of getting their work done while improving service to internal customers. Also consider that employees may fear simplifying tasks out of concerns that their jobs may not be needed any more. Do what you can to assuage these concerns by pointing out the many opportunities for HR to contribute at a more strategic level, once administrative tasks are automated.

The key is to be innovative and think process improvement. Consider that every piece of paper that crosses your desk might represent an opportunity to streamline your work and free up your time. For HR in particular, often burdened with paper-pushing activities, the intranet represents a way to break free from some of the administrative tedium to focus more on the strategic imperatives affecting the organization.

FAQs

What are the critical elements of effective employee communication?

Karen Horn:

Critical elements include

1. Having an integrated strategy. There is little difference (if any) between internal and external communication today. Technology has changed how quickly and easily information — and opinions — can be accessed.

2. Having a foundation of key messages. Key messages have to be in simple language. If they are not, people won't spend the time to interpret or try to understand them.

3. Understanding the delivery vehicles and how they are really used in the organization. I am amazed by how many communicators still focus on messages and cannot tell you anything about the delivery vehicles or have not done their homework to see if the vehicles are the right ones and are effective. Like any other business process, it is important to know how the product gets to the customer.

What is the role of the HR professional in communication?

Karen Horn:

The HR professional's role depends on two key things: topic and intention of the specific communication, and the role of the HR professional in the organization (such as compensation expert or client-facing/business partner).

HR professionals are expected to be knowledgeable about anything that has to do with people and the HR department. So, at the time the communication was being developed, HR professionals might have been subject matter experts, a test audience, or at least knowledgeable about the communication. All of these roles require that HR professionals provide input and/or have advanced knowledge about most communication related to people. (Note I do not say "HR communication." I refuse to use that term unless the communication is about the human resource *function*. The term HR communication is misused about 90 percent of the time.)

A strong partnership between communication and HR professionals is essential.

Is it a good idea to have a policy on employee use of the Internet? What about an e-mail policy?

Wendy Bliss:

Workplace access to the Internet has created temptations that employees may be unable to resist, and many employers are aware of the potential for cyber-lollygagging and other misuse.

E-mail presents similar issues. Although e-mail can contribute to more effective business communication, it can also lead to decreased productivity if employees spend too much time at work on personal e-mail or overload the organization's computer network. Moreover, in the last few years, employees' e-mail has been used as evidence against the employer in dozens of cases of harassment and discrimination. E-mail also makes it easy for employees to share an organization's trade secrets or other confidential information with the wrong parties.

To lay the foundation for proper online activities and e-mail use — and to minimize potential legal or productivity problems — employers should create and implement Internet and e-mail policies that

- Remind employees that all company computer equipment and electronic communication systems belong to the employer.
- Reserve the organization's right to monitor employee Internet use and e-mail.
- Describe what work-related and personal uses are permissible.
- Specify any limits on employees' use of the Internet and e-mail.
- Describe and prohibit usages that are improper. An example is accessing or sending material that is defamatory; sexually explicit; or racially, religiously, or ethnically offensive. Other improper activities are downloading copyrighted material, transmitting trade secrets or confidential information, and any other illegal uses.
- State that violations of the policies may result in discipline, up to and including discharge.

Policies should be widely publicized through multiple channels such as the employee handbook and in computer log-on banners. Notifying employees in writing and getting their written consent to the policies are essential. Simply educating employees on appropriate usage also can reduce workplace abuse.

Can/Should employers monitor employee e-mail?

Wendy Bliss:

Clearly, there are reasons for employers to monitor workers' e-mail, and such monitoring has become a common practice.

As a general rule, an employer may monitor an employee's electronic communications, including e-mail, if the employee has consented or if the communications are work related and occur in the ordinary course of the employer's business. However, such monitoring must comply with the federal Electronic Communications Privacy Act of 1986 and with applicable state or local laws.

Monitoring raises the issue of how to balance the employer's need to conduct business safely and productively against employees' rights to privacy at work. Employees typically believe that their e-mail communications are private unless the organization makes clear that is not the case. Consequently, to prevent employee relations problems and claims of invasion of privacy, employers that monitor e-mail should develop and communicate a clear and specific written policy, as outlined above.

There have been attempts to enact federal legislation that would require employers to notify employees of the practice of electronic monitoring, and it appears that increased federal regulation in this area is likely.

What are the implications of social media on employee communication?

Karen Horn:

Social media has eliminated any boundaries between "internal" and "external" communication. While some of us would argue that this has been true for many years, technology has changed how quickly and easily information can be accessed. Now, virtually all information is available to anyone within seconds.

Social media requires us to be better communicators. There are more choices and more tools. We need to understand them all and how our employees use them, we need to be more succinct in our messages, and we need to understand how the vehicles are used with our people. It is a great time to be a professional communicator.

What should be included in a policy on employee use of social media?

Ann Kiernan:

A comprehensive model Internet and E-mail Policy and Procedure, including for blogs and social networking, is available from Fair Measures, Inc.

Here is an excerpt:

If an employee chooses to identify himself or herself as a [Company] employee on a social network or in a chatroom, bulletin board, web site, Twitter, or blog, he or she must adhere to the following guidelines:

- Remember that you are personally responsible for the content you publish on blogs, wikis, or any other form of user-generated media. Be mindful that what you publish will be public for a long time.
- Make it clear to readers that the views expressed are yours alone and do not necessarily reflect the views of [Company].
- Do not disclose any information that is confidential or proprietary either to [Company] or to any third party that has disclosed information to [Company].
- Follow our reference policy, which states that no employee is allowed to give a reference for any current or former [Company] employee on any social network or in a chatroom, bulletin board, web site, Twitter, or blog.
- Uphold [Company's] value of respect for the individual, and avoid making negative or defamatory statements about [Company] employees, clients, partners, affiliates, and others, including competitors. Do not use ethnic slurs, personal insults, or obscenity, and do not engage in any conduct that would not be acceptable in [Company's] workplace.

Sample 10

Table of Contents: Employee Handbook

INTRODUCTION

CEO Letter of Introduction

Introduction to Company

Company Mission

New Employee Orientation

EMPLOYMENT

Employee Relations

Equal Employment Opportunity

Nondiscrimination and Anti-harassment

Hiring of Relatives

Employee Medical Examinations

Immigration Law Compliance

Conflict of Interest

Disability Accommodation

EMPLOYMENT STATUS AND RECORD

Employment Categories

Access to Personnel Files

Reference Checks

Performance Management

Job Descriptions

COMPENSATION AND BENEFITS

Employee Benefits

Time Off with Pay

Jury Duty

Savings Plan

Credit Union

Employee Assistance Plan (EAP)

Salary Administration

Promotions and Transfers

Benefits Continuation (COBRA)

TIMEKEEPING/PAYROLL

Timekeeping (nonexempt)

Paydays

Employment Termination

WORKPLACE PROCEDURES

Safety and Accident Prevention

Smoking

Overtime

Special Situations (nonexempt)

Expense Reimbursement

Vehicle Insurance—Official Business

Moonlighting/Second Job (conflict of interest)

Political Activity

LEAVE OF ABSENCE

Family and Medical Leave

Personal Leave

Military Leave

Funeral Leave

EMPLOYEE CONDUCT AND DISCIPLINARY ACTION

Standards of Conduct and Discipline

Progressive Discipline Guidelines

Alcohol and Drug Use

Attendance and Punctuality

Personal Appearance

Company Property

Restrictions on Solicitation

Problem Resolution/Grievance Process

Lessons from the Trenches

Working Solo

Lynn King was Director of Human Resources at Sweetbriar College in Virginia from 1998 to 2007 and has been in HR for about 25 years. "I started shortly after college," King says. "I just applied for a position that was posted as a personnel assistant. It was an organization that was just being formed — sort of a spin-off from a university — so there was an afterthought to create this personnel assistant position. At first, it was thought that it would be mostly clerical."

The organization grew tremendously, from 67 employees when King started to several hundred only a few years later. "Basically, I was able to grow with the job," King says. "I was the only HR person for the first five years." When King left that position, she took on a greater challenge — working for a small college that, she says, "had never really had an HR function before.

"The exciting part was that it was all developmental. They had someone handling benefits, but no other HR function. Either it was all decentralized, or they just didn't do it."

Gathering Your Resources

The biggest challenge, King says, "was pulling resources together.

"I came to an office empty except for furniture. People assume because you've been in the field for a number of years that you have all this stuff memorized — and you don't. One of my first questions was a records-retention question, and I had no place to look it up!"

King used the Internet extensively to set up the office and found that it was "invaluable." She also bought some resource guides on personnel issues. And, she adds, "establishing a relationship with an attorney was important — they didn't really have one." King also found that connecting with other people in human resources was important. "E-mail discussion lists have been very helpful to me."

Managing Expectations

One of the drawbacks of being a sole practitioner in an HR start-up, King says, "is that people may not have reasonable expectations about what a single HR person can do. They may think, 'This person is going to do all my interviewing, hiring — and plan the company picnic,' and you may not be able to do it all.

"It's important to establish your role early on. For me, one of the things I had to do was decide how much I was going to do for them and how much I was going to enable them to do themselves." Learning the priorities of senior staff members — and other key players — helped King determine where to start. "Meet with senior staff," she advises. "Interview them. Find out what their priorities are. That's what determined my direction here."

One of the drawbacks of being in a solo environment, King says, is "the lack of other HR professionals to work with. If you're used to working as part of a team, you know you can bounce things off people." You can build those networks in other ways, though. "I've found it helpful," she says, "to work with committees or small groups of people. Before, I might have worked with other HR staff to develop something; now I'm more inclined to draw in other staff."

Benefits of Being Small

Still, there are also big benefits to a small environment. "Ownership is one of the things that appealed to me about moving to a smaller organization," King admits. "Previously, I was supervising staff and spending more time supervising than doing, and not being as creative as I liked. When you're in a larger HR office and you're one person dealing with one area, you only see a piece of the organization. Here, I'm able to get a picture of the whole organization."

Workplace Safety and Security

A total of 5,071 fatal work injuries were recorded in the United States in 2008, down from a total of 5,657 fatal work injuries reported for 2007. While the 2008 results are preliminary, this figure represents the smallest annual preliminary total since the Census of Fatal Occupational Injuries program was first conducted in 1992. Final results for 2008 will be released in 2010.

Based on these preliminary counts, the rate of fatal injury for U.S. workers in 2008 was 3.6 fatal work injuries per 100,000 full-time equivalent workers, down from the final rate of 4.0 in 2007. Key findings of the 2008 Census of Fatal Occupational Injuries include the following:

- Fatal work injuries in the private construction sector in 2008 declined by 20 percent from the 2007 total, twice the all-worker decline of 10 percent.
- Fatal workplace falls, which had risen to a series high in 2007, also declined by 20 percent in 2008.
- Workplace suicides were up 28 percent to a series high of 251 cases in 2008, but workplace homicides declined 18 percent in 2008.
- The number and rate of fatal work injuries among 16- to 17-year-old workers were higher in 2008.
- Fatal occupational injuries involving Hispanic or Latino workers in 2008 were 17 percent lower than in 2007.
- Fatalities among non-Hispanic Black or African American workers were down 16 percent in 2008.
- The number of fatal workplace injuries in farming, fishing, and forestry occupations rose 6 percent in 2008 after declining in 2007.
- Transportation incidents, which accounted for approximately two-fifths of all the workplace fatalities in 2008, fell 13 percent from the previous series low of 2,351 cases reported in 2007.

Overall, 90 percent of the fatal work injuries involved workers in private industry. Service-providing industries in the private sector recorded 46 percent of all fatal work injuries in 2008, while goods-producing industries recorded 43 percent. Ten percent of the fatal work injury cases in 2008 involved government workers. The number of fatal work injuries in the private sector decreased 11 percent in 2008, and fatalities among government workers, including resident military personnel, decreased 4 percent. Fatality rates were lower in 2008 for both goods-producing industries and service-providing industries, but remained unchanged for civilian government workers.

While workers in construction incurred the most fatalities of any industry in the private sector in 2008, the number of fatalities in construction declined 20 percent, from 1,204 cases in 2007 to 969 cases in 2008. Fatalities involving workers in the construction of buildings were down 21 percent from 2007, with most of the decrease occurring in residential building construction (down 28 percent to 93 cases). Fatalities in heavy and civil engineering construction were down 14 percent, and the subsector with the largest number of fatalities, specialty trade contractors, had 19 percent fewer fatalities in 2008 than in 2007.

Employees are entitled to a safe and healthful work environment. But employees play a role in ensuring their own safety. HR professionals not only can help guide and develop safety policies, procedures, and practices, but also can ensure that these practices are communicated effectively and that employees are aware of their personal responsibilities for ensuring a safe work environment.

This chapter provides an overview of federal and state laws that affect employee safety and provides suggestions for the establishment of a safety program, including the formation of a safety committee, training and compliance with federal and state laws on workplace safety, and dealing with the issue of violence in the workplace.

Employer Responsibility for Employee Safety

Employers have a legal responsibility to protect the safety of their employees. SHRM's statement on Workplace Health, Safety, and Security suggests the following employer responsibilities:

- Employers should focus safety and health efforts primarily on hazards that pose the greatest risk of health and safety to the greatest number of employees.
- *Employees* as well as *employers* should be adequately trained in safety and health and be held responsible for safety.
- If an employer admits that a violation has occurred and does not contest the abatement period, the employer should correct the violation within the prescribed period.
- Employers should be encouraged to obtain input from employees on workplace health and safety issues.

- Employers should have a written workplace health and safety policy.
- Safety changes that the employer makes to the workplace should be based on sound science; address real, not hypothetical, risks; and recognize that the workplace, like other aspects of life, cannot be made risk-free.
- Where organizations have procedures for resolving problems, including alternative dispute resolution procedures, employees should use these procedures to resolve workplace safety problems before they file a complaint with Occupation Safety and Health Administration (OSHA).

While many employers will naturally be concerned about the safety of their employees, federal and state laws are in place to ensure that employee safety issues are addressed on the job. Workers' compensation insurance programs, mandated by individual state laws, exist to ensure that injured employees are able to obtain medical attention and receive reasonable compensation for any damage resulting from an on-the-job injury.

In 1970, the federal government entered the safety arena with the enactment of the Occupational Safety and Health Act (OSH Act). Under the OSH Act, employers are subject to the "general duty clause" and "general industry standards," which mandate that they provide a safe work environment.

The Americans with Disabilities Act (ADA) of 1990, which protects qualified persons with disabilities from unlawful discrimination in employment, also may influence how employee injuries are handled. An employer must make reasonable accommodations for persons with disabilities unless doing so would place undue hardship on the employer. Since the ADA became law, almost 70 percent of the discrimination charges filed by employees have been for failure to accommodate workers who have suffered occupational injuries. Employers that fail to consider the interplay of the ADA along with other laws (such as workers' compensation) may expose themselves to unnecessary liability.

In 1998, two proposals to streamline OSHA and make administration more employer-friendly passed Congress and were signed into law. These were the first significant amendments to the Act since its inception. The amendments codified OSHA's consultation program to assist small businesses and their employees in improving workplace safety and health and prohibited OSHA from using the number of inspections, citations, and penalties as a basis to measure a company's performance.

In early 2001, OSHA began moving forward on three major initiatives involving ergonomics, record-keeping, and the safety and health program rule. Industry- and task-specific ergonomic guidelines were not yet developed by year-end 2002. A timetable for new record-keeping regulations was released in 2001 and included requirements for maintaining and reporting illness and injury information. By February 2003, employers were expected to post 2002 calendar year data on the OSHA 300A form; employers may remove the 2002 posted data on May 1, 2003.

Beginning January 1, 2004, employers were required to check a hearing loss column to record work-related cases meeting the new recording criteria established by OSHA. The new criteria went into effect in 2003.

OSHA's safety and health program rule, in draft form at the end of 2002, requires all employers outside the areas of construction and agriculture — regardless of size and prior safety record — to establish a workplace safety and health program.

In early 2001, OSHA began moving forward on three major initiatives involving ergonomics, record-keeping, and the safety and health program rule. OSHA has developed industry- and task-specific guidelines for some, but not all, industries. These guidelines are voluntary and are designed to assist employers in recognizing and controlling ergonomics-related risk factors. As of January 1, 2004, employers have been required to check a hearing loss column to record work-related cases meeting the new recording criteria established by OSHA.

OSHA mandates that certain materials must be posted in prominent locations in the workplace to keep employees informed about OSHA. These include a Job Safety and Health Protection poster, summaries of petitions for variances from standards or recordkeeping procedures, and copies of OSHA citations for violations of standards.

OSHA's safety and health program rule requires all employers outside the areas of construction and agriculture — regardless of size and prior safety record — to establish a workplace safety and health program.

Starting a Safety Program

Federal and state laws require employers to take steps to ensure a safe working environment for employees. Not only do accidents and injuries affect the company's bottom line through increased workers' compensation costs, higher insurance, and lost workdays, but an unsafe work environment can take a toll in terms of employee satisfaction and productivity as well. It is to everyone's benefit to ensure a safe environment.

Employee safety is a major management function. The National Safety Council estimates the indirect costs of injuries and accidents — such as product and equipment damage, management investigation and reports, customer order delays, and co-worker inefficiencies — at more than 12 times the direct costs. Having a good safety and accident prevention program can be the key to remaining profitable.

Requirements for Preventing Workplace Accidents and Injuries

Every accident has a cause. Once the cause is known, preventing future accidents is possible. Because each workplace is different, safety programs will also differ, but regardless of the size of a business, there are four requirements for preventing workplace accidents and injuries:

1. Management commitment and employee involvement.
2. Planning and organizing.
3. A safety committee.
4. A worksite audit.

Management Commitment and Employee Involvement. Top management needs to be committed to the organization's safety efforts and must demonstrate its commitment to the safety program. HR cannot undertake this initiative on its own. In starting a safety program, management must not only be informed about safety but also demonstrate a positive attitude about maintaining a safe workplace. If management is not willing to show its commitment, the program will not be successful. Employers need to demonstrate concern for employees' health and safety. This concern can be demonstrated in a number of ways, as follows:

- Participation by employees in the development of the workplace safety program, including ongoing membership on the company's safety committee.
- Development of a policy statement on workplace safety and demonstrated commitment to upholding the policy.
- Prominent posting of required safety notices (such as the OSHA workplace poster), as well as internally developed policy statements, safety tips, and so forth.
- Discussion of job safety and health issues at employee meetings and in conversations with employees.
- Positive reinforcement and recognition of employee safety efforts.

Workplace objectives related to safety should be given as much attention and commitment as comparable objectives related to sales and productivity. Objectives can readily be expressed in objective terms — for instance, "We will increase the number of accident-free workdays from X to Y," or "We will have 20 percent fewer lost workday incidents this year."

With accountability clearly established and commitment to safety demonstrated through management's own actions and initiatives, the organization will have greater success in engaging all employees in its safety improvement initiatives.

Planning and Organizing. As with any other business activity, safety and accident prevention require comprehensive planning by both management and employees. The strategic planning process for safety is similar to other management planning processes. Safety committee members should be involved in ongoing strategy and planning, including an audit of the work environment; the establishment of specific goals for improvement; delegation of responsibility to specific departments, individuals, or workgroups; and the setting of goals, objectives, milestones, and target dates. Nowhere is the slogan "If you do not plan to succeed, you plan to fail" more true than in the area of safety.

By identifying the areas of the company that are most at risk and concentrating on those areas, the organization can demonstrate success in achieving its safety goals. In addition, employees can be rewarded for improving safety and contributing to a safe work environment.

The Safety Committee. Safety committees are essential to an effective safety effort; however, their effectiveness and value depend largely on how they are organized and managed. Safety committees should be designed to fill a specific need. For example, a small employer will likely have only one committee with a few members, while a large company will have a safety committee, maybe even more than one, in each plant or facility.

There has been some confusion about safety committees, which fall under the heading of employee participation committees, and employee improvement teams, which are made up of elected representatives of the employees and which legally exist to represent the employees. Employee participation committees, if designed properly, do not usurp the authority of the legally elected representatives of the employees. Safety committees can be beneficial, create a loyal and committed workforce, and lead to substantially increased productivity and quality. A few general rules apply to safety committees.

- Members of safety committees must not represent other employees.
- Safety committee deliberations must avoid discussions of financial rewards for safety improvement.
- Safety committees may assume management responsibilities such as safety inspections and accident investigations.
- Although employee safety is a management right, if employees are represented by a union, management should involve the union in the design and implementation of the safety committee.

HR professionals may want to discuss forming a safety committee with experienced employee relations professionals or HR consultants. The SHRM HR Knowledge Center can provide reprints of articles written by employee relations specialists and labor lawyers about improvement teams and employee participation committees.

The safety committee should clearly explain that the sole objective of the committee is to prevent accidents. It should cover membership, terms, selection, responsibilities and accountabilities, specific duties, specific activities and functions, and overall authority. It is generally accepted that activities involving the safety of employees are not a subject of bargaining. Normally, an employer can assert that management has reserved this right for itself. Be careful, however; many companies abdicate their right to use discretion in this area through past practice of not using that right.

Management should appoint all members of any safety committee. Although safety committees can be made up of employees from each functional area, the members should not be described as representing a department or a group of employees. If possible, a maintenance engineer or a member of the facilities staff should be a member of the committee, to provide technical expertise to help the committee make safety improvement decisions.

Although the HR person or another management official often functions as the committee chair, this is not a requirement. In any case, the chair should be a responsible person capable of running a meeting, setting priorities, and keeping committee activities at a high level. If the chair is not an experienced meeting facilitator, he or she should receive training in this area. Initially, the HR professional may consider being the chair to serve as a role model; later, a supervisor or employee may step into the role. The safety committee can perform a variety of functions. Following are some suggestions for functions of the safety committee:

- Investigate serious or dangerous accidents.
- Conduct area safety inspections and observe employee work habits to detect unsafe acts.
- Monitor housekeeping levels and initiate corrective action.
- Review and evaluate protective equipment needs.
- Review the safety program and recommend improvement.
- Periodically review safety rules and recommend changes.
- Review and evaluate existing hazards and new installations with the intent to eliminate or reduce any known hazards.
- Send information gained in training sessions to all employees.
- Review accident and injury data on an ongoing basis.

Regular meetings of the safety committee are important to ensure that safety is an issue that receives continued attention. Posting the agenda and minutes of these meetings is an additional way to communicate the company's commitment to a safe work environment.

The Worksite Audit. A preliminary step in starting a safety program and meeting OSHA requirements is the worksite audit. This is a formal safety assessment to provide information about areas where safety activities are adequate, where they can be improved, and where they require immediate attention. The OSHA Handbook for Small Businesses contains a self-inspection format that can be adapted for use in different companies. As an alternative, you may want to retain a professional safety consultant to assist in conducting the audit. (Choosing consultants and other advisers is discussed in Chapter 10.) Regardless of whether you conduct your own audit or obtain outside advice, you have the responsibility to know what hazards are present in the workplace. Once the initial audit system is set up, conducting subsequent safety audits will be a relatively simple process.

Sample 11 at the end of this chapter offers an abbreviated safety audit questionnaire (the entire original questionnaire consists of 400 questions). Each question would be assigned a weight. A summary report would be generated to indicate where the company is strong and where it needs to improve safety activities.

Safety Inspections

Safety inspections are the main tools for detecting unsafe conditions. Regular safety inspections ferret out unsafe conditions. There are two kinds of safety inspections: incidental inspections and planned inspections.

Incidental Inspections. The incidental inspection is largely a matter of keeping your eyes open. Most supervisors inspect their areas this way. Such inspections are useful, but they are usually superficial and erratic. When supervisors become engrossed in other matters, incidental inspection virtually ceases.

Planned Inspections. The planned inspection is deliberate and thorough. The supervisor knows the area and knows what tools, equipment and machines, structures, and supplies require inspection. There is a checklist for recording inspection items and findings. Inspection of this kind leaves nothing to chance. Unsafe conditions are much more likely to be spotted.

To initiate safety inspections, the first step is to conduct a safety inspection inventory to ascertain, for example, who is responsible for what areas, what items in each area require regular inspection, what conditions should be checked, how frequently the items should be inspected, who should inspect the items, and which items require special equipment and techniques for inspection.

Most companies develop a list of the tools, equipment, machines, structures, and supplies that require regular inspection, based on knowledge of unsafe conditions that have occurred in the past. When a tool, machine, structure, or piece of equipment is inspected, attention should be paid to the parts that can create unsafe conditions. The employer should decide exactly what parts of each tool should be inspected regularly. Figure 8.1 lists a number of ideas for developing a safety inspection inventory.

The National Safety Council's Handbook for Industrial Operations is another excellent source of inspection ideas.

FIGURE 8.1. Safety Inspection Inventory

- **Atmospheric conditions:** dust, gases, fumes, sprays, illumination
- **Buildings and structures:** windows, doors, floors, stairs, roofs, walls
- **Containers:** scrap bins, disposal receptacles, barrels, carboys, gas cylinders, solvent cans
- **Electrical equipment:** switches, cables, outlets, connectors, grounds, connections
- **Elevators, escalators, and lifts:** cable, controls, safety devices
- **Firefighting equipment:** extinguishers, hoses, hydrants, sprinkler systems, alarms
- **Hand tools:** bars, sledges, wrenches, hammers; also, power hand tools
- **Hazardous supplies and materials:** flammables, explosives, acids, caustics, toxic chemicals
- **Material handling equipment:** conveyors, cranes, hoists, forklifts
- **Personal protective equipment:** hard hats, safety glasses, respirators, gas masks
- **Personnel supporting equipment:** ladders, scaffolding, high platforms, catwalks, sling chairs, staging
- **Power source equipment:** gas engines, steam engines, electrical motors
- **Pressurized equipment:** boilers, vats, tanks, piping, hosing
- **Production and related equipment:** any equipment that processes materials into more finished products, such as mills, shapers, cutters, borers, presses, lathes
- **Structural openings:** shafts, pits, sumps, and floor openings, including those usually kept covered
- **Storage facilities and areas:** racks, bins, cabinets, shelves, tanks, closets; also yard and floor storage areas
- **Transportation equipment:** automobiles, trucks, railroad cars, motorized carts, buggies
- **Walkways and roadways:** aisles, ramps, docks, walkways, vehicle ways
- **Warning and signaling devices:** crossing lights, blinker lights, sirens, claxons, warning signs
- **Miscellaneous:** items that do not fall into any of the above categories

Safety Training

OSHA requires that all employees be trained for safety in specific areas. Employees also need education on the technical aspects of their jobs and on various safety topics. Employers must provide and document OSHA-required training to avoid being cited and fined. Beyond concern over legal liability, though, if employers do not provide technical, job-specific training, employees will not know how to avoid accidents and will not have the basic skills to identify hazards and avoid injury.

When an employee moves into a new position, an orientation on safety as it relates to that position should be provided. The object of the orientation should be to acquaint the employee with safety matters specifically related to the activities of the new position. The following areas represent some good areas to focus on in a safety orientation process:

- *Major area hazards.* Explain any major area hazards the new employee will be exposed to and what precautions are expected.
- *Personal protective equipment.* Protective equipment should be issued to the employee, and its use explained.
- *Housekeeping and clean-up responsibilities.* Acquaint the employee with his or her housekeeping and clean-up responsibilities. Poor housekeeping is a major cause of accidents and injuries; employee responsibility for housekeeping should be clearly defined.
- *Critical safety rules.* Safety rules should be explained immediately.

A specific orientation, related to the unique aspects of the employee's job, is critical. A general caution to be careful is not enough. The following safety instructions can serve as a good starting point for identifying areas to address before the employee assumes his or her responsibilities:

- *Potential accidents.* Possibilities of fire, explosion, toxic gases, electrical contacts, chemical contacts, cave-ins, falls, or other potentially serious accidents should be discussed and precautions agreed upon.
- *Unsafe practices.* Some jobs may tempt employees into unsafe practices — for example, throwing materials down instead of lowering them, failing to lock out equipment, and neglecting to rope off areas.
- *Protective equipment.* When jobs require special protective equipment, the assigning supervisor should see to it that the employees get the equipment.
- *"Other-fellow" precautions.* Many repair, service, and construction jobs require special precautions be taken to protect workers in the area.

Training involves ongoing communication. Organizations use a variety of activities to help encourage employees to maintain active safety awareness. For example,

- Regular meetings focusing on safety issues. These might be all-employee meetings, department meetings, or shift meetings. Meetings may be entirely focused on safety, or safety issues might be added as regular agenda items for group discussion.
- Contests that engage employees in discussion and consideration of safety issues. Simple quizzes involving safety tips or hazard recognition can be a way to have fun sharing information. Prizes may be awarded based on a drawing of entries from employees who answered the questions correctly. Contests might also involve safety challenges between departments.
- Recognition. The company should be committed to recognizing employees' safety efforts. These efforts can be simple — a commendation from the CEO, or coffee and cookies provided after a safety milestone has been reached.

There are many ways to keep safety at the forefront of employee concern. The keys are commitment and hands-on participation from top management, effective training and communication, and an effort to recognize and reward positive safety outcomes.

Record-Keeping Requirements

OSHA requires employers to keep certain records related to employee safety. These records often identify causes and can be used by OSHA to begin control procedures to prevent similar accidents. Employers may keep all information on computers at a central location and may use alternatives to federal forms, as long as the information is compatible and the data can be produced for OSHA and state officials when needed. Forms and guidelines are available on OSHA's web site at www.osha.gov or from the OSHA publications office at (202) 693-1888.

OSHA record-keeping requirements are shown in Figure 8.2. These requirements may seem onerous, but they are the minimum. These basic OSHA records include only injury and illness cases and should be expanded to include data that can pinpoint unsafe conditions or procedures. Certain OSHA standards that deal with toxic substances and hazardous exposures require additional records. In addition to maintaining the required records and filing the appropriate reports, throughout the year the records should be reviewed to see where injuries are occurring and to identify high-exposure and high-risk areas where attention should be directed.

FIGURE 8.2. OSHA Record-Keeping Requirements

- Obtain a report on every injury requiring medical treatment (death, disabling, or medical aid).
- Record each injury on OSHA Form 300.
- Prepare a supplementary record of occupational injuries and illnesses for recordable cases either on OSHA Form 301 or on Workers' Compensation First Report of Injury.
- Every year, prepare the annual summary, OSHA Form 300A; post it by February 1 and keep it posted until April 30. Posting it next to the OSHA workplace poster and the business safety policy is a good idea.
- OSHA requires employers to retain these records for at least five years, but most companies keep them for the life of the business. If the business is sold, the records must be transferred to the new owner.

In 2002, OSHA revised its record-keeping rule to collect better information, to improve employee awareness and involvement in recording and reporting job-related injuries and illnesses, to protect employees' privacy, to simplify record-keeping for employers, and to permit increased use of computers and telecommunications technology.

At the time of the revision, OSHA and the Department of Labor's Bureau of Labor Statistics (BLS) withdrew previously issued OSHA guidelines and all letters of interpretation regarding the former rule's injury and illness record-keeping requirements. The new BLS *Recording and Reporting Occupational Injuries and Illnesses* (revised 29 CFR Part 1904) includes complete information for record-keeping required by OSHA.

There are three OSHA record-keeping forms: Form 300 is the Log of Occupational Injuries and Illnesses, on which are recorded the occurrence, extent, and outcomes of cases. Form 300A is the Summary of Occupational Injuries and Illnesses, which is used to summarize the Log at the end of the year. Form 301, Supplementary Record of Occupational Injuries and Illnesses, provides additional information on each of the recorded cases.

Accident Investigations

Many employers use the First Report of Injury required by state workers' compensation systems as the sole accident investigation form. An alternate form is provided at the end of this chapter (Sample 12) and can be revised to meet specific needs. Most companies with successful accident and injury prevention programs use a comprehensive form. A similar form is available from the National Safety Council.

The workers' compensation system normally limits awards for occupational injuries and illnesses; consequently, the employer is strictly liable, and fault does not enter the process. However, a comprehensive accident investigation must identify specific causes and inquire into what employees either did or failed to do that caused the accident or injury. This report requires detailed, precise data, which may find the employer negligent in not preventing the accident. If there is additional litigation outside the workers' compensation area, the accident investigation report may be discoverable by opposing counsel. However, without comprehensive accident investigation documentation, the number of injuries and accidents will never be reduced.

The ultimate purpose of an accident investigation is to collect information that can be used to prevent a recurrence of the accident. The investigation should look for answers to the following questions:

- Who experienced the accident?
- When did the accident occur?
- Where did the accident occur?
- What position was being worked?
- What job was being done?
- What occurred?
- What were the causes of the accident?
- How can recurrence be prevented?
- Were there witnesses to the accident? Who were they?

Two common problems in accident investigation are reluctance to acknowledge responsibility and lack of proper concern for minor accidents. Supervisors who are nominally responsible for accidents are often reluctant to acknowledge accident causes that reflect on their own indifference, lack of action, or other contributing responsibility. Supervisors may investigate accidents with a defensive attitude and a readiness to blame the employee involved. A practical solution is to have injury accidents analyzed by an investigating committee consisting of one or more neutral supervisors plus the supervisor who is nominally responsible. Many companies use their safety committees for accident investigation. These committees usually conduct more thorough investigations than an individual investigator does.

There is often an understandable, but mistaken, lack of concern for minor accidents. Even in the case of minor accidents, a supervisor's lack of concern for injury prevention teaches employees that they do not have to be concerned about their own safety and that conditions that cause injuries do not have to be corrected.

Accident investigation reports usually are reviewed and filed by the supervisor. Sometimes they are discussed in management staff meetings and safety committee meetings. Occasionally, mechanical or engineering issues are identified and repairs and modifications made. Seldom, however, are the reports used to their full potential.

The report form in Sample 13 at the end of this chapter lists critical items that can be extracted from the accident report to calculate the type, number, and causes of injuries.

This form provides ongoing information about where accidents and injuries occur and their causes. While workers' compensation insurance carriers have loss prevention departments that are supposed to provide assistance in reducing accidents, often their reports are not very detailed and they do not summarize injuries and accidents annually. Most companies require more timely data.

A multilocation construction employer requested help with its safety efforts, specifically on required record-keeping for multiple locations and how to use the data. The employer was part of a risk pool in which several companies had joined together to purchase workers' compensation insurance as a group. This usually results in lower premiums. However, if one member of the pool has a high claims experience, the other members share the increased cost. Accurate accident and injury information is essential for this arrangement to work, but this company had only its own first report of injuries and the workers' compensation insurance administrator's loss control data.

From this small amount of data, information was reconstructed to support safety improvement recommendations. First, from the loss data, accident incidence and severity rates were calculated for each location, as shown in Sample 14 at the end of this chapter.

It is apparent where the problem with accidents and injuries existed. Although not shown here, the severity rate (the number of days lost to injuries per 200,000 hours worked) also was calculated. This calculation can identify serious hazards. However, the difference between the significance of a first-aid or near-miss accident and a serious disabling injury is slight. Most safety professionals strongly believe that for every serious injury, the injured employee has done the same thing, the same way, and not been injured. Successful safety and injury prevention programs should focus as much on near-miss incidents as they do on exposure to serious, possibly disabling injuries.

For more information on accident investigation, contact the National Safety Council or a safety practitioner or consultant.

Case Management

In spite of a company's best efforts and preventive measures, employees may be injured. Since the passage of the ADA in 1990, there has been some movement toward bringing injured employees back to work as soon as possible; in fact, refusal to bring an employee who is partially disabled back to work may be a violation of the ADA. But under the Family and Medical Leave Act (FMLA) of 1993, a partially disabled or injured employee cannot be forced to return to work on "light duty" before 12 weeks have elapsed.

The sooner an injured employee returns to work (either to full duty or to an accommodated position), the more likely the employee is to return to full productivity. Conversely, if an employee is off work more than several weeks, the outlook for returning to full efficiency is diminished significantly. This issue is of significant concern for HR professionals.

Many employers use an internal case management process. Case management is the immediate review of any occupational injury requiring medical attention with the objective of reducing unnecessary medical cost, time lost from work, and permanent partial disability expenses.

Here is a hypothetical case scenario from one company. Steve, a maintenance employee, inadvertently puts his forefinger into a conveyor drive chain and the tip is cut off. Instead of having a co-worker take Steve to the hospital, the manager, Loretta, accompanies him to the emergency room, to comfort Steve and to get firsthand information on what occurred. The emergency room physician sutures the severed fingertip and prescribes medication. Steve and Loretta discuss with the doctor the treatment, possible therapy, and prohibitions on returning to full duty. Steve and Loretta agree, and the physician concurs, that Steve should stay in the shop, performing bench work, for the next week. After the next doctor's appointment, Steve and Loretta will discuss any temporary disability and plan his return to full duty.

Both return to the plant, and while Loretta completes the accident investigation report, Steve gathers bench work that has backed up and starts full-valued work. The total cost of this accident is less than $500, including the indirect cost of the manager's time at the emergency room.

In another organization, the scenario might have been different. Steve might have been taken to the emergency room by a co-worker. Without a manager to discuss his return to work on light duty, Steve might be given a week off to recuperate. Loretta might have been busy and might not have completed the accident investigation report for a few days. Steve would be missed on the job, but since he had a doctor's excuse, the time off would not have been questioned. At the very least, there would have been no discussion until the doctor returned Steve to full duty. The direct costs (medical and temporary partial disability) could easily have exceeded $5,000; the indirect costs, twice that.

This simple case study illustrates how a proactive response to an accident can save an organization a significant amount of money. Even more important is the result when there is a permanent partial disability and the employee cannot meet the full requirements of the job. As discussed previously, the ADA requires employers to accommodate disability unless there is an undue hardship to the employer. This law applies to hiring, but the largest number of complaints under the ADA have been against employers that refuse to accommodate disabilities resulting from occupational injuries.

The issues of safety, workers' compensation, and the ADA are too complicated to discuss fully here, but the following factors should be considered in starting a safety program:

- The employer must have a policy that covers early return to work and subsequent adaptations to the permanent disabilities of employees who are injured while working.
- While the ADA does not require job descriptions, every position should be analyzed so that only the essential job functions are included as requirements in the company's job description. Employers should be sure that such requirements accurately reflect the job being performed and that these requirements are reviewed and updated regularly. Physical requirements, such as the amount of weight someone must be able to lift, are just one example of how job descriptions contribute to the safety program.
- Managers must receive a comprehensive education on safety, early return to work, and ADA issues. If managers do not understand the requirements and are not committed to the process, it will fail. Many discrimination charges have been filed against companies for misjudgment on ADA-related matters.
- All employees must be given an orientation on the early return to work process. The objectives and process must be clearly understood by all.
- Managers' performance evaluations should be based in part on how well they reduce the number of injuries and accidents, comply with the ADA, and manage the case management process.
- HR professionals should regularly monitor accident and injury reports and identify areas where employees are not returned to work immediately after an occupational injury.

Case management is not a fully developed process in most companies, but many consultants offer case management services. The most successful case management processes are those that require both the manager and the line supervisor to participate. This is especially true when considering ADA and FMLA issues. Only persons very familiar with the operations and the work culture should be making decisions about whether the employer can adapt a position to a particular employee's temporary partial disability.

Violence in the Workplace

Workplace violence — including assaults and suicides — accounted for 16 percent of all work-related fatal occupational injuries in 2008. Homicides are perennially among the top four causes of workplace fatalities for all workers. Workplace violence has been on the decline, but in spite of these improvements, it is still important to take steps to ensure that your work environment is a safe one.

Factors that may increase a worker's risk for workplace assault, as identified by the National Institute for Occupational Safety and Health, are these:
- Contact with the public.
- Exchange of money.
- Delivery of passengers, goods, or services.
- Having a mobile workplace such as a taxicab or a police cruiser.
- Working with unstable or volatile persons in health care, social services, or criminal justice settings.
- Working alone or in small numbers.
- Working late at night or during early morning hours.
- Working in high-crime areas.
- Guarding valuable property or possessions.
- Working in community-based settings.

What can you do?
- Find out how safe your employees feel at work. Are there times, places, or situations that make them feel vulnerable or at risk? Why?
- Take steps to improve security. If there are areas of risk in your company, take steps to minimize those risks. Local law enforcement agencies may be a good resource to you in this process.
- Consider various deterrents such as bright lighting, convex mirrors, deep service counters, alarm systems or panic buttons, and the use of security guards.
- Develop and clearly communicate a zero tolerance policy for workplace violence. Make sure that employees are aware of the policy and that they feel comfortable bringing forward any violence-related issues. Enforce the policy stringently.
- Be sensitive to issues that can lead to violence, such as high levels of stress, excessive overtime, or fear of layoffs or downsizing.
- Train managers to recognize warning signs. Managers can be your first line of

defense against workplace violence. Make sure that they're familiar with your policy and that they recognize and are comfortable with their role in detecting and responding to issues of potential or actual violence.

FAQs

What are the warning signs for workplace violence?

Wendy Bliss:

There are some common characteristics of potentially violent employees. These individuals often change jobs frequently or have a history of violence or aggression. They tend to be loners, have low self-esteem, be suspicious of others, exhibit a "victim" mentality, or have limited outlets for anger. Violent workers often abuse drugs or alcohol, own weapons, or exhibit excessive fascination with weapons. They may hold fanatical political or religious beliefs and show extreme interest in media reports of violence. Historically, perpetrators of violent acts at work have tended to be white males between the ages of 25 and 40, but experts caution that violent employees cannot be pigeonholed into a single demographic profile.

HR professionals and supervisors should be aware of these common characteristics. More important, they should be alert for warning signs of violence. These signs include strong verbal cues such as angry outbursts, excessive profanity, expressed wishes or threats to hurt co-workers or management, or comments about suicide. Other warning signs are changes in behavior such as marked shifts in work patterns (uncharacteristic tardiness, absenteeism, becoming more accident-prone), extreme disorganization, and depression. Other red-flag employee behaviors are holding grudges (especially against supervisors), escalating misconduct, exhibiting harassing or intimidating behavior, exhibiting obsessions, or sabotaging property.

Sample 11

Safety Audit Questionnaire

- Do you have an accident investigation procedure?
- Does the procedure require that injuries, occupational illnesses, property damage, accidents, and near misses be reported?
- Does it require that supervisors be trained in investigation and reporting?
- Is there a standard form for accident investigation?
- Do employees participate in accident investigations?
- Is the atmosphere one of fact-finding rather than fault-finding?
- Does your accident investigation program require
  a) a complete investigation by the immediate supervisor, with the results recorded on a standard form?
  b) that injury and alleged causal information on all injuries treated by first aid be recorded?
  c) that serious accidents and near misses be called to the attention of the group manager to ensure full investigation?
- Is a monthly check made of the following areas to learn the number of accidents reported?
  a) First aid stations and medical treatment center.
  b) Maintenance shops, storerooms, and equipment storage areas.
  c) Fire control center.
- Is there a procedure for ensuring that remedial action (and follow-up of that action) as recommended in the investigation report is carried out?
- Do you have an organized system to ensure that all remedial action listed on major loss accidents has been taken? If yes, does it include
  a) A periodic report from the area supervisor on the status of incomplete remedial actions?
  b) Follow-up by the appropriate person, with item-by-item check-off as actions are completed?
- How frequently is management made aware of the progress of remedial action taken on major or high-potential-loss accidents?
- Is the progress of remedial action expressed in written form?
- Is it also expressed orally at meetings?
- Are summaries of the vital information on major injuries or illnesses written and distributed to department managers within 24 hours of the occurrence?
- Are summaries of the major property damage accidents and fires written and distributed to department heads within 48 hours of the occurrence?
- Are the considerations and declarations of investigation review meetings recorded?
- How often is an audit made of the percentage of accidents investigated?
- Are the findings communicated in written form to all managers?
- Is there a system to evaluate the quality of accident investigation reports? If yes, how often is this done and recorded?
- Are these evaluations communicated to all levels of management?

Sample 12

Accident Investigation Form

PERSONAL INFORMATION

Name: Employee no.:   Age:

Location: Department:

Time of   Date of   Date injury   Date lost   Date returned
accident: accident: reported: time started: to work:

Position title: Years of   Specific activity being performed:
                                         experience:

Nature of injuries and injured body parts:

ACCIDENT DESCRIPTION AND RELATED INFORMATION

Exact location where accident occurred:

Job employee was doing at the time injured:

Describe exactly what occurred:

Sample 12, continued

ANALYSIS OF ACCIDENT CAUSES

What did the injured (or other person) do or fail to do that contributed directly to the accident? Be specific.

Check the items below judged to be responsible for what was done or not done, thereby contributing to the accident. More than one may apply. Write in any information or direct causes not listed.

- ❑ Unaware of job hazards
- ❑ Inattentive to hazards
- ❑ Unaware of safe method
- ❑ Low level of job skill
- ❑ Tried to gain or save time
- ❑ Tried to avoid extra effort
- ❑ Acted to avoid discomfort
- ❑ Indirect cause(s) other than those listed

- ❑ Influence of emotions
- ❑ Influence of fatigue
- ❑ nfluence of illness
- ❑ Influence of intoxicants
- ❑ Defective vision
- ❑ Defective hearing
- ❑ Other personal handicap
- ❑ Unable to judge nature of indirect causes

What defective or otherwise unsafe condition(s) of tools, equipment, machinery, structures, work area, etc., contributed to the accident?

Check the items below judged responsible for the development or existence of any defective or otherwise unsafe conditions that contributed to the accident. Check all conditions that apply. Write in the information for indirect causes not listed.

- ❑ Worn out from normal use
- ❑ Abuse or misuse by user(s)
- ❑ Overlooked by regular inspections
- ❑ Regular inspections not required
- ❑ Housekeeping or clean-up failure
- ❑ Regular clean-up not required
- ❑ Inadequate ventilation
- ❑ Congestion—lack of space
- ❑ Indirect cause(s) not listed above

- ❑ Unsafe design
- ❑ Faulty construction
- ❑ Inadequate illumination
- ❑ Lubrication failure
- ❑ Exposure to corrosion/rust
- ❑ Exposure to vibration
- ❑ Exposure to extreme temperature
- ❑ Tampering: unauthorized removal
- ❑ Unable to judge cause of contributing condition

Sample 12, continued

ACTIONS TO PREVENT ACCIDENT RECURRENCE

Mark the corrective actions planned or already taken to prevent accident recurrence at the time of this report. More than one item may apply.

❏ Reinstruct employees involved
❏ Reprimand persons involved
❏ Discipline persons involved
❏ Reinstruct others doing job
❏ Temporary reassignment of person
❏ Permanent reassignment of person
❏ Action to improve inspection
❏ Action to improve housekeeping
❏ Order job safety analysis conducted

❏ Revise job safety analysis
❏ Equipment repair or replacement
❏ Action to improve design
❏ Action to improve construction
❏ Installation of guard or safety device
❏ Correction of unnecessary congestion
❏ Improve personal protective equipment
❏ Start new pre-job instruction
❏ Use other materials
❏ Communicate safety concern

❏ Other than above, please specify:

Describe details of any primary corrective action for disabling-injury or near-disabling-injury accidents.

Recommend any corrective actions needed to prevent accident recurrences that are beyond your authority to implement. Describe the basic idea.

MISCELLANEOUS INFORMATION

Names of witnesses:

Was a job safety analysis conducted? ❏ yes ❏ no   Was revision ordered? ❏ yes ❏ no

Investigated by: Reviewed by:

Date: Date:

Sample 13

Cumulative Accident Report Form

BODY PARTS ANALYSIS

Month	Head	Eyes	Neck	Back	L/arm	L/hand	Fingers	R/arm	R/hand	L/leg	L/foot	R/leg	R/foot
Jan													
Feb													
March													
April													
May													
Totals													

CONTRIBUTING FACTORS

Month	Unaware of job hazards	Inattentive to hazards	Unaware of safe methods	Low level of skill	Saving time	Avoiding extra effort
Jan						
Feb						
March						
April						
May						
Totals						

Sample 14

Accident Loss Data, by Location

Location	Hours	Lost Time Cases	Lost Time Rate	Medical Aid Cases	Medical Aid Rate	First Aid Cases	Priority
Phoenix, AZ	xxx,xxx,xxx	20	8.00	31	12.4	35	Third
San Francisco, CA	xxx,xxx,xxx	12	4.80	15	6	20	
Los Angeles, CA	xxx,xxx,xxx	11	4.40	17	6.8	19	
Colorado Springs, CO	xxx,xxx,xxx	31	12.40	45	18	59	First
Kansas City, MO	xxx,xxx,xxx	30	12.00	34	13.6	39	Second
Overland Park, KS	xxx,xxx,xxx	8	3.20	10	4	8	
St. Louis, MO	xxx,xxx,xxx	6	2.40	19	7.6	40	
Minneapolis, MN	xxx,xxx,xxx	7	2.80	23	9.2	36	
Omaha, NE	xxx,xxx,xxx	5	2.00	10	4	17	
Springfield, MO	xxx,xxx,xxx	7	2.80	11	4.4	20	
Las Vegas, NV	xxx,xxx,xxx	15	6.00	11	4.4	23	

Management Reports

We have all heard statements made by CEOs and upper management to the effect that our employees are our most valuable resource, and most HR practitioners would agree with that statement. The problem lies in proving the value of the organization's human resources — often a very challenging thing to do.

While HR professionals encourage management to see a payoff from the company's investments in its human resources, management may have difficulty seeing that relationship.

The reason for this conflict may be the age-old problem that human resources is not viewed as a strategic part of the organization. Instead, management expects human resources to be oriented toward administrative and maintenance activities. This perception creates a dilemma between the HR professional's understanding of what needs to be accomplished and top management's purpose in creating the HR function. In these situations, the HR professional must satisfy strategic management objectives while building a foundation of basic HR activities. If human resources does not identify key objectives, implement activities carefully, and report on its achievements using actual dollar measurements, it will not be able to retain the support of management.

HR functions are successful when these three business objectives are achieved:

1. Accomplishing the purposes of the employer.
2. Supporting other functions interdependently.
3. Returning more in profitability than is expected.

A management consultant once said, "Without a yardstick, there is no measurement; without measurement, there is no control." This chapter will present some ideas and advice for measuring human resources and proving that its activities add value. Techniques for measuring employee satisfaction with human resources and management will also be discussed, as well as techniques for gaining feedback from employees through employee suggestion programs.

When Human Resources Does Not Meet Business Needs

How does the newly appointed HR professional know which HR management activities are not meeting business needs? As with any other business function, certain signs are present when activities are weak and ineffective. The following are possible signs of problems:

- Advanced HR activities are being conducted, while HR maintenance activities are overlooked. Management may have initiated excellence in customer service processes, total quality management, or manufacturing receiving processes. But if managers have not been trained in recruiting, hiring, and equal employment opportunity requirements, or if the organization is experiencing high turnover, human resources is not meeting the business's needs.

- There are no budgets or control mechanisms in place. When an HR function cannot justify its existence with quantifiable numbers, it will not have the trust and support of top management. Even simple measures, such as cost-per-hire or turnover rate, accompanied by comparisons with costs at other companies, show management that human resources is attuned to the bottom line.

- Nothing seems wrong, but processes are not working. Processes and programs are implemented according to professional standards, but they do not work. One example is a reward and recognition strategy that has no effect on internal inequities. Other examples are performance standards that are not focused on customer value-added activities or a recruitment and selection strategy that fails to have a positive impact on turnover. The company may have a technically perfect compensation and benefits program, a nationally recognized performance evaluation program, or an expensive recruiting process. But if people are complaining and turnover is high, HR is not doing its job.

- There is no payoff from the investment. No matter how technically correct or professionally sophisticated a program is, if it has no payoff, it is not making a positive contribution to the company's success; consequently, it has no value to the organization. An example might be a substantial investment in management and employee training programs that do not demonstrate any tangible improvements.

- Nothing is measured. The excuse is that you cannot measure results in dollars; the results are intangible. Or that human resources is a soft profession — you cannot quantify it. These statements are self-defeating, and they contribute to HR's ongoing struggle to be seen as a strategic partner. Strategic departments in any organization understand that they must demonstrate their value to the organization. HR is no different. You must measure the results of your efforts to demonstrate, specifically, how you add value to the organization. If there are no measurements, there is no value.

Evaluating HR Effectiveness

As discussed in Chapter 1, strategic planning is an important component of a successful HR operation. HR professionals need to align their objectives with the objectives of the organization, and they need to demonstrate that the activities they are engaged in have a positive impact on the organization.

Part of the strategic planning process is a SWOT analysis — a critical look at the department's Strengths, Weaknesses, Opportunities, and Threats. The results of this analysis are then incorporated into the department's general operational objectives.

Figure 9.1 shows a sample objective and related strategies for a small, public-sector HR function. Each of the strategies identified is then supported with specific action plans developed by the director and his or her staff. For example, the strategy *Increase staff time devoted to providing services to internal clients* might result in the action plan shown in Figure 9.2.

FIGURE 9.1. HR Function Objective and Strategies

Objective:
Improve the efficiency and productivity of the human resource department.

Strategies:
- Increase staff time devoted to providing services to internal clients.
- Automate 25 percent of all transactional processes.
- Simplify two work processes by 20 percent each.
- Improve internal client satisfaction by 20 percent.
- Reduce turnover by 20 percent.

FIGURE 9.2. Action Plan

Activities	Responsibility	Completion Date	Resources/Costs
1. Analyze time by major activity of each staff member. Develop summary report.	Director	1 Jun 10	Staff time
2. Gather data from internal clients on their requirements.	Staff members	15 Jun 10	Staff/client time
3. Brainstorm and prioritize improvement ideas for each staff area.	Team	1 Jul 10	Staff time
4. Set pilot productivity improvement goals for staff members.	Team	15 Aug 10	Staff time
5. Present interim monthly reports at staff meeting.	Team	Ongoing	Staff time
6. Review/revise plan as necessary.	Team	1 Sep 10	Staff time
7. Identify improvements and calculate cost savings.	Team	1 Dec 10	Staff time
8. Set improvement goals for 2011.	Team	1 Dec 10	Staff time

Increasing staff time dedicated to working with internal clients results in measurable achievements. Is there a cost-improvement justification? If the staff time is spent on activities that add value to the internal client, the answer is obviously yes. Can an actual dollar amount be attached to the savings? Again, the answer is yes.

HR professionals use many techniques to identify savings and HR improvements. Some use a formula based on the cost of adding a salaried professional. Others use the value provided to the client. Still others might use the improvement in the efficiency of the internal client.

Increasing staff time devoted to providing services to internal clients might be justified by identifying the number of additional staff required to maintain the same level of service. Human resources might want to focus on value and identify the increased efficiency and satisfaction of the internal client.

Identifying money saved when the result is lower turnover or better hiring decisions is also possible. A 1998 William M. Mercer study indicated that companies estimated the average cost of turnover at anywhere from $10,000 to $30,000 per employee. Clearly, efforts to reduce turnover can have a rapid return in dollars.

The director of a public-sector HR function used a form similar to that in Sample 15 at the end of this chapter to gather data from internal clients.

The data were summarized in a monthly report that included comparisons with the same month in the previous year, the previous year's summary, and a current year-to-date summary. The report focused not on numbers but on areas of improvement and areas in which there was no improvement. The report was distributed to the top management team.

Clearly, there are many opportunities for HR professionals to quantify the value of their contributions to the organization. The value of data cannot be overemphasized. Making recommendations to management without solid information to back up those recommendations — whether the issue is a change in the benefits program, the addition of staff, or a policy change — is ill advised. The more ways in which you can tangibly demonstrate the value of each of the services that HR provides, the more successful you will be in becoming a strategic partner and seeing your recommendations put into action.

Measuring the Organization's Climate

Just as the HR function should evaluate customer satisfaction based on its internal clients, it should also measure employee satisfaction with the company. Normally, this is accomplished by using some form of organizational climate (attitude) survey. Two sample questionnaires are included at the end of this chapter (Samples 16 and 17).

Climate surveys are popular, but the maximum advantage is seldom gained from them. In fact, members of management often are surprised at employees' responses and disappointed with the results, because they have unrealistic ideas about how satisfied employees are with the job management is doing. From employees' point of view, communication of results is not handled well. Employees are frequently dissatisfied with the priority management places on the identified issues. Organizational climate surveys can be valuable tools, but they regularly fail in use.

It is important to be open to feedback and encourage your staff members to welcome feedback as a way of improving performance and value to the organization. Your relationship with management and employees is an important element in developing credibility. Your responsiveness, accessibility, and timeliness of response are important. Perception is everything. While you may believe that you are providing service in the most efficient manner possible, if your internal customers perceive otherwise, you have a problem.

In addition to measuring the perceived value of services provided by HR staff members, organizational climate surveys can provide broader insights into the organization's opinions on HR-related issues (such as benefits, culture, etc.).

Following are some important considerations for conducting an organizational climate survey:

- Use a climate survey that is designed specifically for the company and that includes only those items that management has the interest and the resources to change. Do not ask employees if they are satisfied with their benefits package unless you are prepared to change the benefits package if their answer is a resounding no.

- Do not ask what you already know. If you know that your company's managers are not conducting performance evaluations in a timely manner, do not ask employees if their performance evaluations are conducted in a timely manner. If you have quantifiable data available, or other sources of information about issues or attitudes, don't waste your time — and your employees' time — with a survey.

- Start with clear objectives. Before you conduct any survey, know what you want to know — and what you will do with the information after the survey is completed. What information do you hope to obtain? How will you use that information? Do not ask questions just for the sake of asking. Make sure your surveys are focused and actionable. And don't just repeat the same survey year after year because it is part of your ongoing practices. The work environment changes rapidly, and your survey tools need to reflect those changes and be continually focused on gathering information that will be actionable and meaningful.

- Choose an appropriate sample. While you can obtain statistically valid results by surveying a segment of your employee population, there are often good reasons to include all members of the group whose feedback you are seeking in the survey. Prime among these is the feeling of exclusion. Employees not included in the sample may feel left out and resentful, not understanding statistical sampling. On the other hand, don't survey your entire employee population if the information you are seeking can be obtained from specific employee segments. For example, if you are concerned about high turnover in a specific department, focus on that department. If you do use a sample, make sure it is chosen by someone well versed in statistical sampling.

- Involve the organization's managers in the process, and ensure that they understand why the survey is being conducted, how the results will be used, and what expectations the organization has of them in responding to employee feedback. Unless they are adequately prepared and involved, members of management may dismiss the results when the survey replies do not meet their expectations.

- Maintain confidentiality to ensure that employees will be candid and honest. To guarantee anonymity and to ease employee concerns about the confidentiality of their responses, you may choose to use an outside consultant or resource to gather and summarize survey responses.

- Plan to share the results of the survey with employees. Employees will be as anxious to see this information as management is. Be prompt and up front in sharing the feedback. Any delay can be interpreted by employees as an indication that management and human resources are trying to hide something.

- Consider benchmarking your survey results against those in your company's industry or against specific job classes. While some companies benchmark against other companies, this can be misleading because of the differences in management philosophy, culture, and work environments. In addition, you should definitely benchmark against your own results from previous years to show gains and areas for improvement.

- Choose an appropriate time. Timing can be an important factor when conducting a survey. Do not survey employees during the holidays, during major corporate downsizing or restructuring, or during extremely busy work periods. At the same time, if you are surveying in response to an immediate need or to gauge response to a specific issue, conduct the survey as quickly as possible after the event or issue.

- Determine whether each question on a survey instrument is properly worded. Unless it is a standardized instrument, human resources should ascertain what each question is asking, what area it addresses, and what the possible responses might be. This will ensure that there are no misunderstandings. Test your survey before you distribute it. It is easy to overlook the obvious when developing a survey. Before you roll out any survey instrument to the population at large, test the tool on a group of employees — 10 to 12 samples should give you a good idea of whether the survey was easy to understand and follow, whether questions were meaningful, and whether you inadvertently missed a key point.

- Consider automating your surveys if all employees have computer access. Intranet-based surveys provide convenience not only for employees but also for HR staff. Employees can enter their responses, and the survey tool compiles, analyzes, and reports results. Online surveying can be a good way to take the pulse of employees quickly, and employees enjoy the interactivity of the survey tools. Or consider a combination of methods — pencil and paper, intranet, and telephone surveying — to gather data.

- Do something! Always share results with employees and always act on the information you obtain. Never survey employees without sharing the aggregate results — and letting them know how you intend to respond to the data you have gathered.

Employee Suggestion Programs

Suggestion programs are common in corporate America — but too many of these programs are poorly managed and not effectively tied to the strategic needs of the organization. Consequently, employee input tends to focus more on complaints than on useful suggestions; management staff resent the time they must spend responding to what they often perceive as worthless input; and those managing the program feel overwhelmed by the administrative burden of gathering, logging, and responding to the comments they receive.

There are successful employee suggestion programs, however, that yield valuable results. What makes a suggestion program successful? A number of things. Successful employee suggestion programs are

- Supported by upper management. As with any major initiative, without the support of upper management, even the best-run program is destined to fail. To get top management on board, gather examples of successful programs implemented by other companies, conduct research to find information on the value of allowing employee input, and develop methods of measuring your own program's success.

- Developed with clearly defined goals and objectives. What results do you want to obtain through your program? A program designed as a way to manage the rumor mill will look very different from a program designed to help the company save money on expenses.

- Easily accessible by all employees. For your program to be useful, employees need to have ready and convenient access. This may mean that you offer a number of alternatives for submitting suggestions — traditional suggestion boxes, a suggestion hotline, e-mail suggestions, and so on. Consider all employees when establishing your program.
- Easy to use. A four-page form that must be filled out and submitted in triplicate probably will not generate an overwhelming amount of input. If your objective is to limit suggestions and to educate employees on preparing sound business cases, that approach may be all right. But if your goal is to involve as many employees as possible and to generate numerous ideas, keep it simple.
- Low risk. Employees are often hesitant to share their ideas. They may feel that nobody cares, that their ideas will be considered stupid, or that somebody else may already have thought of the same idea. They may fear that they will somehow get in trouble for making a suggestion that may step on someone's toes. Or they may fear retribution from their direct supervisor. For all of these reasons, it is a good idea to allow employees the option of submitting ideas and comments anonymously. The less an employee has to risk in submitting an idea, the more likely he or she will be to submit it.
- Easy to administer. Many programs fail simply because the administrative burden is too great and the time and effort involved to maintain the program are viewed as excessive.
- Responsive. Employees need to hear whether their ideas have been acted upon, and they need to see tangible evidence that their suggestions are valued and are making a difference. Quick follow-up to any suggestion or comment submitted is a must. The follow-up can be as simple as "We've received your suggestion and will evaluate it within the next 30 days." Attempt to acknowledge suggestions within 48 hours and make final responses within 30 days. If the submitter has identified himself or herself, respond to the employee. Share the input and responses with employees at large.
- Measurable. To continue to generate management support for your employee suggestion program, you need to develop some means of measuring the value the program provides. This measurement does not have to be extensive or administratively burdensome. For example, a goal might be to improve the score that employees give on an employee satisfaction survey in response to the comment "I feel that my suggestions are valued." Or you may choose to measure the number of suggestions that are implemented. The key is to make your measurements match your goals and objectives.

Here are some additional tips for establishing an employee suggestion program:

- Be specific in terms of what types of ideas you want from employees, and provide guidelines to help them submit suggestions that are focused and clearly presented.
- Make it easy for managers to respond. The burden on management to respond to suggestions can be overwhelming. The administrators of the program can help ease this burden by developing lists of frequently asked questions, drafting suggested responses to certain comments, and so forth.
- Share suggestions and responses with the staff at large. A simple Q&A format in your employee newsletter can be a great way to share suggestions and responses. This helps to cut down on duplicate suggestions and comments and offers an excellent way to educate and inform employees on issues they are concerned about.
- Manage employee expectations. Make sure employees know what to expect when they contribute a suggestion. Where will their suggestion go? How long will it be before they receive a response?

A well-designed and well-implemented employee suggestion program can provide a great deal of value for an organization. Not only will many of the suggestions received result in cost savings or improved efficiencies, but allowing employees an avenue for sharing ideas, concerns, and comments can provide valuable information to management about employee perceptions, misconceptions, and developing issues.

Employees have suggestions. They have concerns. They have complaints. They will have these suggestions, concerns, and complaints whether you have a formal suggestion program or not — you are just less likely to hear about these issues if you do not have a program.

FAQs

What are some good, quantitative measurements to determine HR's effectiveness?

Paul Falcone:

Following are some examples of questions that metrics and analytics can answer:

Recruitment

- What percentage of our jobs are filled internally?
- What percentage of those internal hires were minorities and females?
- What percentage of new hires survive/thrive beyond the first year?

Development

- What does our average employee look like in terms of average tenure, pay, age, ethnicity, and gender?
- How many hours of training are assigned to new versus experienced employees, and how can we link production results to our training efforts?
- What is the average trend in performance appraisals over time?
- What is the key differential in merit pay awards between high-performing and lower-performing employees?
- What trends in unscheduled absenteeism, intermittent Family and Medical Leave Act leave, and workers' compensation costs are we seeing on a year-over-year basis?

Retention

- What is the retention rate for critical human capital (e.g., 4 and 5 scores on the annual performance review)?
- What types of disciplinary interventions are we seeing, and what are the top three reasons employees are disciplined and/or terminated?
- What trends are we seeing in voluntary turnover, what's the number one reason for leaving, and how many of our employees are defecting to the competition?

Return on Investment

Return-on-investment calculations combine measurable human capital metrics with financial results and are the "brass ring" of the metrics function. Jacques Fitzenz in *ROI of Human Capital* and David Ulrich in *The HR Scorecard* recommend calculating the following:

- Human capital ROI.

- Human capital value-added.
- Human economic value-added.
- Human capital market value.

Why do we need quantitative measurements to measure the effectiveness of HR?

William G. Bliss:

The quick answer is to provide information that is of value to management. This information must be timely, relevant, and actionable. What purpose will a turnover report serve if it focuses on information that is six months old?

All information should be compared to a benchmark. For example, if the report shows a cost-per-hire of $4,000, it also needs to provide information about the average cost-per-hire in the community, in the industry, or for the type of position being filled. Otherwise, management cannot assess whether that $4,000 is a great figure or something to be concerned about.

Many organizations tend to view HR as a cost center. HR is better viewed as a profit center — as a function that can make money for the business by developing and implementing programs and processes that add value to the bottom line. Examples include cost-effective recruiting and retention programs, compensation and benefits plans that *really* attract and retain employees, and training experiences that have a measurable impact on employee performance.

Consider measuring the following information:

Reactive

- Employee turnover and the cost of that turnover; reasons for turnover.
- Time required to fill open positions.
- Cost required to fill open positions.
- Absenteeism and time off.
- Projected rise in benefits costs.
- Comparison of your compensation rates to your competitors', for both type of position and industry.
- Unemployment cost; workers' compensation cost.
- Internal promotions over a given time period.

Proactive

- Goals and objectives to address the company's strategic objectives from an HR perspective.
- What the competition is planning to do in the future.

- The impact of legislative actions on your company and a proactive plan to address that impact.
- A plan to become an employer of choice in your industry and geographic region.

Is an HR audit a good idea? If so, what should it include?

Erin O'Connor:

Most HR audits start out looking at the various functions in HR. There are a couple of top priorities — legal compliance being first and foremost. You want to make sure you are complying with all of the laws and regulations applicable to you, which will depend on your location, your size, your state, city. That is probably the most comprehensive and complex audit.

There are several other audits I would do. I would look at the performance management system and decide whether it is actually achieving the objectives of a performance management system and, if not, how to address that. I would look at compensation infrastructures to determine whether pay systems are appropriately aligned with the strategic objectives of the organization. I would look at recruitment and staffing to make sure the people who are coming into the organization meet the long-term objectives of the organization.

I would go through each of these areas and determine whether they are aligned with the strategic objectives of the organization.

Sample 15

Internal Customer/Client Satisfaction Survey

	Satisfied	Somewhat Satisfied	Dissatisfied
1. Did we deliver the service on time?	❑	❑	❑
2. Are you satisfied with the quality of the service?	❑	❑	❑
3. Did we keep you up-to-date on the service?	❑	❑	❑
4. Did we treat you in a helpful/professional manner?	❑	❑	❑

5. <u>Is there anything else we can do for you?</u>

_____

_____

6. Please describe the value our service provided for you.

_____

_____

_____

_____

_____

Sample 16

Employee Survey

Note: Read these answer categories carefully, then answer each of the following questions by using the answer number you think is most appropriate. Feel free to make comments in the space below each statement or on the back of the survey.

Answer numbers:

1) To a very little extent,

2) To a little extent,

3) To some extent,

4) To a great extent,

5) To a very great extent.

1.	To what extent is this organization quick to use improved work methods?	1	2	3	4	5
2.	To what extent are work activities sensibly organized?	1	2	3	4	5
3.	To what extent are decisions made at the levels at which the most adequate and accurate information is available?	1	2	3	4	5
4.	To what extent does this organization tell your workgroup what it needs to know to do the best possible job?	1	2	3	4	5
5.	How much does this organization try to improve working conditions?	1	2	3	4	5
6.	When decisions are made, to what extent are the persons affected asked for their ideas?	1	2	3	4	5
7.	Overall, how satisfied are you with your supervisor?	1	2	3	4	5
8.	Overall, how satisfied are you with your job?	1	2	3	4	5
9.	To what extent is your supervisor willing to listen to your problems?	1	2	3	4	5
10.	To what extent does your supervisor encourage persons in your workgroup to work as a team?	1	2	3	4	5
11.	To what extent does your supervisor encourage people to exchange opinions and ideas?	1	2	3	4	5
12.	How much does your supervisor encourage people to give their best effort?	1	2	3	4	5

Sample 16, continued

13. To what extent does your supervisor maintain high levels of performance in the group? 1 2 3 4 5

14. To what extent does your supervisor provide help, training, and guidance so that you can improve your performance? 1 2 3 4 5

15. To what extent does your supervisor ask for opinions and ideas from members of your workgroup? 1 2 3 4 5

16. To what extent does your supervisor have skills for getting along with others? 1 2 3 4 5

17. To what extent does your supervisor have information about how workgroup members see and feel about things? 1 2 3 4 5

18. To what extent does your supervisor have an interest in and concern for workgroup members? 1 2 3 4 5

19. To what extent does your supervisor have confidence and trust in you? 1 2 3 4 5

20. To what extent do you have confidence and trust in your supervisor? 1 2 3 4 5

21. To what extent does your workgroup produce the amount of work expected of it? 1 2 3 4 5

22. To what extent is your workgroup efficient in doing the work that is expected of it? 1 2 3 4 5

23. To what extent is your workgroup's work high in quality? 1 2 3 4 5

24. How much do persons in your workgroup encourage each other to work together as a team? 1 2 3 4 5

25. How much do persons in your workgroup emphasize a team goal? 1 2 3 4 5

26. How much do persons in your workgroup exchange ideas and opinions? 1 2 3 4 5

27. To what extent do persons in your workgroup encourage each other to give their best effort? 1 2 3 4 5

28. To what extent do persons in your workgroup maintain high standards of performance? 1 2 3 4 5

29. To what extent do persons in your workgroup help you find ways to do a better job? 1 2 3 4 5

30. To what extent do persons in your workgroup offer each other new ideas for solving job-related problems? 1 2 3 4 5

31. To what extent does your workgroup plan together and coordinate its efforts? 1 2 3 4 5

Sample 16, continued

32. To what extent does your workgroup feel responsible for meeting its objectives successfully?   1   2   3   4   5

33. To what extent do you have confidence and trust in the persons in your workgroup?   1   2   3   4   5

34. When conflicts arise between workgroup members, to what extent are mutually acceptable solutions sought?   1   2   3   4   5

35. When solutions are reached, to what extent do the opposing group members accept and implement them?   1   2   3   4   5

36. To what extent do you enjoy performing the actual day-to-day activities of your job?   1   2   3   4   5

37. To what extent does doing your job give you a sense of personal satisfaction?   1   2   3   4   5

38. To what extent does your job let you do a number of different things?   1   2   3   4   5

39. To what extent does your job use your skills and abilities —let you do the things you do best?   1   2   3   4   5

40. To what extent does doing your job well lead to things like pay increases and bonuses?   1   2   3   4   5

41. To what extent does doing your job well lead to things like recognition and respect from those you work with?   1   2   3   4   5

42. To what extent does your job provide good chances for getting ahead?   1   2   3   4   5

43. To what extent are you clear about what people expect you to do on the job?   1   2   3   4   5

44. To what extent do people expect too much from you on your job?   1   2   3   4   5

45. To what extent are there times when one person wants you to do one thing and someone else wants you to do something else?   1   2   3   4   5

46. To what extent do you go through a lot of red tape to get things done?   1   2   3   4   5

47. To what extent do you get hemmed in by long-standing rules and regulations that no one seems to be able to explain?   1   2   3   4   5

48. To what extent do different work units plan together and coordinate their efforts?   1   2   3   4   5

49. To what extent does your work unit receive cooperation and assistance from other units?   1   2   3   4   5

Sample 16, continued

50. To what extent do you produce the amount of work that is expected of you?   1   2   3   4   5

51. To what extent are you efficient in doing the work that is expected of you?   1   2   3   4   5

52. To what extent do you produce work that is high in quality?   1   2   3   4   5

53. To what extent is this organization effective in getting you to meet its needs and contribute to its effectiveness?   1   2   3   4   5

54. To what extent does this organization do a good job of meeting your needs as an individual?   1   2   3   4   5

55. Overall, how satisfied are you with this organization?   1   2   3   4   5

Sample 17

Internal Customer Survey
Human Resources Department

The Human Resources Department wants to know how well we are serving our internal customers. We would very much appreciate it if you would take the time to fill out this survey.

Please feel free to suggest improvements in any area.

Some notes about the survey:

- Because we have a variety of internal customers, not all items may apply to all customers. Respond to those that affect you; select "N/A" for those that do not apply to you.

- On items with a rating scale, a 1 would indicate "poor," 3 would indicate "satisfactory," and 5 would indicate "excellent."

- While a signature is not mandatory, knowing your name or department will help us analyze the results and target areas for improvement.

I. GENERAL ITEMS

We in the Human Resources Department . . .

A. ACCESS AND AVAILABILITY	N/A	Poor				Excellent
1. Are available to meet personally with you. Comments or suggestions for improvement:	N/A	1	2	3	4	5
2. Are available to speak by phone with you. Comments or suggestions for improvement:	N/A	1	2	3	4	5
3. Are available on the days and hours you need. Comments or suggestions for improvement:	N/A	1	2	3	4	5
4. Are available at a location convenient to you. Comments or suggestions for improvement:	N/A	1	2	3	4	5
5. Respond to your questions in a timely manner. Comments or suggestions for improvement:	N/A	1	2	3	4	5

B. RELIABILITY						
1. Exhibit solid understanding of HR issues. Comments or suggestions for improvement:	N/A	1	2	3	4	5
2. Provide accurate, helpful information. Comments or suggestions for improvement:	N/A	1	2	3	4	5

C. CUSTOMER RELATIONS						
1. Treat you with courtesy and respect. Comments or suggestions for improvement:	N/A	1	2	3	4	5
2. Honor requests of confidentiality. Comments or suggestions for improvement:	N/A	1	2	3	4	5

Sample 17, continued

D. COMMUNICATION OF INFORMATION	N/A	Poor			Excellent	
1. Adequately communicate changes in benefits, company policies. Comments or suggestions for improvement:	N/A	1	2	3	4	5
2. Provide information when you need it. Comments or suggestions for improvement:	N/A	1	2	3	4	5
3. Provide information that is accurate and requires no rework. Comments or suggestions for improvement:	N/A	1	2	3	4	5

II. PROGRAMS AND SERVICES

This section deals with a variety of programs and services offered through the Human Resources Department. Please rate your satisfaction level with the way they are handled. Use a scale of 1 to 5, with 1 being "not satisfactory," 3 being "fairly satisfied," and 5 being "extremely satisfied." Use the lines beneath each item to indicate how these programs or services could be improved.

	N/A	Poor			Excellent	
a. Job applicant screening. Comments or suggestions for improvement:	N/A	1	2	3	4	5
b. Job-posting process. Comments or suggestions for improvement:	N/A	1	2	3	4	5
c. Preemployment drug screening. Comments or suggestions for improvement:	N/A	1	2	3	4	5
d. New employee orientation. Comments or suggestions for improvement:	N/A	1	2	3	4	5
e. OPTIONS open enrollment. Comments or suggestions for improvement:	N/A	1	2	3	4	5
f. OPTIONS open enrollment form. Comments or suggestions for improvement:	N/A	1	2	3	4	5
g. Service award luncheon. Comments or suggestions for improvement:	N/A	1	2	3	4	5
h. 25th Edition recognition dinner. Comments or suggestions for improvement:	N/A	1	2	3	4	5
i. Workers' compensation claims. Comments or suggestions for improvement:	N/A	1	2	3	4	5
j. Help Hotline seminars. Comments or suggestions for improvement:	N/A	1	2	3	4	5
k. Savings Plus programs. Comments or suggestions for improvement:	N/A	1	2	3	4	5

Sample 17, continued

		N/A	Poor				Excellent
l.	Annual benefits statement.	N/A	1	2	3	4	5
	Comments or suggestions for improvement:						
m.	Annual mammography screening.	N/A	1	2	3	4	5
	Comments or suggestions for improvement:						
n.	Child Care Referral Line.	N/A	1	2	3	4	5
	Comments or suggestions for improvement:						
o.	VP/LS handbook.	N/A	1	2	3	4	5
	Comments or suggestions for improvement:						
p.	Human Resources lending library.	N/A	1	2	3	4	5
	Comments or suggestions for improvement:						
q.	Retirement planning information.	N/A	1	2	3	4	5
	Comments or suggestions for improvement:						
r.	Benefits information in Home Edition.	N/A	1	2	3	4	5
	Comments or suggestions for improvement:						
s.	Advice on personnel situations.	N/A	1	2	3	4	5
	Comments or suggestions for improvement:						
t.	Manager and supervisory training.	N/A	1	2	3	4	5
	Comments or suggestions for improvement:						

III. GENERAL SUGGESTIONS

Use this space to indicate any suggestions for improved productivity or customer service.

(Optional)
Your Name:

Your Department:

THANK YOU!

Lessons from the Trenches

Making Your Mark

"Start-ups are murder," says John Lewis, SPHR. "They'll take you through the wringer mentally and physically." Lewis was the Human Resource Manager of Wurzburg Inc. in Memphis, Tennessee, from 1988 to 2008.

What you do in those important early stages is critical, Lewis says. "You can shoot yourself in the foot, and it can take you years to recover if you start off on the wrong track."

His advice? "Lay low" until you have a firm understanding of the company's culture and mission. If you come in trying to make too many changes too quickly, he cautions, "you're going to set up barriers of resistance. You have to kind of soft-pedal your way in."

While each HR practitioner's experience will be different, depending on the company, he offers a number of tips from his experience.

- Understand the culture. "A new person setting up an HR department has to get a finger on the corporate culture. Who does what? Who has the title and who has the actual power?" At Wurzburg, Lewis says, he learned that the mission was to "take care of the family." Everything else came second.
- Look for areas where you can make your mark. If the company has operated without an HR department in the past, you have to give management some reasons why they need you. "One of the really good places that you can make a major impact and get the attention of top management is in the area of benefits. Any time you save a small company money, you get management's attention very quickly."
- Avoid stepping on toes. Chances are that other people in the company handled HR activities before you came on board. Somebody took applications. Somebody conducted interviews. Somebody took care of benefits. "You're going to have to be careful," Lewis says. "Power is going to come into play if other people have been doing these jobs. Even though they may be overloaded, they're probably going to be somewhat reluctant to surrender these tasks. You're going to have to win their confidence that you're there to be a help — not to be a hindrance." The key to easing this transition, he says, is winning the confidence of these employees and assuring them that you are not there to strip them of power.

- Rank and prioritize. You cannot do everything at once, so you need to determine where you can have the most impact quickly. "You're going to have to lay out a battle plan about how you're going to organize and what your objectives are," Lewis says. "A written plan can be a great asset."
- Find a way to satisfy management. Start by finding out who all the players are and what the management that hired you wants you to do. You are going to have to get them on your side. "Enlist their support and help them so they can see where you're headed. If they haven't had a formalized program, they don't know what to expect, and if you don't have a plan, they're going to be throwing stuff at you all the time."
- Communicate and educate. "Your job is not only to organize but also to teach upper-level management what HR is," Lewis says. "More than likely, they don't have the slightest idea."

Outsourcing and Consultants

If you operate in a small HR department, or if you are the sole HR practitioner in your organization, the sheer volume of activities that fall under the purview of HR can be overwhelming. How can you possibly get everything accomplished?

Fortunately, there are a number of options available to you, from the outsourcing of various HR functions, to contracting with private consultants, to various online resources and other opportunities to augment and extend the services provided by your HR department.

This chapter discusses outsourcing and working with consultants.

Outsourcing and Working with Consultants

Even if it were possible to have, on staff, people with the experience and expertise you need to handle every facet of HR management, it would not be practical. Fortunately, HR professionals can choose from a virtually endless supply of resources that allow them to outsource many of the functions they do not have the time or the in-house staff resources to handle. Whether you want to develop a training program on sexual harassment, revamp your benefits program, update your employee handbook, or automate your payroll processes, there are firms and consultants ready to lend a hand.

It is easy to see the value that outsourcing can have, especially for small or solo HR departments. If you are thinking of contracting with external resources to help meet your HR challenges, the following information can help you make an informed choice.

Where Do You Begin?

Whether working with an outside organization, an independent consultant, or a freelancer, the first step is determining specifically what it is you need to have done. Sit down with the appropriate people internally, making sure to involve all stakeholders, to explore what you need and the deliverables you are looking for. This is valuable information that you can use as a guideline when selecting an external vendor as well as when evaluating the final product or outcomes.

Involving the right people in the selection process is critical. Identify a project leader and team members, as appropriate, to help manage and facilitate the process. This input and involvement will be critical to the success of the project.

The many companies, individuals, and options available to meet your needs can be overwhelming. Doing a thorough needs assessment and clearly outlining the results you are looking for will help you make an informed and cost-effective choice.

Ultimately, you want to select a company or resource that is going to stand the test of time. You want to know that this vendor is going to be around for a while and that you will be able to get the support you need. How do you determine this? Look for a company that already has an established history. Check out the company's web site. Talk to colleagues at other companies. Ask questions like these:

- How long has your company been in business?
- How many employees do you have?
- What is your annual sales volume?
- How many other customers do you have? (The answer can help you gauge the level of support and attention you will receive.)
- Who are your clients? (Ask for — and follow up with — references.)

What Do Consultants Do?

A consultant offers advice and service in a professional or technical skill area *at some fixed fee or on a contractual basis.* Consultants give advice or complete a specific project for an agreed-upon fee. By understanding what consultants can and cannot do, human resources can most successfully take advantage of the services they provide.

One of the great values consultants provide is their ability to look objectively at a company and its issues and to recommend solutions or direction based on this analysis. Consultants can and will do exactly what you ask them to do — but do not overlook the potential for gaining valuable insights by involving consultants strategically in your efforts.

Deciding Whether Outside Help Is Needed

Most HR practitioners have good experiences working with external resources, but some have had serious problems. When the client is responsible for the failure, it is usually a result of not doing the proper planning, not understanding the outsourcing process, or not communicating clearly with the consultant.

Before you search for a consultant, you need to ask yourself what your needs and expectations are. Unless you know specifically what results you are looking for, it can be a waste of time and resources to contract with a consultant. In addition, without a clear idea of your goals, you won't be able to determine the type of outside service most appropriate for your needs.

Be realistic and accept the fact that you simply cannot do it all yourself. Turning to a consultant or other outside source of service is not a sign of failure. It is a positive step that can help you maximize the contribution of HR to the company. Remember that you are responsible for seeing that the critical human relations issues in your organization are managed effectively. That does not mean that you, personally, need to take a hands-on approach to every issue. Learning to manage outside resources effectively can greatly enhance your value to the organization.

Figure 10.1 lists some arguments for and against using a consultant.

Once a company decides to start an HR function and hires someone (you!) to lead the charge, management can be anxious to see results. Sometimes management can be too anxious, given the limited resources the lone HR practitioner often has at his or her disposal — primarily time. While you may have all the necessary technical skills, implementation of the many programs, processes, and services needed for a fully functional HR department can be time-consuming and difficult. Consultants and other outside resources can be extremely helpful in getting the process off to the right start quickly. Outsourcing can be an effective technique for controlling staffing needs.

FIGURE 10.1. Arguments For and Against Hiring a Consultant

For
- Skills not available in-house.
- Don't have the time in-house.
- Need outside perspective.
- Don't know what needs to be done.
- Need a second opinion.
- Consultant may be more efficient.
- It's a short-term project.

Against
- Company may not be receptive.
- Not ready to hear bad news.
- Support resources not available in-house.
- Not the right time.

Before you select an external vendor or consultant, you should consider some possible problems. Some potential problems — and solutions — are outlined in Figure 10.2.

FIGURE 10.2. Problems and Solutions When Using Outside Resources

Problem	Solution
Manager dominates the relationship and insists on doing things the same way.	Hire a firm or consultant with the courage and skills to challenge the status quo.
General reluctance to use external resources.	Prepare a cost-benefit analysis. Start with pilot projects to test fit and build trust. Get references from other clients.
Loss of employee commitment.	Involve employees from the start and communicate with them.
Selecting the wrong firm or hiring the wrong consultant.	Look for an external resource that offers a good blend of general knowledge and practical experience. Get references.
Bailing out too quickly when problems arise.	Ensure frequent progress meetings and ongoing communication. Give early feedback.
Lack of financial resources.	Negotiate the project fee as a percentage of savings, if possible. Stage the project over time.

The Outsourcing Process

Once the decision has been made to turn to external resources for help on a project, a number of steps must be taken.

- Compile a list of potential resources. There are literally thousands of firms and consultants available to choose from. Your initial task is to clearly identify the results you want and then select the appropriate individual or organization to help you obtain those results. The process is similar to that involved in hiring an employee; you are matching specific job-related criteria or performance objectives to the qualifications of individuals available to assist you. Talk to your business colleagues and other contacts who may have recommendations for you, or do research through organizations such as SHRM.
- Hold on-site interviews. Once you have compiled a list of potential resources that may be appropriate for your needs, start making contacts. Invite three or four firms or consultants to come to your company for on-site interviews. Ask, specifically, to meet with the individual or individuals you will be working with directly. Before the meeting, prepare a detailed list of questions designed to help you learn how the firm will approach the project, what steps it will take to meet your goals, what format the firm's report or recommendations will take, and how certain the company or consultant is that it can address your needs. Do not overlook the importance of fit. Working effectively with external resources requires a positive relationship.

- Check references. Ask for names of other HR departments that have used the services of the firm or consultant. Do some detective work on your own as well — online forums can be a great way to get information about the experiences of other HR professionals. Talk to at least three references, preferably those that have used the consultant on similar projects.

- Pin down the financial terms of the arrangement. Be specific about your requirements, and expect the firm or consultant to be specific about costs as well. Get these expectations in writing. Do not sign any agreement until you have examined it thoroughly to determine that it accurately and adequately reflects your understanding of the services you will receive and the results you can expect. Look for such things as additional expenses you may not have anticipated (travel, copying, long-distance phone charges, etc.). Consider having your legal counsel review the contract before you sign it.

- Communicate. Your role in this business relationship is to communicate your expectations adequately and to cooperate with the firm or individual you hire along the way. Allow the consultant ready access to the data and individuals that he or she will need to do the job effectively. Inform the consultant immediately of any business changes or issues that might affect the project. Foremost, be up front in your communications. If you feel the project is floundering, or if you have questions about any aspect of the relationship, speak up!

- Evaluate results. Once the project is done and the bills are paid, you will want to evaluate the results of the project. Were your expectations met? If not, why? If they were, to what degree? The information you gain from this debriefing will help you in your next outsourcing relationship.

- Do not be reluctant to terminate the relationship if it's not working. Include language in the consulting agreement about the circumstances under which either party can terminate the agreement, the notice required (generally 30 days), and how the project fee would be prorated.

Most HR professionals, even experienced generalists, will need outside assistance at times. HR professionals, especially in large companies, often have a staff or a network of peers who regularly discuss common problems. For the newly appointed HR professional, getting advice and assistance has clear advantages, whether it is through other experienced HR professionals or by tapping into the advice and assistance of competent external resources.

Online Resources

In the old days, if you wanted news, you looked in the newspaper. If you wanted information on a specific product, you called a vendor. To find the vendor, you might ask friends or colleagues for recommendations or note advertisements in trade and professional journals. If you wanted to network with colleagues, you attended seminars and conferences. If you wanted to hire an employee, you put an ad in the local newspaper. The old days are gone. Today, you can do all of these things, and more, from the comfort of your office. The Internet has changed the way we work as dramatically as the advent of the personal computer.

There is no doubt that the Internet has a lot to offer. There are new resources to discover virtually every day that can help you be more efficient and effective in your job.

Networking

Not that long ago, networking meant belonging to local business organizations, participating in business and professional groups, and maintaining a Rolodex or Microsoft Outlook contacts list. Today, networking means much, much more. The Internet has expanded the personal network of HR professionals to include not just the practitioner down the street but also people — literally — from around the globe.

Social media tools and online forums are widely available, offering, for example, the opportunity to network with colleagues and participate in active and lively discussions about every conceivable management and HR-related issue.

Forums allow HR professionals with similar interests to post messages, share information, ask questions, and discuss issues online. There are literally hundreds of forums on the Internet. The SHRM web site (www.shrm.org) offers numerous forums for questions and discussion.

Online Articles and Research

While much of the information on the Internet is commercial, if you know where to look you can also find valuable news, information, and resources — the same resources that used to require a trip to the library. For HR practitioners, the resources are many; fortunately, a few stand-out sites provide access to the vast majority of useful and reliable information.

About.com. About.com (www.about.com) GuideSites provide useful online resources by various categories — including HR. At http://humanresources.about. com, you will find news and links to information on benefits, compensation, consultants, government, health and safety, labor relations, legal issues, screening and testing, training, and more. The guides at About.com do the work for you — scanning the Internet for useful information and compiling it into their About.com GuideSites.

Google. Google has acquired the text of the HR discussion group that was at Deja. com.

HR.com. HR.com (www.hr.com) is a content-rich site with information catego-rized into several communities, including compensation and benefits, HR informa-tion systems, HR management, labor relations, legal, organizational development, staffing, and training and development. The home page offers daily news and weekly columns on timely HR issues.

Safety Info.com. Safety Info.com (www.safetyinfo.com) is a subscription-based site that offers a wide variety of information on health and safety issues, includ-ing a "Weekly Safety Brief" and a "Weekly Safety Poster," extensive information on safety programs, audit guides, training outlines, Occupational Safety and Health Administration (OSHA) standards, Environmental Protection Act and Department of Transportation information, clip art and photos, and numerous articles on health and safety issues.

Society for Human Resource Management. One of the sites most frequently ref-erenced by HR practitioners is the SHRM web site at www.shrm.org. This site is the premier HR resource. While portions of the site are viewable only by members, there is plenty of information for nonmembers. Of particular interest is the extensive and useful list of links to other HR references, broken down by topic area.

For members, the site offers the Commerce Clearing House Monthly Summary of State Law Changes; a Consultants Referral Directory; HR Disciplines for questions and discussion; and the SHRM HR Knowledge Center, an online resource offering a variety of databases with answers to HR questions, news articles, links and short research articles.

SHRM also offers a variety of publications and sponsors conferences and seminars in most major cities across the United States.

Access to Current Government and Legal Information

The federal government offers a wide range of information on the Internet, in-cluding forms available for downloading and updates on laws and regulations.

At the IRS site (www.irs.gov), you can download forms and find answers to questions. "The Digital Daily," the IRS's online e-publication, provides daily news updates. At the Social Security Administration's site (www.ssa.gov), you will find information on employment support for people with disabilities, Medicare informa-tion, current rules and regulations, and laws and legislation. The Bureau of Labor Statistics (BLS) web site (www.bls.gov) offers surveys and reports on employment, compensation and working conditions, productivity and technology, and employ-ment projections. You will also find publications like the *Monthly Labor Review* and *Occupational Outlook Handbook*, as well as research papers on a variety of topics relevant to HR professionals.

The Department of Labor (DOL) web site (www.dol.gov) is a comprehensive source of information including laws and regulations, statistics and data, and useful news items about current issues that affect employers and employees. Press releases are also archived, providing a quick source of information on DOL announcements and activities. The library link includes congressional testimony, speeches, publications, and online access to workplace posters. Quick links take you to related DOL agencies like the BLS and OSHA (with data on occupational injury and illness incidence rates).

If you operate in multiple states, you may find the Commerce Clearing House web site (www.cch.com) useful — it provides easy access to state regulations and laws.

Other Resources

A wide variety of resources are available to help HR practitioners bolster their productivity, find support, or reaffirm what they already know. Here are a variety of creative options from HR practitioners in the trenches:

- Build a network of colleagues from other organizations whom you can turn to for advice and counsel. Just getting together on occasion for lunch, or another social event, can provide you with information or a shoulder to lean on.
- Find out about the availability of local HR organizations, employer groups, or Chamber of Commerce support.
- Organizations like the Bureau of National Affairs (www.bna.com) and Commerce Clearing House (www.cch.com) provide comprehensive legal information on CD-ROM that can be used to develop manuals and policies or to research state codes.
- Look for local resources. Some states have independent agencies that offer support in a variety of areas, including legal services.
- The Economic Research Institute (www.erieri.com) provides salary survey and other information on CD-ROM that is updated quarterly.
- Network, network, network. Join SHRM, Professionals In Human Resources Association, National Human Resources Association, or any of your local HR organizations. These people and relationships are invaluable when you need advice or referrals.
- Use the Internet.
- Have a good law firm on retainer that specializes in labor relations.
- Visit other companies and glean wisdom from their HR practices.
- Read extensively.

FAQs

What is a PEO?

Debra Squyres, SPHR:

PEO stands for professional employer organization. PEOs provide small and medium-size companies with outsourced HR services, specifically employment and HR management services. PEOs are not staffing companies. Traditionally, PEOs manage functions such as payroll, employer tax compliance, employee benefits, workers' compensation, and government compliance, but those services have steadily expanded to include optional services such as talent acquisition, employee training, and performance management.

The web site of the National Association of Professional Employer Organizations (www.napeo.org), explains that PEOs bring value via:

- Relief from the burden of employment administration.
- A wide range of human capital strategy and guidance services offered by a team of experienced professionals.
- Improved employment practices, compliance, and risk management to reduce employer-related liability.
- Access to a comprehensive employee benefits package, allowing smaller companies to be competitive in a tight labor market.
- Assistance in improving productivity and profitability.

Are PEOs becoming more or less popular because of the economy?

Debra Squyres, SPHR:

Historically, PEOs have experienced about the same amount of growth in down periods as they did during flat or slow growth periods. Over the last five years, the industry has seen double-digit increases year over year despite the recent economic framework. During a downturn, clients turn to PEOs to improve efficiencies; during an upswing in the economy, clients are attracted to PEOs as a scalable solution to meet their rapid growth needs.

What are the key considerations in selecting a PEO?

Debra Squyres, SPHR:

- Find a legitimate and stable PEO. Select a PEO partner that has been around for some time and that looks stable in its financials as well as in its systems. Look at its history and its credentials. The best PEOs generally have accreditation from the industry's "watchdog" organization, the Employer Services Assurance Corporation. Another good resource for information on quality providers is the National Association of Professional Employer Organizations web site (www. napeo.org).

- Find a PEO that solves issues quickly and effectively. The PEO you choose should have systems in place that result in good service. By service, I mean two things: direct access to someone who can answer your employees' questions, no matter how trivial those questions may seem, and the option of self-service HR tasks via an online platform.

- Understand how you are being charged. There are two basic ways PEOs charge their customers. There is the break-out model, where you are shown what each category costs — workers' compensation insurance, benefits, service fees, etc. And then there is the bundled model, where payments are grouped together in various ways. A transparent set of fees will be easier to understand than a percentage of payroll fee — and the latter can be tremendously expensive if your organization employs highly compensated people that routinely accrue bonuses and salary increases.

- Look for better benefits. Benefits are key to attracting and retaining the talent you need to remain competitive. You simply cannot skimp on them. To make the cut, HR outsourcing candidates should offer a package that provides all the benefits that large companies offer their employees.

- Verify that the employee risk pool matches your company's profile. An HR provider that mixes your relatively low-risk staff with other employers' higher-risk groups of employees almost ensures that your health insurance and workers' compensation rates will rise faster than market rates.

- Ensure that the service provider meets all state regulatory requirements. Regulations vary from state to state, so ensure that the PEO you pick complies with the laws in your area. If you have employees in multiple states, make sure your PEO can easily handle HR for those states.

- Find out how long it takes to transition. Ask about the set-up process. How many days will it take? How much paperwork will it entail? Or is the process mostly online? How much hassle will you have to go through in the transition process?

What are the drawbacks of using a PEO?

Mary Glaeser:

Two drawbacks that can be overlooked are the conflict of interest for a PEO, which can lead to poor service/representation, and the cost of decoupling with the PEO if you sever the relationship.

Realize that the PEO is a business unto itself, with its own goals and a need to protect itself and stay in business. If you are hit with an employment-related claim, the PEO may or may not help you with the claim. I have seen PEOs blame the client and not become involved, which led to months and months of distraction for the client. Additionally, if the PEO is having financial difficulties, service may suffer. It may want to keep you as a client, but it simply may not be providing the kind of service you want.

If you decide to end the relationship with the PEO, the hassles are tremendous. One of the hidden costs relates to the benefits. As part of a group of employees, your company will have no track record for workers' compensation and employee benefits, so it is likely your rates will be higher. If you are larger than when you first signed on with the PEO, this gets expensive fast, whereas if you had the higher rates when your headcount/payroll was smaller, it would not hurt quite as much.

Lastly, I am not sure what it says to employees when you outsource HR. Does it tell them that they are an important part of your organization and you want to invest in them? Or does it tell employees that they are an administrative hassle that you want to get rid of? I am sure that some of the perception is in the message delivered, but it is something to consider.

What key points should I be sure to include in an outsourcing contract?

William G. Bliss:
- Define the specific scope of the agreement. Is the project to discover, assess, investigate, recommend solutions, implement, or provide advice?
- Define the expected duration of the project.
- Define the expected outcomes or deliverables and how — and when — those outcomes will be delivered.
- Define the costs associated with the project and how they will be incurred. Will you pay a project fee or will the fee be based on time and materials? What about travel, report preparation, or miscellaneous costs? What are the payment terms? Is any money required up front?

- Especially if there is a formal contract, be sure to have your legal counsel review it for liability, hold harmless, and remedy clauses.
- Define the expectations for the handling of confidential or proprietary information.
- Define who owns the product of the project. For example, if outsourcing a training program, who will own the content?

As a consultant, what do you look for from your clients?

William G. Bliss:

I look for someone who:

- Has a general appreciation of what I can and cannot do.
- Is open to a variety of alternatives to address a given issue.
- Understands the real situation in the organization and the real needs of the line departments.
- Can make decisions needed to move the project along.
- Is connected with the businesspeople, including the CEO.
- Is comfortable in facilitating access to the client group and attendance at key company meetings.
- Is open to hearing information that he or she may not want to hear.
- Has realistic expectations.
- Wants to uncover and address the *real* issues, not just the surface ones. If the client does not want to address the underlying or root causes, it is a waste of resources to bring in a consultant.

Appendix A

Federal Requirements Affecting Human Resources

Below are summaries of major federal laws, executive orders, and guidelines that affect human resources, presented in alphabetical order. This is not a comprehensive discussion. There are many other federal requirements that may affect certain industries or that relate only to certain components of HR, and federal contractors are covered by more requirements than are described here.

A number of these requirements apply only to companies that hold federal contracts or that have a minimum number of employees. Appendix B shows the number of employees necessary for an organization to be covered by specific laws.

The purpose of this appendix is to give you a starting point for determining compliance with the law for your company. But you will need detailed information for each law to ensure full compliance.

The date after each entry is the date that it originally was enacted or promulgated. Some laws have been amended, and others are linked to cases that affect how they are interpreted. The text describes the requirements as they currently exist, including all amendments.

Age Discrimination in Employment Act (ADEA) (1967); Older Workers Benefit Protection Act (1990)

The ADEA prohibits discrimination against workers ages 40 and older in any employment or employment-related decision. The Act applies to most employers with 20 or more employees. With few exceptions, employers cannot force an employee to retire. Incentives for early voluntary retirements are allowed, but specific conditions must be met to avoid violation of the Act.

In the event of a violation, employees may be awarded back pay, reinstatement, retroactive seniority, and attorneys' fees. Liquidated damages equal to the amount of pecuniary losses suffered may be awarded if the violation is willful.

The Older Workers Benefit Protection Act (OWBPA) is an amendment to the ADEA. This amendment is designed to ensure equality of treatment between older and younger workers under employee benefits plans. The OWBPA amendment allows voluntary incentive programs for early retirement, but those programs must be nondiscriminatory. It also provides that an employee who waives age discrimination or ADEA claims or rights must do so knowingly and voluntarily — and that the waiver must be consistent with specific guidelines.

- See www.eeoc.gov/laws/types/age.cfm for more information.

Americans with Disabilities Act, Title I (ADA) (1990), as amended by the ADAAA (2008)

Title I of the ADA prohibits private employers with 15 or more employees, state and local governments, employment agencies, and labor unions from discriminating against qualified individuals with disabilities in job application procedures; hiring; firing; advancement; compensation; job training; and other terms, conditions, and privileges of employment.

When an individual's disability creates a barrier to employment opportunities, the ADA requires the employer to consider whether a reasonable accommodation could remove the barrier.

The ADA is enforced by the Equal Employment Opportunity Commission, and the penalties are the same as for violations of Title VII of the Civil Rights Act, with maximum amounts for intentional discrimination mandated by the Civil Rights Act of 1991.

The ADAAA expanded the definition of the term "disability" to include more individuals with less-severe disabilities. The ADAAA also makes it more likely that employees will qualify for reasonable accommodations than was the case under the original ADA.

- See www.ada.gov/pubs/adastatute08mark.htm for more information.

Civil Rights Act, Title VII (1964); Civil Rights Act (1991)

In virtually every employment circumstance, Title VII prohibits discrimination and harassment on the basis of race, color, religion, sex, or national origin. Title VII must be considered when reviewing applications or resumes; interviewing candidates; testing job applicants; and considering employees for promotions, transfers, or any other employment-related benefit or condition. The Pregnancy Discrimination Act of 1978 amended Title VII to provide that pregnant women must be treated the same as other nonpregnant, similarly situated employees. Thus, the Act requires that an employer's policies for taking leave, health benefits during leave, and reinstatement after leave apply equally to pregnant women and other employees.

Remedies of back pay, reinstatement, and retroactive seniority may be required of any employer for all types of discrimination, whether intentional or unintentional.

In cases involving intentional discrimination, employees may seek a jury trial, with compensatory and punitive damages up to the maximum limitations established by the Civil Rights Act of 1991. According to the number of employees, these maximums are 100 or fewer employees, $50,000; 101–200 employees, $100,000; 201–500 employees, $200,000; and more than 500 employees, $300,000.

- See www.elinfonet.com/titleVIIsum.php for more information.

Consolidated Omnibus Budget Reconciliation Act (COBRA) (1985)

COBRA mandates that employers continue health care coverage for employees enrolled in the company's benefits plan for a certain number of months (usually 18) after the employees would otherwise lose those benefits. The usual reasons for loss of benefits are termination of employment or a reduction in hours that makes employees ineligible for the benefits plan. All persons covered by a plan, including spouses and children, are eligible for COBRA. The employee must pay the premiums, and the employer may charge the employee 2 percent of the premium for administrative costs. The Act mandates how long employees have to elect to participate under COBRA, when employers must respond to requests for COBRA coverage, and what notices employers must provide.

Under the Employee Retirement Income Security Act (see below), employers may be fined for failure to provide notice to employees or beneficiaries. The fine is $100 per day per violation until notice is provided. Under the Internal Revenue Code, an excise tax of $100 per day per violation may be applied for each qualified beneficiary during the noncompliance period. A qualified beneficiary who did not receive coverage can bring a lawsuit against the employer.

Note: While the **American Recovery and Reinvestment Act (ARRA) (2009)** provides for premium reductions for health benefits under COBRA, this change primarily impacts employees rather than employers.

- See www.dol.gov/ebsa/compliance_assistance.html for more information.

COBRA Extension

The U.S. Senate passed the Fiscal Year 2010 Department of Defense Appropriations Act in December 2009. The federal spending bill included provisions to extend and expand the COBRA subsidy program. The bill expanded the COBRA premium subsidy period from nine to 15 months. It also changed the end date for eligibility for the subsidy from December 31, 2009, to February 28, 2010.

- See www.dol.gov/ebsa/newsroom/2009/ebsa122109.html for more information.

Consumer Credit Protection Act (1968)

This Act establishes limits on how much of an employee's income can be subject to garnishment and establishes standards for state garnishment laws. It also prohibits employers from firing employees because of garnishment of wages for any one indebtedness, although employers may dismiss employees for garnishments for two or more separate debts where there is a consistently applied policy or practice of doing so. However, if those being dismissed are mostly women or minorities, employers should take care to prevent a disparate impact on those groups. Penalties for noncompliance are a fine of up to $1,000, one year of imprisonment, or both.

- See www.dol.gov/compliance/laws/comp-ccpa.htm for more information.

Drug-Free Workplace Act (1988)
(Federal Contractors Only)

Under this Act, all firms that do business with the federal government must have written drug-use policies.

Federal contractors with contracts of $100,000 or more must follow certain requirements to certify that they maintain a drug-free workplace. Contractors are required to issue a statement prohibiting the illegal manufacture, distribution, dispensation, possession, or use of any controlled substances in the workplace and specifying the consequences for violating the policy. They must establish a drug-abuse awareness process that informs employees about the dangers of drug abuse, explains the employer's policy and the availability of employee assistance programs, and specifies the action that will be taken if an employee is convicted of a drug violation that occurred in the workplace.

Note: The **Federal Acquisition Streamlining Act (1994)** amended the Drug-Free Workplace Act by raising the threshold for covered contracts from $25,000 to $100,000.

- See www.dol.gov/elaws/asp/drugfree/screen4.htm for more information.

Employee Polygraph Protection Act (1988)

The Employee Polygraph Protection Act prohibits most private employers from requiring employees or candidates for employment to submit to a lie detector test. The only times an employer may ask (but not require) an employee to take a polygraph test are in the conduct of an ongoing investigation into theft, embezzlement, or similar economic loss, or if the employee had access to property that was lost and the employer has a reasonable suspicion that the employee was involved. Employees who take a polygraph test may not be discharged or suffer any other negative consequences solely on the basis of the test without other supporting evidence. The Act strictly mandates how polygraph tests may be administered and how the results may be used. Additionally, employers are required to post notices summarizing the protections of the Act in their places of work.

The Act provides for up to $10,000 in civil penalties. Aggrieved candidates for employment may obtain employment; aggrieved employees may be awarded reinstatement, back pay, and benefits.

- See www.dol.gov/compliance/laws/comp-eppa.htm for more information.

Employee Retirement Income Security Act (ERISA) (1974)

ERISA applies to companies that offer benefits and sets requirements for the provision and administration of employee benefits plans, such as health care benefits, profit-sharing, and pension plans. ERISA requires companies to file a form (Form 5500) annually with the Internal Revenue Service (IRS) that discloses basic information about each benefit plan, such as plan expenses, income, assets, and liabilities. ERISA also requires employers to submit a Summary Annual Report to plan participants and beneficiaries. The IRS and the Department of Labor jointly enforce ERISA requirements. Willful violations result in criminal and civil penalties.

- See www.dol.gov/ebsa/compliance_assistance.html for more information.

Equal Pay Act (1963)

This Act is an amendment to the Fair Labor Standards Act. The Equal Pay Act prohibits employers from discriminating between men and women by paying one more than the other "for equal work on jobs the performance of which requires equal skill, effort, and responsibility, and which are performed under similar working conditions."

Penalties for noncompliance include back pay for up to two years, or three years if the violation was willful, and liquidated damages in an amount equal to back pay. Fines of up to $10,000 or imprisonment for up to six months are also possible for willful violations.

- See www.dol.gov/oasam/regs/statutes/equal_pay_act.htm for more information.

Executive Orders 11246 (1965), 11375 (1967), 11478 (1969) (Federal Contractors Only)

These orders apply to all companies that hold federal contracts exceeding $50,000 and that have a workforce of more than 50 employees. These employers are required to prepare an Affirmative Action Plan covering recruitment of minorities and women. The plan must be prepared according to regulations issued by the Office of Federal Contractor Compliance Programs. In addition to the specific requirements of these orders, federal contractors must comply with all equal employment opportunity regulations and guidelines.

- See www.dotcr.ost.dot.gov/asp/execorders.asp for more information.

Fair Credit Reporting Act (1970)

This Act governs the use of consumer reports in all employment decisions. Under the Act, a "consumer report" refers to information collected by a consumer reporting agency that bears on an individual's creditworthiness, credit standing, credit capacity, character, general reputation, personal characteristics, or mode of living. Amendments made in 1997 substantially increased employers' administrative obligations under the Act. These amendments have been interpreted to broaden the coverage of the Act beyond traditional credit reports to include any investigation conducted by an outside professional agency, including a reference check.

- See www.yale.edu/hronline/careers/screening/documents/ FairCreditReportingAct.pdf for more information.

Fair Labor Standards Act (FLSA) (1938)

The FLSA defines the nature of the employment relationship and regulates child labor, minimum wage, overtime pay, and record-keeping requirements. It determines which employees are exempt from the Act (not covered by it) and which are non-exempt (covered by the Act). Its guidance establishes wage and time requirements when minors can work, sets the minimum wage that must be paid, defines what constitutes work time, and mandates when overtime must be paid.

The FLSA is administered by the Wage and Hour Division of the Department of Labor. Employers that violate the Act unintentionally ("nonwillfully") may be penalized up to two years' back pay to the employee. Employers that intentionally ("willfully") violate the Act may be penalized up to three years' back pay to the employee, and multiple willful violations can subject an employer to fines and imprisonment.

- See www.dol.gov/whd/flsa/index.htm for more information.

Family and Medical Leave Act (FMLA) (1993)

The FMLA allows employees who have met minimum service requirements and worksite requirements to take up to 12 weeks of unpaid leave for specified purposes. The service and work requirements are as follows: 12 months employed by the company with 1,250 hours of service in the preceding 12 months, and employment at a worksite with at least 50 employees working within a 75-mile radius.

The purposes for which FMLA leave may be taken are

1. A serious health condition,
2. Care for a family member (parent, child, or spouse) with a serious health condition,
3. The birth of a child and care for the child after birth, or
4. The acceptance of a child for adoption or foster care and the care for the child after placement.

There is no complete list of medical conditions that are considered "serious health conditions." Employers must consider the following six general criteria:

1. Hospital care,
2. Absence plus treatment,
3. Pregnancy,

4. Chronic conditions requiring treatments,
5. Permanent/long-term conditions requiring supervision, and
6. Multiple treatments (non-chronic conditions).

The FMLA requires employers to

- Allow their eligible employees who meet any of the four conditions to take up to 12 work weeks of unpaid leave in a 12-month period;
- Provide continued health benefits during leave;
- Upon return from leave, restore employees to the same positions or to equivalent positions with the same pay, benefits, and terms and conditions of employment; and
- Appropriately notify employees of their rights and responsibilities under the Act.

On January 16, 2009, revised FMLA regulations became effective. The new regulations are consistent with proposed revisions outlined in February 2008.

Congress passed the FMLA to address the issue of families struggling with competing demands of work and family. The law was signed by President Clinton on February 5, 1993. The FMLA allows employees to take unpaid leave of absence from their jobs and provides a minimum level of job security for them upon return.

With the revisions in 2009, the intent of the regulations remains the same. Changes in the new FMLA regulations primarily affect and clarify three areas: 1) the definition of serious health condition, 2) certification requirements related to serious health conditions, and 3) changes in both employer and employee notification requirements.

The new rules also provide clarification with regard to medical certification. Employers must request medical certifications within five days (formerly two days) of determining that the employee's need for leave is FMLA-related. If an employee is not responsive to the request, or if the response is incomplete or insufficient, an employer may demand that the employee cure the deficiency and may deny leave if the deficiency is not cured.

Noncompliance may entitle employees to recover back pay and benefits with interest, as well as reinstatement and/or promotion. Attorneys' fees and costs also may be awarded.

- See www.dol.gov/whd/fmla/index.htm for more information.

The U.S. Department of Labor formulated new regulations to implement the recent expansion signed in December 2009 by President Obama of the FMLA for military family caregivers, veterans, and others.

- See www.businessknowhow.com/manage/fmla_changes-2008.htm for more information.

Federal Insurance Contributions Act (FICA) (1935)

This Act establishes Social Security and Medicare taxes on employers and employees, with the intent of providing a source of retirement income. The wage base on which FICA taxes are computed is established each calendar year. The employee's portion of the tax is deducted from the paycheck and then matched by the employer's portion of the tax.

- See www.law.cornell.edu/uscode/26/usc_sup_01_26_10_C_20_21.html for more information.

Genetic Information Nondiscrimination Act (GINA) (2009)

GINA took effect November 21, 2009, and prohibits employers from discriminating against employees or applicants based on their genetic information. The Act also restricts how and when employers may acquire or disclose employee genetic information. Companies that sponsor a health and wellness program are encouraged to consult with an experienced labor and employment attorney.

- See www.eeoc.gov/eeoc/newsroom/release/11-20-09.cfm for more information.

Health Insurance Portability and Accountability Act (HIPAA) (1996)

HIPAA makes health insurance more portable from one job to another. The Act helps employees who change jobs to maintain their health care coverage without being subject to the same restrictions as someone who did not have coverage from a previous employer.

HIPAA Overview

Generally, HIPAA provides more protections for employees of small organizations. Firms with 50 or fewer employees are guaranteed access to health insurance.

For all employers, no insurer can exclude a worker or family member from employer-sponsored coverage based on that person's health status. Effective July 1, 1997, insurers are required to renew coverage to all groups, regardless of the health status of any individual member.

HIPAA's group-market rules apply to every employer-sponsored group health plan that has at least two participants who are current employees. States have the option of applying these rules to groups of only one employee. Some states have elected to do this. Among its specific protections, HIPAA

- Limits (but does not eliminate) exclusions of preexisting conditions from coverage.
- Prohibits group health plans from denying an employee coverage or charging extra for coverage based on past or present poor health of the employee or family member.

- Guarantees the right to purchase health insurance to certain small employers and certain individuals who lose job-related coverage.
- In most cases, guarantees that employers or individuals who purchase health insurance can renew the coverage regardless of any health conditions of individuals covered under the insurance policy.

HIPAA does not
- Require employers to offer or pay for health coverage for employees or family coverage for spouses and dependents.
- Guarantee health coverage for all workers.
- Control the amount an insurer may charge for coverage.
- Require group health plans to offer specific benefits.
- Permit people to keep the same health coverage when they move to a new job.
- Eliminate all exclusions of preexisting conditions.
- Replace the state as the primary regulator of health insurance.

HIPAA Privacy Rule

Virtually every employer that offers health benefits or health services to employees is affected by a privacy rule issued by the U.S. Department of Health and Human Services in April 2001, designed to protect the privacy of patients' health records.

This HIPAA Privacy Rule, effective April 14, 2003, governs the handling of "protected health information." Protected health information (PHI) is information that identifies an individual's physical or mental health condition, the health care that the individual has received, or payments for such care.

Employers that sponsor self-insured health plans, that offer health care, or that receive, transmit, or manage PHI, generally in relation to group health plan policies, need to ensure that they and their insurance companies and health care providers are in compliance with this rule. Employers should
- Designate a privacy officer to plan, implement, and oversee compliance.
- Develop a compliance program and policies where access to employee PHI is granted on a "need to know" basis.
- Make sure management staff is aware of the scope and implications of the rule — and of the consequences of noncompliance, which can involve fines of $100 a day, for each affected employee.
- Train employees about privacy obligations.
- Obtain written warranties from their insurers and company-sponsored health care providers that those vendors are in compliance with this rule.

The Department of Health and Human Services has published guidance covering the HIPAA Privacy Rule. This document can be viewed at www.hhs.gov/ocr/hipaa/privacy.html.

Immigration Reform and Control Act (1986)

This Act requires that new hires provide appropriate documents (from a defined list) to employers to verify their identity and their legal right to work in the United States. The burden of verifying that a new employee is eligible to work in the United States falls on the employer. The Act also makes it illegal for employers to discriminate on the basis of national origin, citizenship, or intention to obtain citizenship.

- See www.eeoc.gov/facts/qanda.html for more information.

Labor-Management Relations Act (Taft-Hartley) (1947)

The Taft-Hartley Act established a list of union labor practices that are unfair and unlawful. The Act also ensures an employer's right to talk about the pros and cons of a union freely, as long as the company does not threaten employees or make promises to them. When a threatened or actual strike is believed to "imperil the national health or safety," the Act gives the Attorney General the power to obtain an 80-day cooling-off period. It also declares closed union shops illegal and permits union shops only after a vote of a majority of the employees. It forbids jurisdictional strikes and secondary boycotts.

- See http://vi.uh.edu/pages/buzzmat/tafthartley.html for more information.

National Labor Relations Act (NLRA) (1935)

The NLRA provides that all employees have the right to form, join, and assist labor organizations and to bargain collectively with their employers. The National Labor Relations Board enforces the Act, and the body of decisions and regulations from the Board has formed an extensive set of standards for electing and decertifying unions, for negotiating bargaining agreements, and for defining activities as fair or unfair labor practices.

Violations of the Act are subject to a wide variety of penalties, depending on the type of violation.

- See www.nlrb.gov/about_us/overview/national_labor_relations_act.aspx for more information.

Occupational Safety and Health Act (OSH Act) (1970)

The OSH Act includes a "general duty clause" that requires all employers to maintain a workplace that is free from recognized hazards that would cause injury or death to employees. Most employers must comply with the specific Occupational Safety and Health Administration (OSHA) workplace safety and health standards that apply to their workplaces and the hazards they present. OSHA requires employers to maintain a log of certain injuries and illnesses, report certain deaths and multiple hospitalizations, and post supplementary records on an annual basis. Employers may not discharge employees who refuse to do a job that they reasonably believe places them at risk of injury or exposes them to a hazardous workplace condition. The standards are voluminous and may be obtained from the Government Printing Office.

Penalties for noncompliance include civil penalties up to $1,000 for individual violations, up to $10,000 for repeated and willful violations, and back pay and reinstatement for employees who suffer discrimination.

- See www.osha.gov/pls/oshaweb/owasrch.search_form?p_doc_type=oshact for more information.

Rehabilitation Act (1973)

This Act applies to employers with federal contracts or subcontracts that exceed $10,000. It requires them to take affirmative action to hire, retain, and promote qualified individuals with disabilities.

- See www.dol.gov/ofccp/regs/compliance/ca_503.htm for more information.

Uniform Guidelines on Employee Selection Procedures (1978)

These Guidelines address the use of employee selection practices — such as interviewing, testing, and training — and their impact on discrimination based on race, color, religion, sex, or national origin.

Specifically addressed is adverse impact, as measured by the "80 percent test," also known as the "four-fifths rule." This test states that if a selection practice results in less than 80 percent of a protected group being selected, as compared with the most frequently selected group, this may constitute evidence of discrimination. Assume, for example, that white candidates are most frequently selected for a job. In a test for that job, if 60 percent of American Indian candidates pass while 90 percent of white candidates pass, this result could be evidence of discrimination. There are other criteria that are significant, including the makeup of the labor force in the area.

The Guidelines also require employers to maintain records, for an unspecified period of time, on selection procedures, on any adverse impact noted, and on the workforce broken down by race and ethnic groups.

- See www.dol.gov/dol/allcfr/title_41/Part_60-3/toc.htm for more information.

Uniformed Services Employment and Reemployment Rights Act (1994)

This Act, which replaced the Veterans' Reemployment Rights Act, broadly prohibits employers from discriminating against individuals because of past, present, or future membership in a uniformed (military) service, including periods of voluntary training and service. It requires reinstatement on the job after periods of active service.

Penalties for noncompliance include back pay and benefits, as well as liquidated damages if the conduct was willful.

- See www.osc.gov/userra.htm# for more information.

Vietnam-Era Veterans Readjustment Assistance Act (1974)
(Federal Contractors Only)

This law was enacted as a result of concerns about the reentry of Vietnam-era veterans into the workforce. The Act requires contractors and subcontractors with federal contracts of $25,000 or more to practice affirmative action in hiring and promoting certain veterans. Covered employers must list certain vacancies with the local government employment service and must file an annual "VETS-100" report outlining the hiring of certain veterans.

The **Jobs for Veterans Act (2002)** amended the Vietnam-Era Veterans Readjustment Assistance Act by raising the threshold for covered contractors from $25,000 to $100,000 for contracts entered into after December 1, 2003.

- See www.dol.gov/compliance/laws/comp-vevraa.htm for more information.

Worker Adjustment and Retraining Notification Act (1989)

This Act requires employers with 100 or more full-time employees to provide 60 days' written advance notification of plant closings and mass layoffs. Notification must go to employees, bargaining units, and state and local government officials.

For noncompliance, employers are liable for attorneys' fees, back pay, and lost benefits (including medical expenses that otherwise would have been paid) for up to 60 days.

- See www.doleta.gov/programs/factsht/warn.htm for more information.

NEW AND PENDING LAWS

As of the writing of this edition, the following legislation or bureaucratic rule changes were pending but had not yet been passed or enacted. Below is a listing of, brief description of, and links to several pending laws or rule changes that may impact your company's HR decisions, should they become law.

Employee Free Choice Act (EFCA)

The EFCA bill would amend the National Labor Relations Act to permit the use of union cards as a substitute for secret ballots.

- See www.aflcio.org/joinaunion/voiceatwork/efca/10keyfacts.cfm/ for more information.

Employment Non-Discrimination Act (ENDA)

ENDA would prohibit discrimination against employees on the basis of sexual orientation or gender identity for civilian, nonreligious employers with more than 15 employees.

- See http://edlabor.house.gov/hearings/2009/09/hr-3017-employment-non-discrim.shtml for more information.

Healthy Families Act

The Healthy Families Act would require employers with more than 15 employees to provide workers with up to 56 hours or seven days of paid sick leave each year. For every 30 hours worked, workers would accrue one hour of paid sick leave.

- See http://womensissues.about.com/od/intheworkplace/f/HealthyFamiliesAct.htm for more information.

Appendix B

Federal Labor Laws by Number of Employees

1-14 Employees

- Title VII of the Civil Rights Act of 1964 (for employment agencies and labor organizations). See 15-19 for other employers.
- Consumer Credit Protection Act of 1968
- Employee Polygraph Protection Act of 1988
- Employee Retirement Income Security Act (ERISA) of 1974 (if company offers benefits)
- Equal Pay Act of 1963
- Fair and Accurate Credit Transactions Act of 2003 (FACT)
- Fair Credit Reporting Act of 1969
- Fair Labor Standards Act of 1938
- Federal Insurance Contributions Act of 1935 (FICA) (Social Security)
- Health Insurance Portability and Accountability Act (HIPAA) of 1996 (if company offers benefits)
- Immigration and Nationality Act of 1952
- Immigration Reform and Control Act of 1986
- Mental Health Parity Act of 1996 (MHPA)
- National Labor Relations Act of 1947
- Newborns' and Mothers' Health Protection Act of 1996
- Occupational Safety and Health Act of 1970
- Sarbanes-Oxley Act of 2002
- Uniform Guidelines on Employee Selection Procedures of 1978
- Uniformed Services Employment and Reemployment Rights Act of 1994

11-14, add

- OSHA Recordkeeping (maintain record of job-related injuries and illnesses)

15-19, add

- Americans with Disabilities Act of 1990

- Genetic Information Nondiscrimination Act (GINA) of 2008
- Lilly Ledbetter Fair Pay Act of 2009
- Title VII of the Civil Rights Act of 1964
- Pregnancy Discrimination Act (PDA)

20-49, add
- Age Discrimination in Employment Act of 1967
- Consolidated Omnibus Benefits Reconciliation Act (COBRA) of 1986
- 50 or more, add
- Family and Medical Leave Act of 1993
- EEO-1 Report filed annually with EEOC if organization is a federal contractor
- Mental Health Parity Act of 1996 (for employers who offer mental health benefits)

100 or more, add
- Worker Adjustment and Retraining Notification Act of 1988
- EEO-1 Report filed annually with EEOC if organization is not a federal contractor

Federal Contractors, add
- Executive Order 11246 of 1965
- Vocational Rehabilitation Act of 1973
- Drug Free Workplace Act of 1988
- Vietnam-Era Veterans Readjustment Act of 1974
- Davis Bacon Act of 1931
- Copeland Act of 1934
- Walsh-Healy Act of 1936
- Service Contract Act (1965)
- Contract Work Hours and Safety Standards Act (CWHSSA)

Source: "Federal Labor Laws By Number of Employees," Society for Human Resource Management. Available at www.shrm.org/LegalIssues/FederalResources/FederalStatutesRegulationsandGuidanc/Documents/FederalLawThresholds.pdf.

Appendix C

Timeline of Health Care
Reform Impacts

2010	President Obama Signs Health Care Reform Legislation	
Insurance Market Reforms for Existing Plans (Comply beginning with the plan year that starts Oct. 1, 2010, or for calendar year plans, Jan. 1, 2011)	Children not eligible to enroll on another employer's plan can be covered by their parents' plan through age 26.	
	Lifetime and annual limits will be prohibited	
	Children under 19 years old may not be excluded due to pre-existing conditions.	
	Plans cannot rescind coverage.	
	All plans must comply with new disclosure requirements (timing for this requirement is unclear).	
Insurance Market Reforms for New Plans	Preventive care must be covered.	
	Maximum annual out-of-pocket amounts set for participants.	
	Preventive and wellness benefits must be covered with no deductibles or other cost-sharing.	
	New standards apply to appeals processes.	
	Plan participants may choose any participating primary care provider.	
	No prior authorization or referral may be required prior to ob-gyn visits.	
	No prior authorization may be required for emergency care services.	
	Group health plans may not discriminate in favor of highly compensated employees.	
	Individuals in clinical trials must be covered.	
	Insurers must maintain a medical loss ratio of not less than 85 percent for large groups or 80 percent for individual and small group markets. Those that do not meet the standard must pay rebates to policyholders.	
Retiree Reinsurance	June 21: A temporary reinsurance plan for employers covering retirees who are not eligible for Medicare starts. The plan ends in 2014.	
Small Businesses	Tax credits of up to 35 percent of premiums will be available to small businesses that offer health coverage. To qualify, businesses must have fewer than 25 employees and average annual wages of less than $50,000.	
High-Risk Pool	A national high-risk pool will be established for uninsured individuals with pre-existing conditions.	

2011

Long-Term Care Coverage	The Community Living Assistance Services and Supports Act, which provides limited long-term care coverage through the workplace for employees, takes effect.
Consumer-Directed Health Plan Changes	For consumer-directed health plans (CDHPs), the penalty for nonqualified distributions from a health savings account (HSA) increases to 20 percent. Over-the-counter drugs are no longer reimbursable under health flexible spending accounts (FSAs), health reimbursement arrangements (HRAs) or HSAs unless prescribed.

2012

Employer Reporting	Employers must disclose the value of employer-provided health benefits for each employee on the employee's annual Form W-2. The first report goes out in 2012 for coverage provided in 2011.
Insurance Market Reform	A fee will be assessed to fund comparative effectiveness research. It is payable by insurers and self-insured plans.

2013

Health FSA Changes	Health flexible spending arrangement contributions are capped at $2,500.
Medicare Payroll Taxes and Retiree Drug Subsidies	Employees' share of the Medicare tax on wages in excess of $200,000 (or $250,000 for joint tax filers) increases.

Employers will no longer be permitted to take an income tax deduction for the Medicare Part D retiree drug subsidies they receive from the federal government. |
| Employer Notifications | March 1: Employers must notify employees of state health insurance exchanges, whether the employer's plan meets minimum coverage requirements and how to access information regarding premium subsidies that may be available for exchange-based coverage. |

2014

| Employer Mandate | Employers that offer health coverage must offer a free choice voucher for employees who choose to purchase coverage through exchanges. The voucher must be equal to the amount paid to provide coverage to participants in the company health plan.

Employers with 200 or more employees must auto-enroll workers in the health care plan.

Employers with 50 or more employees that do not offer health coverage and that have one full-time employee receiving a subsidy will pay a penalty of $2,000 per each full-time employee (minus the first 30 employees).

Employers with 50 or more employees that do offer health coverage and have one full-time employee opting out of that coverage and instead receiving a federal subsidy will pay a penalty of $2,000 per employee. |
| --- | --- |
| Insurance Reforms for Plans in Effect Prior to March 23, 2010 | Waiting periods longer than 90 days for health coverage are prohibited for plan years beginning on or after Jan. 1, 2014.

Employers may offer wellness program incentives/penalties of up to 30 percent of premium to employees. The amount can increase to 50 percent after government agencies conduct a study on wellness programs. Health risk assessments may not include questions on gun ownership. |

2014, continued		
	State Health Insurance Exchanges	States must create Small Business Health Options Programs or "SHOP Exchanges." Small employers may be able to provide coverage through an exchange plan.
	Individual Mandate	Individuals must purchase health insurance. Employees who earn less than four times the federal poverty level and pay more than 8 percent of their income for the employer-sponsored coverage will have the option of purchasing health insurance through health care exchanges.
2017		
	State Health Insurance Exchanges	States may begin to allow large employers to provide coverage through an exchange plan.
2018		
	Excise Tax	Insurers and employers who self-insure will be charged a nondeductible 40 percent excise tax on cost of employee health coverage that exceeds $10,200 for single coverage and $27,500 for family coverage. Multiemployer plans would be treated as providing family coverage. Thresholds are increased for high-risk workers and retirees. The tax will be indexed for inflation.

Source: "SHRM Health Care Reform Timeline: The Latest Developments and When They Take Effect," Society for Human Resource Management. Available at www2.shrm.org/HC_Timeline/scroller3.html.

Appendix D

Resources and Reading List

(Many of these resources are available through the SHRMStore at www.shrm.org/shrmstore.)

101 Sample Write-Ups for Documenting Employee Performance Problems: A Guide to Progressive Discipline & Termination, 2d ed., Paul Falcone (AMACOM/SHRM, 2010).

539 Ready to Adapt Human Resource Letters, Memos, Procedures, Practices, Forms ... and More: The Comprehensive, All-in-One HR Operating Guide, R.J. Landry (SHRM, 2006).

Anger and Conflict in the Workplace: Spot the Signs, Avoid the Trauma, Lynne McClure (Impact Publications, 2000).

Assessing External Job Candidates, Jean M. Phillips and Stanley M. Gully (SHRM, 2009).

Assessing Internal Job Candidates, Jean M. Phillips and Stanley M. Gully (SHRM, 2009).

Beyond the Myths and Magic of Mentoring, Margo Murray (Jossey-Bass, 2001).

Dealing with Problem Employees: A Legal Guide, Amy DelPo and Lisa Guerin (Nolo, 2007).

Designing and Using Organizational Surveys, Allan H. Church and Janine Waclawski (Jossey-Bass, 2001).

Downshifting: How to Work Less and Enjoy Life More, John D. Drake (Berrett-Koehler, 2001).

Employee Management for Small Business, Lin Grensing-Pophal (Self-Counsel Press, 2009).

The Employee Recruitment and Retention Handbook, Diane Arthur (AMACOM, 2001).

The Employers Immigration Compliance Desk Reference, Greg Siskind (SHRM/ILW, 2009).

Employment Termination Source Book, Wendy Bliss and Gene R. Thornton (SHRM, 2006).

The Essential Guide to Family and Medical Leave, Lisa Guerin and Deborah C. England (Nolo, 2009).

The Essential Guide to Federal Employment Laws, 2d ed., Lisa Guerin and Amy DelPo (Nolo/SHRM, 2009).

The Essential Guide to Workplace Investigations, 2d ed., Lisa Guerin (Nolo/SHRM, 2010).

Financial Intelligence for HR Professionals: What You Really Need to Know About the Numbers, Karen Berman and Joe Knight (Harvard Business School Press, 2008).

First Break All the Rules: What the World's Greatest Managers Do Differently, Marcus Buckingham and Curt Coffman (Simon & Schuster, 1999).

Hire for Fit, Don Anderson (Oakhill Press, 2001).

Hiring Source Book, Catherine D. Fyock (SHRM, 2004).

HR and the New Hispanic Workforce: A Comprehensive Guide to Cultivating and Leveraging Employee Success, Louis E.V. Nevaer and Vaso Perimenis Ekstein (Davies-Black/SHRM, 2007).

The HR Answer Book: An Indispensable Guide for Managers and Human Resources Professionals, Shawn Smith and Rebecca Mazin (AMACOM, 2004).

HR Competencies: Mastery at the Intersection of People and Business, Dave Ulrich, Wayne Brockbank, Dani Johnson, Kurt Sandholtz, and Jon Younger (SHRM, 2008).

HR from the Heart: Inspiring Stories and Strategies for Building the People Side of Great Business, third edition, Libby Sartain with Martha I. Finney (AMACOM, 2003).

The HR Scorecard: Linking People, Strategy and Performance, Brian E. Becker, Mark A. Huselid, and Dave Ulrich (Harvard Business School Publishing, 2001).

HR Transformation: Building Human Resources From the Outside In, Dave Ulrich, Justin Allen, Wayne Brockbank, and Jon Younger (McGraw-Hill, 2009).

Human Resources Kit for Dummies, Max Messmer (For Dummies, 2006).

The Legal Context of Staffing, Jean M. Phillips and Stanley M. Gully (SHRM, 2009).

Love 'Em or Lose 'Em: Getting Good People to Stay, Beverly Kaye and Sharon Jordan-Evans (Berrett-Koehler, 2008).

Managing Off-Site Staff for Small Business, Lin Grensing-Pophal (Self-Counsel Press, 2010).

Never Get Lost Again: Navigating Your HR Career, Nancy E. Glube and Phyllis G. Hartman (SHRM, 2009).

Performance Appraisal Source Book, Mike Deblieux (SHRM, 2003).

Reinventing Talent Management, William A. Schiemann, (Wiley/SHRM, 2009).

Seven Habits of Highly Effective People, S.R. Covey (Free Press, 2004).

Smart Policies for Workplace Technologies: Email, Blogs, Cell Phones and More, Lisa Guerin (Nolo/SHRM, 2009).

Solving the Compensation Puzzle: Putting Together a Complete Pay and Performance System, Sharon K. Koss (SHRM, 2008).

Stop Bullying at Work: Strategies and Tools for HR and Legal Professionals, Teresa A. Daniel (SHRM, 2009).

The Strategic Human Resource Leader: How to Prepare Your Organization for the Six Key Trends Shaping the Future, William J. Rothwell, Robert K. Prescott, and Maria W. Taylor (Davies-Black, 1998).

Strategic Interviewing: How to Hire Good People, Richard Camp, Mary E. Vielhaber, and Jack L. Simonetti (Jossey-Bass, 2001).

Strategic Staffing: Comprehensive System for Effective Workforce Planning, 2d ed., Thomas P. Bechet (AMACOM/SHRM, 2008).

Successful Manager's Handbook, Susan Gebelein (2004).

Supervisor's Guide to Labor Relations, T.O. Collier Jr. (SHRM, 2001).

Weathering Storms: Human Resources in Difficult Times, Society for Human Resource Management (SHRM, 2008).

Appendix E

FAQ Contributors

A special thank-you goes to the following HR professionals, who gave me their stories "From the Trenches," helped with FAQs, and assisted with so many other aspects of this book. They were great resources.

Tom Adam
Advanced Research Intl.

Barbara Adams
HR Architects Group

Wendy Bliss, JD, SPHR
Bliss & Associates

William G. Bliss
Bliss & Associates

K. Tia Burke
Christie, Pabarue, Mortensen and Young

Michael A. Couch
Michael Couch & Associates, Inc.

Demont Daniel, CSP
PrideStaff

Kevin Doherty
Greenwald Doherty LLP

John Drake, Ph.D.
Drake Inglesi Milardo Inc.

Tom Fitzpatrick
Becker Professional Review

Lynda Ford, SPHR
The Ford Group

Patricia Fragen
Strategic Office Solutions

Hilarie Frank
Union County College

Sheri L. Gilbert
Proskauer Rose LLP

Mary Glaeser

Marian Hall, SPHR
Comcast Cable Communications

Janet Hirsch
Toyota Boshoku America

Karen Horn
Horn Communication

Eddie Isler
Ray & Isler, PC

Sharon Jordan-Evans
Jordan Evans Group

Beverly Kaye
Career Systems International

Eileen Keane
The Link Agency

Ann Kiernan
Fair Measures, Inc.

Lynn King
Sweetbriar College

Paige Klatt, PHR
Springbok Technologies Inc.

Chris Laggini
DLT Solutions, Inc.

John Lewis, SPHR
Wurzburg Inc.

Lynne McClure, Ph.D.
McClure Associates Inc.

Erin O'Connor
Cammack, LaRhette Consulting

Patricia Peirce
CMS Companies

Daryl Rother
Verity Credit Union

Debra Squyres, SPHR
TriNet

Jim Sutton, SPHR
Mirant

Index

About the Author

Lin Grensing-Pophal, M.A., SPHR, is an HR/communication consultant and business journalist with an extensive background in corporate communications and employee relations. As a director in the fields of education, energy, and health care, Pophal has managed all aspects of corporate and marketing communication including employee communication, public relations, advertising, market research, and brand management. Her firm, Strategic Communications, LLC, (www.stratcommunications.com) works with businesses to develop and implement strategic communication solutions for both internal and external audiences.

Pophal is a prolific writer of business management and marketing articles for both general and trade publications and is the author of several books, including: *Managing Off-Site Staff* (2010), *Employee Management for Small Business* (2010), and *The Essentials of Corporate Communications and Public Relations* (2006).